PHILOSOPHICAL
FOUNDATION

Other works by Dr. Surrendra Gangadean & The Logos Foundation:

History of Philosophy: A Critical Analysis of Unresolved Disputes
Theological Foundation: A Critical Analysis of Christian Belief
Philosophical Foundation: Trivium Study Guide
The Logos Papers: To Make the Logos Known

PHILOSOPHICAL FOUNDATION

A Critical Analysis of Basic Beliefs

Second Edition

SURRENDRA GANGADEAN

 PUBLIC PHILOSOPHY PRESS ◆ THE LOGOS FOUNDATION

Phoenix, Arizona

Philosophical Foundation: A Critical Analysis of Basic Beliefs

Copyright © 2022 Surrendra Gangadean
Original publication 2008 Surrendra Gangadean

Republished by Public Philosophy Press 2022
Phoenix, Arizona
publicphilosophypress.com

Printed in the United States of America

Cover design: Beth Ellen Nagle
Typesetting: Matthew P. Hicks & Brian J. Phelps

Library of Congress Cataloging-in-Publication Data pending

Gangadean, Surrendra, 1943–2022.
    Philosophical foundation: a critical analysis of basic beliefs
    Includes bibliographical references, index, and glossary.
    Second edition
    ISBN 978-1-7365424-9-1 (pbk.)

1. Philosophy—Basic Beliefs 2. Rational Presuppositionalism
3. Philosophy—Epistemology 4. Philosophy—Metaphysics
5. Philosophy—Ethics 6. Clarity and Inexcusability I. Title

To Raj and Dev and Shanti

and all whom they represent

CONTENTS

Preface   ix

Acknowledgments   xi

Outline   xiii

Introduction   xxiii

PART I: EPISTEMOLOGY

Chapter 1: Clarity, Philosophy, and Reason   3

Chapter 2: Sources of Skepticism and Fideism   17

Chapter 3: Knowledge, Argument, and Presupposition   49

Chapter 4: On Eternality and Causality   61

PART II: METAPHYSICS

Chapter 5: Material Monism   71

Chapter 6: Spiritual Monism and Anti-Realism   101

Chapter 7: Dualism and Logically Possible Worlds   129

Chapter 8: Theism   139

PART III: ETHICS

Chapter 9: The Good and The Moral Law   165

Chapter 10: Moral Law 1: The Good and God   171

Chapter 11: Moral Law 2: Thinking and Presupposition   185

Chapter 12: Moral Law 3: Integrity and Knowledge   199

Chapter 13: Moral Law 4: Work and Hope   207

Chapter 14: Moral Law 5: Authority and Insight   221

Chapter 15: Moral Law 6: Human Dignity and Rationality 231

Chapter 16: Moral Law 7: Love and Fidelity 245

Chapter 17: Moral Law 8: Value and Talent 255

Chapter 18: Moral Law 9: Truth and Justice 267

Chapter 19: Moral Law 10: Suffering and The Good 277

Conclusion 284

APPENDICES

Appendix 1: Presupposition of *Philosophical Foundation*:
Common Ground and the Principle of Clarity 287

Appendix 2: A Response to Critics of Clarity:
Common Ground Applied to Avoid
Meaningless Disputes 293

Glossary of Terms 311

Suggested Reading 323

Bibliography 327

Index 343

About the Author 349

PREFACE

PHILOSOPHY IS NEEDED BY ALL, so this book is written for all. It is written for those who are beginning to think deeply about basic things and for those who have wandered in the labyrinth a while. It is also written for those who have been avoiding the subject for any number of good and bad reasons.

What is investigated here are answers to the most basic questions we can ask: Can we know anything? What ultimately is real? What ought I to do? The reader may understandably ask: Why another book on the subject—is there anything new under the sun? If we can learn from the past, if we can learn from challenges and conflicts, if we can learn from our suffering, then we can become more conscious and consistent in what we think and do. This book is offered as another step in that direction.

Because of the range of readers, not everything here is intended for all. All can follow the main line of argument, even when names and ideas are mentioned without being introduced. The more advanced reader does not need it, and the beginner is being spared a burden. There has been a continuing dilemma to include more and to exclude more. An outline, introduction, footnotes, glossary, suggested readings, bibliography, and index are added to help.

This book will be read profitably if the reader continually proceeds from what is more basic to what is less basic. Critical thinking is by nature presuppositional; without the more basic in place, what comes after cannot be understood. *Caveat lector.* May the reader be aware.

—SURRENDRA GANGADEAN
Phoenix, Arizona
November 2007

ACKNOWLEDGEMENTS

I am indebted to many who helped to make this book possible:

To dialogue partners who shaped and expressed the ideas and world-views engaged with in the text.

To those whose lives have encouraged the use of reason in the pursuit of the good.

To students whose intellectual perplexities required answers which were relevant and intelligible.

To Kelly and Haley and Brian, and all who helped to bring this work from manuscript to text.

To the one who by daily being and presence has been my confidante.

OUTLINE

PART 1: EPISTEMOLOGY

Chapter 1: Clarity, Philosophy, and Reason

1. On Clarity
    - i. Need for clarity: meaning vs. nihilism
    - ii. Skepticism and fideism lead to nihilism
    - iii. Basic belief and clarity
2. What Is Philosophy? — Five Features
    - i. Area: foundation and goal
    - ii. Attitude: love of wisdom
    - iii. Method: critical use of reason
    - iv. Application: self-examination
    - v. System: world and life view
3. What Is Reason?
    - i. Reason in itself: the laws of thought
    - ii. Reason in its use: formative, critical, interpretive, constructive
    - iii. Reason in us: natural, ontological, transcendental, fundamental

Chapter 2: Sources of Skepticism and Fideism

1. Sources of Skepticism: Popular, Philosophical, and Personal
    - i. Worldview pluralism
    - ii. Pragmatism and skepticism
    - iii. Truth and power
    - iv. Construction and deconstruction
    - v. Relativism and tolerance

vi. Tradition and transcendence

vii. Persuasion and proof

viii. Appearance and reality: common sense and realism

ix. Intuition and certainty: sign and reality

x. Empiricism: knowledge by sense experience

xi. Reason: its uses, its limits, and its limited use

xii. Attitude: the fundamental source of skepticism

2. Sources of Fideism: Popular, Theological, and Personal

i. *Sensus divinitatis*: is knowledge of God immediate or inferred?

ii. Knowledge and accountability

iii. The magisterial vs. the ministerial use of reason

iv. Ontology and epistemology: can reason grasp ultimate reality?

v. Faith and reason

vi. Rason and the *testimonium Spiritu Sancti*

vii. Reason and the particular

viii. Reason and rationalism

ix. Reason and hermeneutics

x. Piety and intellect

xi. Reason and the mysteries of the faith

xii. Reason and personality

3. Twelve Informal Fallacies: Persuasion by Pseudo-Arguments

Chapter 3: Knowledge, Argument, and Presupposition

1. Definition of Knowledge—Challenges and Responses

2. Knowledge by Reason and Argument

i. First act of reason: concept—essence, word, and ambiguity

ii. Second act of reason: judgment—contradictions and contraries

iii. Third act of reason: argument—validity and soundness

3. Presupposition: Our Most Basic Belief

    i. Most basic concept and most basic belief: about what is eternal

    ii. Two basic beliefs: all is eternal and only some is eternal

    iii. Classification of worldviews by basic beliefs

    iv. Presuppositions are held more or less consciously and more or less consistently

Chapter 4: On Eternality and Causality

1. There Must Be Something Eternal

    i. Proof by *reductio* argument: no being from non-being

    ii. Analysis of being from non-being

2. There Are No Uncaused Events

    i. Analysis of appeal to uncaused events

    ii. Uncaused events and being from non-being

PART II: METAPHYSICS

Chapter 5: Material Monism

1. Introduction: Definition, Forms of Encounter, Historical Background, and Worldview Implications

2. The First Argument Against Material Monism: The Material Universe Is Not Self-Maintaining

    i. In general: the problem of entropy

    ii. In its parts: the sun and the stars

    iii. As a whole: the big bang oscillating universe and inflationary universe

3. The Second Argument Against Material Monism: Based on the Analysis of Thought

    i. The mind is not the brain: thinking is not motion of atoms in the brain

    ii. Many forms of reductionism and problems with reductionism in general

4. The Third Argument Against Material Monism: Based on the Analysis of Perception

    i. The mind is not the brain: a neural impulse is not a mental image

    ii. Three objections to the analysis of perception and response to each

5. The Fourth Argument Against Material Monism: The Naturalistic View of Origins Is Not Based on Science

    Three issues in the controversy concerning origins:

    i. Is the question of origins a matter of science or religion or philosophy? Assumptions not argued for in science and religion vs. philosophy

    ii. Which assumption best interprets the data: uniformity or non-uniformity?

        a. Geological data: seven phenomena

        b. Biological data: the four stages from non-life to human life

        c. Astronomical data: cosmological order and age of the cosmos

    iii. Is a compromise position—theistic evolution—possible? Four problems

Chapter 6: Spiritual Monism and Anti-Realism

1. Introduction

    i. Definition, forms of encounter, and spiritual monist worldview

    ii. Reincarnation: reasons for and against

2. Idealism and Anti-Realism: Is Reality Mind Dependent?

    i. The brain in the vat/matrix problem

    ii. Berkeley: *esse est percipi*

    iii. Kant on causality and the noumenal world

    iv. Shankara: absolute non-dual (*advaita*) Vedanta

    v. Ramanuja: qualified non-dual Vedanta

vi. Nagarjuna: the middle way

vii. Pragmatism and the enterprise of knowing

viii. Deconstructing postmodernism

ix. Kierkegaard's view of faith in Abraham—an alternative existential analysis

Chapter 7: Dualism and Logically Possible Worlds

1. Dualism—Introduction

   i. The appeal of dualism and objections to its appeal

   ii. Persistence of dualistic attitudes in popular theism

   iii. Plato: ordinary dualism and objections

   iv. Aristotle: dependent dualism and objections

2. Logically Possible Worlds

   i. New forms of skepticism: being beyond properties; becoming without being; beyond excluded middle

   ii. Logically possible worlds and the actual world; reason and imagination: science fiction and fantasy literature

Chapter 8: Theism

1. Introduction: Problems of Fideism and Definition of "God" in Theism

2. Preliminary Problems Regarding Creation *Ex Nihilo*

3. The Problem of Evil in David Hume's *Dialogues Concerning Natural Religion,* and beyond Hume

4. Hume's Five Solutions and Response to Each

5. The Free Will Solution and Four Objections

6. An Ironic Solution

   i. The nature of the problem of evil: a problem for man as a rational being

   ii. The definition of "good" and "evil" in light of the clarity of general revelation

   iii. The parable of the prodigal son, explained and applied to world history

iv. Why is there moral evil?: purpose and resolution in world history

v. Why is there natural evil?: purpose and resolution in world history

vi. Irony in the problem of evil restated

PART III: ETHICS

Chapter 9: The Good and the Moral Law

1. The Definition of Ethics and Explanation of the Definition

2. The Necessary Conditions for Rational Justification in Ethics

3. There is a Moral Law Which Is Clear, Comprehensive, and Critical

Chapter 10: Moral Law 1: The Good and God

1. Origin: by nature we make choices of means and ends

2. Analysis: the good is the end in itself; rational justification for the ground of the good

3. Moral Law 1: the good is determined by human nature as created by God

4. Applications: what is opposed by the nature of the good, grounded in God the creator

5. Consequences inherent in affirming or denying the good and its ground

Chapter 11: Moral Law 2: Thinking and Presupposition

1. Origin: by nature we think; by nature we distinguish the finite and the infinite

2. Analysis: thinking is presuppositional; we think of the less basic in light of the more basic

3. Moral Law 2: we are not to think of the infinite (God) in light of the finite (man)

4. Applications: misconceptions of the divine nature which have divided theists

5. Consequences inherent in affirming or denying presuppositional thinking about the nature of God

Chapter 12: Moral Law 3: Integrity and Knowledge

1. Origin: each person is by nature a unity in being, not a divided being

2. Analysis: integrity as a concern for consistency is necessary and sufficient for knowledge

3. Moral Law 3: we should have integrity: we should be consistent, not divided, in our thoughts and actions

4. Applications: integrity is opposed to all inconsistency in what we say and do

5. Consequences inherent in affirming or denying integrity

Chapter 13: Moral Law 4: Work and Hope

1. Origin: to bring into being and to sustain in being requires work

2. Analysis: the end of work is the good; the nature of the good; the certainty of hope

3. Moral Law 4: we are to work with hope for the good

4. Applications: true hope is opposed to false hope and to no hope concerning the good

5. Consequences inherent in affirming or denying work and hope

Chapter 14: Moral Law 5: Authority and Insight

1. Origin: we are born ignorant; we need to be taught the good and the means to it

2. Analysis: authority is rational, based on insight which is historically cumulative

3. Moral Law 5: authority based on insight must be honored; authority without insight must be changed where possible

4. Applications: what is opposed is false authority in principles, in persons, and in institutional practices

5. Consequences inherent in affirming or denying authority based on insight

Chapter 15: Moral Law 6: Human Dignity and Rationality

1. Origin: we are born human with a dignity which distinguishes us from animals

2. Analysis: human dignity consists in the capacity to understand; human society is a society of rational beings

3. Moral Law 6: we are to affirm human dignity; we are to treat others as having the ability and responsibility to understand

4. Applications: what is opposed is all forms of denial of human dignity

5. Consequences inherent in affirming or denying human dignity

Chapter 16: Moral Law 7: Love and Fidelity

1. Origin: human beings are born of a sexual union of one man and one woman

2. Analysis: sexual union is a natural sign and seal of love; a full union is monogamous and lasting; love in marriage seeks the good for and with the other (spiritual fidelity)

3. Moral Law 7: there is an order for marriage which protects love and fidelity

4. Applications: what is opposed in ordinary infidelity is rooted in all forms of spiritual infidelity

5. Consequences inherent in affirming or denying love and fidelity

Chapter 17: Moral Law 8: Value and Talent

1. Origin: no one values all things alike; value is a function of supply and demand

2. Analysis: demand is a function of one's view of the good; supply is a function of talent; the nature, origin, and development of talent

3. Moral Law 8: we are to develop our talent in pursuit of the good in service to others

4. Applications: what is opposed is the neglect, abuse, and hindrance of the use of talent

5.   Consequences inherent in affirming or denying the use of talent in pursuit of the good

Chapter 18: Moral Law 9: Truth and Justice

1.   Origin: we are born equal; in justice equals are treated equally

2.   Analysis: the nature of justice; truth is necessary and sufficient to correct and to prevent injustice

3.   Moral Law 9: we are to know and speak the truth to prevent injustice

4.   Applications: what is opposed is what hinders the pursuit of truth to prevent injustice

5.   Consequences inherent in affirming or denying the pursuit of truth for justice

Chapter 19: Moral Law 10: Suffering and The Good

1.   Origin: we are born changeable; we can change in our belief concerning the good

2.   Analysis: suffering arises when we believe we cannot possess what we conceive to be the good; on the nature of the good, moral evil, and natural evil

3.   Moral Law 10: we are to be content in pursuing what truly is the good

4.   Applications: what is opposed is all forms of discontent rooted in misconceptions about the good

5.   Consequences inherent in affirming or denying what truly is the good

INTRODUCTION

PHILOSOPHICAL FOUNDATION ARGUES THAT some things are clear, that the basic things are clear, that the basic things about God and man and good and evil are clear to reason. This thesis concerning what is clear is affirmed over against skepticism[1] in Western Philosophy and fideism[2] in Western Theology.

Ordinary skepticism is a natural response to fideism, when the latter makes claims about God while offering no proof. Philosophical skepticism is likewise a natural response to the many claims of proof that have failed.[3] Fully consistent skepticism holds that no knowledge at all is possible. Taken strictly, this would imply that even basic conceptual distinctions, such as the distinctions between being and non-being and true and false, are not clear. But the denial of all meaningful distinctions is self-defeating[4] and is a counsel of despair.[5] Examined closely, however, this intellectual despair is seen to be rooted in uncritically held assumptions. One need not avoid skepticism by

---

1. Skepticism in Western Philosophy can be seen in Sextus Empiricus (*ca.* A.D. 200), David Hume (d. 1776), and in current Postmodernism. There are many degrees of consciousness and consistency with which skepticism is held, from ordinary, to philosophical, to fully consistent skepticism. I am particularly concerned with fully consistent skepticism which denies that some things are clear (implying that nothing is clear), including the basic things about God and man and good and evil.

2. Fideism is belief about basic things without proof, either because proof is not considered relevant or necessary or possible. Fideism applies also to proofs that are attempted, but which fail for any number of reasons.

3. I am referring here to the ontological, cosmological, and teleological arguments for the existence of God, which have been found wanting when they have been used as three independent proofs. An alternative approach is to use revised versions of each of these three proofs as three parts of one cumulative proof.

4. Since no distinction is clear and all distinctions are meaningless, then no assertion is meaningful and therefore no assertion is possible, including the skeptic's own assertion. Some skeptics have seen this and have moved to silence.

5. The skeptic is in intellectual despair; he has (too soon) given up hope for knowledge of basic things in saying "knowledge is impossible."

xxiv PHILOSOPHICAL FOUNDATION

adopting the antinomy[6] of fideism. One can respond to the assumptions leading to skepticism by critically examining these assumptions or presuppositions for coherence of meaning. Twelve assumptions of skepticism will be examined and found wanting, as well as twelve assumptions of fideism, after which, the question of *how* knowledge is possible will be considered.

Generally speaking, knowledge claims[7] have been based either on experience (empiricism) or on reason (rationalism). Experience has been appealed to in many forms: experience of others in the past— tradition and testimony; experience of all—common sense; experience of one's own mental states—intuition; and theories which can be verified by experiment—science. Yet the assumption present in interpreting any experience[8] often goes unnoticed and is itself a form of fideism.

Reason itself can become an occasion of skepticism when it is first used as a source of truth, rather than as a test for meaning (Descartes: "I think therefore I am"; Jefferson: "We hold these truths to be self-evident . . ."). Reason can also become an occasion for skepticism when it is used constructively only (for coherence within a worldview, or in theoretical mathematics, or in positing logically possible worlds) and not first used critically as a test for meaning of actual basic beliefs.

The attempt to mitigate skepticism by appeal to what works (pragmatism) merely begs the question about value judgments and about rational justification for one's view of the good (the highest value). This work argues that knowledge is possible by reason and argument applied presuppositionally, beginning with one's most basic belief.

---

6. An antinomy is not a contradiction, but a polar opposite (often a contrary). Both parts of an antinomy are false because both share a common (false) assumption. Skepticism believes that basic things are not clear because they have been unproven or are unprovable; fideism believes that basic things are not clear and does not attempt or achieve proof. Both skepticism and fideism share the assumption that basic things are not clear. An antinomy is going to the right or to the left, when neither the way left nor right should be taken.

7. A person making a knowledge assertion, in contrast to declaring one's opinion, must be ready to give a reason for the truth of that assertion, especially where objections are raised to the truth of that assertion.

8. No experience is meaningful without interpretation. For example, to say, "The sun rises in the east" or "The material world exists," assume that appearance, given in one's experience, *is* reality. This assumption is not self-evidently true. Appearance is being uncritically interpreted to get to statements about reality.

This work also argues against fideism, which is either implicitly or explicitly present in the history of Christian thought. Most human beings live by tradition. The beliefs of tradition, which are not based on sight, are based on an implicit trust in custom (what one is accustomed to). Beliefs held by custom are not beliefs based on proof. Beliefs not based on proof are commonly said to be a matter of one's faith. Fideism is a more conscious affirmation of faith, understood as belief not based on proof. Fideism minimally maintains that proof for the existence of God is either not necessary, or not possible, or not relevant. Yet historic Christianity teaches that Christ died for our sins and that the inexcusability of unbelief is grounded in the clarity of general revelation (Romans 1:20). If this is the case, then anyone affirming sin and inexcusability can reasonably be asked to show how God's eternal power and divine nature are clear from the things that are made. Further, repentance of this root sin of not seeking and not understanding would seem to require all believers to seek to understand what is clear about God.

While there has been occasional acknowledgement by some believers of the clarity of general revelation, the proofs offered historically have been less than adequate. To show that there is something higher than the mind (Augustine), or that there is a first cause of motion (Aquinas), is not to show God the Creator. The teleological argument by itself shows only a designer, not the Creator. The ontological argument (Anselm) by itself shows at best that there must be something eternal, not that *only* some (God) is eternal. A recent form of the transcendental argument argues from the Triune God of the Scriptures, rather than from general revelation. It fails to see that reason is both transcendental (self-attesting as the laws of thought) and ontological (applies to *being* as well as to thought)—this includes God's being— God's being is not both eternal and non-eternal, at the same time and in the same respect.

There is need then for the philosopher and the theologian[9] to begin their work on the necessary assumption that some things are clear.

---

9. Philosophy addresses questions of natural religion, based on general revelation (what can be known of God by all men, everywhere, at all times). Theology address questions of revealed religion based on special revelation (what can be known of God by transmission of testimony only). Thus, in ways that are complementary, both dimensions of religion and of revelation are encompassed in philosophy and theology.

Since thinking by nature is presuppositional (we think of the less basic in light of the more basic), if anything is clear, then basic things must be clear. Failure to critically analyze our most basic assumption for meaning has been the recurrent source of both skepticism and fideism.

In Part One of this work, I analyze the presuppositional nature of philosophy and reason, and identify several sources of skepticism and fideism. I conclude by arguing that we can have knowledge by reason and argument, and show how we can know there must be something eternal.

In Part Two, I offer a sequence of arguments to show that only some is eternal: matter exists and matter is not eternal; the soul exists and the soul is not eternal. I address the principal counterarguments to God as Creator in the problem of origin and the problem of evil. By combining revised forms of the ontological, cosmological, and teleological arguments, the eternal power and divine nature of God can be clearly seen.

In Part Three, by distinguishing virtue, happiness, and the good, longstanding ethical disputes are clarified. Rational justification for the good—the end in itself, man's chief end—is provided, which then becomes the basis of deriving the moral law from human nature. As a result, it can be shown that there is a moral law which is clear, comprehensive, and critical.

Philosophy is concerned with foundational matters. It deals with the most basic questions we can ask: Is knowledge possible? What is real/eternal? What ought I to do? In principle, only philosophy asks these questions and seeks proof for the answers to these questions. However lacking it has been in achieving consensus in its answers, there is agreement that these are the fundamental questions. This work accepts the task of philosophy in principle and seeks a fuller, more consistent, application of critical thinking to this task.

PART I

EPISTEMOLOGY

Chapter 1

———

CLARITY, PHILOSOPHY, AND REASON

ON CLARITY

SOME THINGS ARE CLEAR. The basic things are clear. The basic things about God and man and good and evil are clear to reason.

Skepticism denies that some things are clear. If nothing is clear, then the distinctions between *a* and *non-a*, being and non-being, true and false, good and evil are not clear. Consistently held, skepticism leads to nihilism—the loss of all meaning.

Human beings are more or less conscious and consistent in understanding the meaning and implications of their beliefs. There are many degrees and kinds of skepticism arising from degrees of consistency in basic belief, as well as from differences among persons. All skepticism is grounded in uncritically held assumptions. These assumptions will be critically examined in preparing to show how some things are clear.

Persons as rational beings need meaning. Integrity, as a basic form of honesty, is a concern for consistency. But, consistently held, skepticism leads to nihilism. The existential burden of nihilism is intolerable; it cannot with integrity be borne. As nihilism increases, integrity decreases. But integrity cannot be abandoned without self-deception and self-justification. Lack of integrity complicates the effort to show what is clear.

Fideism is the most common alternative to skepticism. But it too assumes that basic things are not clear. In fideism, basic beliefs are held without proof. But understanding the meaning of what is clear at the basic level amounts to proof. Belief without proof based on understanding therefore empties belief of meaning. A worldview based on fideism, when challenged over time, must offer proof or, like skepticism, yield to nihilism.

There are many forms of fideism, just as there are many forms of skepticism. One form of fideism believes that, in principle, faith is opposed to proof. Another form of fideism holds beliefs based on arguments which are in fact unsound. Still another form of fideism holds beliefs without proof, without addressing the question of proof. Fideism may occur on both sides of an assertion. Fideism may be both theistic and anti-theistic. It may be naturalistic or supernaturalistic. It may be sophistic or simplistic. Without understanding basic things that are clear, fideism, like skepticism, leads to loss of meaning and to loss of integrity.

What is clear can be known by any person who is seeking to know. Assuming integrity, seeking to know is the necessary and sufficient condition for knowing what is clear. There is no rational justification for failure to know what is clear. One has to neglect, avoid, resist, or deny reason in order to avoid what is clear. A person may fail to know what is clear even while claiming to know what is clear. If one knows what is clear, one should be able to show what is clear, and be able to overcome commonly held objections to what is clear.

If some things are clear, then basic things are clear. Thinking, by nature, is presuppositional. We think of what is less basic in light of what is more basic. If what is more basic is not clear, then what is less basic cannot be clear, and therefore nothing can be clear. If there is agreement on what is more basic, which is clear, there will be agreement on what is less basic.

Basic things are searched out in the most basic questions we can ask. How is knowledge possible? What is real? What ought I to do? How knowledge is possible requires attention to the nature of thought and to reason as the laws of thought. It requires attention to the relation of truth and meaning, and to reason as the test of meaning. It requires attention to experience and to the interpretation of experience in light of one's basic beliefs. "What is real?" requires the distinction between the temporal and the eternal, and attention to the questions whether there must be something eternal or whether it is possible that nothing is eternal. It deals with the question whether all is eternal, in some form or other, or whether only some (i.e., God) is eternal.

One's view of the origin and nature of man will depend on one's view of what is real. The question "What ought I to do?" is based on the reality of choice and of values, which assume the notion of the highest value or the good. One's conception of good and evil will depend on one's conception of human nature. If therefore some things are clear, and the basic things are clear, then the basic things about God and man and good and evil are clear to reason.[1]

While knowing what is clear requires ability to show what is clear, showing what is clear does not require persuading another of what is clear. To show what is clear requires giving a sound argument (valid inference and true premises). Sound arguments are persuasive only if one is committed to reason, and one's response to a sound argument reveals one's commitment. While sound arguments may not persuade, they compel change in the attentive hearer. The hearer must agree or try to show that the argument given is not sound. If this response is not merely a quibble, it will call into question what is more basic that has been taken as common ground. A response may go so far as to question the nature and the authority of reason itself. A basic belief may thus be professed apart from or against reason. This change in position is one way in which a sound argument is compelling.

If basic beliefs are clear to reason, then in a step-by-step process, by good and necessary consequences, less basic beliefs can also be clear to reason. A set of beliefs so derived constitutes a coherent worldview. A worldview seeks to make sense of all aspects of human experience in order to satisfy the human need for meaning.[2] A coherent world-view provides and retains meaning in light of the internal and external challenges of reason.[3] A coherent worldview thus secures the basis of a lasting culture.

---

1. Do not proceed if you do not agree that some things are clear. See Appendix 1 on the Prin-ciple of Clarity and Common Ground, the necessary condition for thought and discourse.

2. What we believe is expressed in what we do. A comprehensive set of beliefs (worldview) is expressed in a way of life. A widely shared worldview is expressed in a widely shared way of life, i.e., a culture. The meaning of a coherent worldview is lasting and therefore secures the basis of a lasting culture.

3. An internal challenge of reason arises when one becomes aware that two beliefs within one's set of beliefs are not logically consistent with each other. An external challenge of reason arises when one is faced with having to give a reason for holding to one set of beliefs rather than an alternative set of beliefs.

WHAT IS PHILOSOPHY?

Philosophy is the discipline which deals with basic questions. In contrast to popular misconceptions and current academic limitations, philosophy deals with fundamental issues applicable to all persons and all aspects of life. It is best understood in terms of its several features: area, attitude, method, application, and system.

1. As an *area*, philosophy is concerned with the *foundation and goal* of human life. Philosophy deals with the foundational questions. How do I know? Is knowledge possible or is everything a matter of opinion and interpretation? On the basis of the answers to these questions dealt with in epistemology, it deals with the question of being,[4] of what exists and what has always existed, or, what is eternal? On the basis of answers to these questions dealt with in metaphysics, it deals with the questions of human origin, human nature, and the human identity. It deals also with the question of human destiny—with the meaning and purpose of life, with the question "What is the good for man?"—questions dealt with in ethics. No other discipline answers these questions—neither the natural sciences, nor the social sciences, nor the arts. While views of human origin and destiny are assumed, implied, or declared by other academic disciplines, as well as in revealed religions, their assumptions of epistemology, metaphysics, and ethics are not critically examined, nor are attempts made to show these assumptions are true over and against alternative views.

Answers to foundational questions are for all people, not just for some. These answers may be held thoughtfully, based on knowledge, or casually, or perhaps even zealously, without the thought process that is necessary for knowledge. The foundation of each discipline must be secured through critical thinking. This is attempted by philosophy in philosophy of science, philosophy of religion, philosophy of art, philosophy of law, philosophy of history, etc. Philosophy is not one discipline among many. It is foundational in principle to all other

---

4. There is a recurrent question as to which is more basic: epistemology or metaphysics? If we were not rational in our *being* we could not think. So, being precedes thought as the subject or thinker of the thought. But in our thought about being, thought precedes being as the object of thought, or what is thought about. Since metaphysics is *thought* about being, epistemology (as thought about thought) is more basic than metaphysics.

disciplines. In practice, more often than not, philosophy may be done inadequately by being insufficiently self-critical and its conclusions therefore are rightly resisted. What this calls for is not the despair of skepticism or resort to fideism, but more critical thinking at a more basic level and therefore more, not less, philosophy.

Philosophy as foundational underscores the idea that thinking is presuppositional—we think of the less basic in light of the more basic. It anticipates all that is to be built upon the foundation, which is one's world and life view. It anticipates the need for strength—for foundation built upon rock, not sand—which can withstand challenges through ages, and support the weight of the fullness of human civilization. It anticipates the needs of one's personal life as well as corporate life for a city with foundations.

2. Philosophy is an *attitude*. It is the *love of wisdom*, which is what the term "philosophy" literally means. Wisdom is practical in that it guides practice, all of what we do, in a coherent way. One has wisdom if one knows the good and the means to the good. The good is the end-in-itself or man's chief end, sought for its own sake, not for the sake of anything else. Love for the good, for what is of highest value, engenders love of wisdom by which we come to possess the good. The good is spoken of as life—meaningful life that is both lasting and full. The corollary of this love of life is fear of meaningless existence, which is death. This fear leads us to seek diligently to understand, and is the beginning of wisdom. Love of the good brings us into the fullness of that wisdom.

But some do not seek wisdom. Apart from random factors in the ordinary course of things, some take no thought about the good or for the future consequences of their current practice. In the view of the simple, there is no need to heed counsel. Some believe they already have wisdom and therefore do not seek wisdom. There is a foolish complacency which makes a person resistant to correction or instruction. In either case, there is no love of wisdom, and no diligent seeking to understand. While some in complacency do not seek, no one, apart from suffering, is diligent in seeking. While the beginning of wisdom is to avoid suffering, only through much suffering do we enter more fully into wisdom.

3. Philosophy is a *method*. It is the *critical use of reason* as the test for meaning. Reason in itself is the laws of thought (the law of identity, non-contradiction, and excluded middle) by which concepts are formed, related in judgments, and then supported in arguments. Meaning is more basic than truth. One has to grasp the meaning of a statement before asserting its truth. For example, what do the following mean: "God is love" or "grod is lube" or "bliks are grue"? Furthermore, if a statement violates a law of thought, it cannot be thought and therefore lacks meaning. For example: "s is both *p* and *non-p*" (at the same time and in the same respect); "a ball is both black and non-black" (at the same time and in the same respect); or, "this statement is both true and not true" (at the same time and in the same respect). What is contrary to the laws of thought cannot be thought and has no meaning, and therefore cannot be true.

In the context of conflicts—philosophical, personal, or political, critical thinking seeks to recognize assumptions and implications and examines a set of beliefs for rational coherence. It is willing to do the required work of identifying uncritically held assumptions, and then testing these basic beliefs and their implications for coherence of meaning. By establishing agreement on what is more basic, disputes about what is less basic can be resolved. The persistence of conflicts shows lack of critical thinking on one or both sides. One may be indifferent to (or despair of) resolving conflicts, before having recognized the nature and power of critical thinking. Strong convictions based on intuition, sense experience, or testimony should not be confused with, and are no substitutes for, convictions based upon rational justification through critical thinking. And the critical use of reason should not be confused with its other uses: formative, interpretative, and constructive (see *Reason in Its Use*, Chapter 1). In critical thinking, reason is the test for meaning.

4. Philosophy is an *application*, that of *self-examination*. The first application of critical thinking is to one's own basic belief. The Socratic dictum, "The unexamined life is not worth living," is basic in philosophy. Self-examination is a mark of integrity—a concern for consistency, which is necessary and sufficient for knowledge. The focus is first on oneself rather than on another, and upon one's own basic belief rather than upon secondary belief. Because we are more or less

conscious and consistent, we may not notice our own uncritically held assumptions, even while advocating self-examination. We may make knowledge claims while denying a necessary condition for the possibility of knowledge.

To question oneself or to let one's self be called into question is difficult, especially if it is done later in life, after one has made significant intellectual commitments and investments. The more one has to change, the more subjectively difficult it is to consider change. Psychological and practical considerations co-op the philosophical concern for truth. New wine cannot be contained in old wineskins. But if basic things are clear, then seeking to know what is coherent at the basic level is not objectively difficult. One is rationally obligated to test contradictory basic beliefs for logical coherence and possibility before adopting one and rejecting the other. Self-examination is the source of rational justification for one's belief. Rational justification satisfies the moral requirements for full participation in human society as the society of rational beings. It likewise gives assurance of truth and firmness of the foundation on which we build our lives.

5. Philosophy is a *system*, a *world and life view*. A worldview attempts to make sense of all aspects of human existence as a coherent whole, building upon the foundation. Differing cultures are expressions of differing worldviews. What makes sense rationally in one worldview may not make sense in another, given differing starting points. Culture wars are the expression of deeper philosophical issues which are seldom discussed. While worldviews differ, they share formal similarities as worldviews. In every worldview there are basic beliefs about epistemological authority, about what is real, and about the good. These are rationally connected and together are used to interpret (give meaning to) one's experience. In seeking to make sense of the world, each view aims at rational coherence.

Worldviews are developed in individuals and cultures over time. They are held more or less consciously and consistently and are subject to challenges of reason by those who stand inside or outside the worldview. If the foundation is inadequate to the task of supporting a coherent worldview, meaning in the culture diminishes and divisions appear. With the decrease of meaning, there is an increase of hedonic excess to fill the emptiness of life. Cultural decay sets in and, eventually, cultural collapse.[5] Many cultures in world history have collapsed after centuries of such challenges. Those that remain are not now so promising. Intellectual apathy, weariness, and cynicism are the prevailing mood today. This mood presents a new level of intellectual challenge and calls for a deeper level of philosophical response.

WHAT IS REASON?

Reason is central to philosophy and to human existence. Yet there are disputes about the role of reason because the nature of reason in its most basic sense has not been kept in focus and made the basis of all else that is said about reason. There are disputes about the relation of faith and reason, reason and enlightenment rationalism, rationalism and scientific empiricism, and reason and immediate knowledge by intuition. To avoid these and like disputes, it is necessary to make clear what reason is in itself, what reason is in its use, and what reason is in us. If there is agreement on what is more basic, there can and will be agreement on what is less basic.

Reason in Itself

First, reason in itself is the laws of thought, which are: the law of identity (*a* is *a*); the law of non-contradiction (not both *a* and *non-a*, at the same time and in the same respect); and the law of excluded middle (either *a* or *non-a*).[6] If there are other laws of thought, they are based on these laws as basic. Their status as laws make thought possible, as the laws of life make life possible. If a law of life (breathing, for example) is violated, life ceases. So, if a law of thought is violated,

---

5. Talk of culture must be understood in relation to worldview, and talk of worldview in relation to the need for meaning. Cultures differ as worldviews differ, and change as worldviews change. Focus on the need for meaning, and the consequences of the lack of meaning, distinguish this view of culture from the views of Toynbee and Huntington, particularly the concept and dynamics of culture: Arnold J. Toynbee, and D.C. Somervell, eds, *A Study of History.* (Oxford: Oxford University Press, 1987) and Samuel P. Huntington, *The Clash of Civilizations* (New York: Simon and Schuster, 1996).

6. The law of excluded middle has sometimes been doubted because of a faulty application (the black or white fallacy, rather than the black or non-black distinction). (See also: application to bald or not-bald in Chapter 2, *Sources of Skepticism*, under *Reason: Its Uses, Its Limits, and Its Limited Use.*)

thought ceases. What is contrary to a law of thought, when seen as such, cannot be thought.

The law of identity identifies and distinguishes *a* and *non-a* at the same time: *a* is *a*; *a* is not *non-a*, which is to say, a thing is what it is. Rock is rock; fish is fish; finite is finite; finite is not infinite; being is being, being is not non-being. To conceive of *a* is to conceive of *non-a* and to distinguish the two. To say *a* is different from, and simultaneously the same as, *non-a* is to lose the meaning of "same" and "different" and as a consequence, if one is being consistent, to lose all meaning. Certain claims, upon analysis, will be seen to be saying *a* is *non-a*—the eternal is non-eternal (that is, temporal), being is non-being. Internal incoherence of a view or mutual contradiction between two views is sometimes accommodated by pronouncing that reason is limited. This point will be revisited many times as we work through recurrent moves and maneuvers which attempt to show the limits of reason.

These laws of thought, beginning with the law of identity, assume the reality of essences, which are permanent qualities by which a thing can be identified and distinguished from all else. They assume the notion of being and properties of being, of permanence (of some sort), and of change and causes of change. The consequence of consistently denying the reality of essences, permanence, change, and causality is to make meaningful thought impossible and is therefore inherently self-defeating. Each law of thought is necessarily implicated in the other. Attempts to qualify any law so as to disqualify it will be examined in the course of showing that some things are clear to reason. Even when attempts are made to limit reason, reason is still commonly understood to be these laws of thought: identity, non-contradiction, and excluded middle. Disagreements or conflicts between thoughts cannot be understood apart from the laws of thought, so these laws of thought are most basic.

Reason in Its Use

Conflicts regarding reason are more related to the use of reason rather than to reason in itself. Several uses of reason should be distinguished. Reason in its use is first formative, then critical, then interpretive, and lastly constructive.

The first use of reason is *formative*—it is used to form concepts, judgments, and arguments, which are the forms of all thought. After examining the sources of skepticism, in order to show how knowledge is possible by reason and argument, concepts, judgments, and arguments will each be explained and analyzed. What needs to be noted here is that, even when arguments are not being given, in every thought reason is being used to form concepts and judgments. And if concepts are not well formed, that is, if *a* is not adequately distinguished from *non-a*, the meaning of *a* is obscured or is lacking. If meaning at the level of concept is lacking, meaning at the level of judgments will also be lacking. Neither speaker nor hearer will understand the meaning of what is being asserted and the assertion of the judgment is made void.

The second use of reason is the *critical* use of reason as the test for meaning. Meaning is more basic than truth. One has to understand the meaning of a statement before judging its truth. Reason is used to understand meaning. What is contrary to a law of thought cannot be thought. It lacks meaning and cannot be understood. A meaningless statement cannot be true. To meaningfully assert any statement requires the use of reason to grasp its meaning and therefore requires the critical use of reason. Assertions without meaning are unintelligible, and meaning without reason is not possible. No assertion without the critical use of reason is meaningful to the speaker or hearer. Many assertions, pronouncements, declarations, and slogans made, often with passionate intensity, turn out, upon a little analysis, to lack meaning. The critical use of reason distinguishes sense from apparent sense and so keeps us from believing nonsense.

A third use of reason is to *interpret*[7] experience in light of one's basic beliefs. No experience is meaningful without interpretation. Common sense and science often fail to distinguish between appear-

---

7. Several factors affect interpretation, the primary one being one's *presupposition*. The degree of consciousness and consistency with which one's presupposition is held depends on one's *personality* inclination (focus upon intellectual, emotional, or practical concerns), one's *background* (cultural factors as they affect one's education in the broad sense), and one's *mood* (one's willingness to seek understanding at any given time). Further, there is the need to understand the alternative position in light of its assumptions, not one's own. There is likewise a need to recognize the many *layers* of context or assumptions used in interpretation. All of this is comprehended under the principle of presuppositional thinking: we think of the less basic in light of the more basic.

ances in the mind and reality outside the mind, between pure data and interpretation of data. Mystical or intuitive experience is neither self-certifying nor meaningful without interpretation. Narratives of literature, history, and scripture likewise are interpreted in light of basic belief, though literalists may deny that any interpretation is taking place.[8] Sometimes an entire belief system (for example, theism) may be deconstructed or re-interpreted in light of another belief system (naturalism) by a hermeneutic of suspicion—as if naturalism were metaphysically neutral. Where interpretation is recognized, the temptation is to despair in saying "all is interpretation" (postmodernism), or (as one often hears), "it is all a matter of interpretation." But since interpretation is in light of one's basic belief, reason can be used critically to test basic beliefs for meaning.

Fourth and last, reason is used to *construct* a coherent world and life view (see *Philosophy as a System*, Chapter 1). In man's basic need for meaning, every dimension of life gets connected. In each worldview, some things must be said and some things cannot be said, given the requirements of reason for system and coherence. The constructive use of reason is not the critical use of reason, but its claims are often passed off as "the deliverance of reason."[9] This claim of the constructive use of reason, made in the name of reason, is what is often called rationalism. In rejecting the pretensions made in the name of reason, many uncritically denounce reason generally and indiscriminately, both in itself and in its other uses. The limits of reason within a given system are not to be identified with the limits of reason *per se*. Reason in itself must be distinguished from reason in its (several) uses and from reason in us.

---

8. The more one becomes aware of one's assumptions, the more one is aware of interpretations taking place. Those inclined to tradition and common sense (naïve realism) are generally less aware of their assumptions and may insist that no interpretation is taking place. Epistemological self-consciousness is increased through dialogue, here approached through critical analysis of basic beliefs of alternative worldviews.

9. Some philosophers, more than others, engage in developing systematically the implications of their basic beliefs (Plato, Spinoza, Hegel). These are often taken as exemplary users of reason, and their teachings as "the deliverances of reason." But the constructive use of reason is not the critical use of reason, especially at the level of basic belief. Plato did not analyze critically his assumptions that the soul and matter are eternal. The system is only as sound as the assumptions. If matter and the soul are not eternal, then the system *as a system* is fundamentally flawed. A flawed system does not negate passion and brilliance in so much as the particulars within the system.

Reason in Us

Reason in us is natural, ontological, transcendental, and fundamental. Reason as the laws of thought in us is *natural*, not conventional. It is universal, the same in all who think. There is not a Greek and a non-Greek rationality; there is not a male and a female rationality; there is not an old and a young, or a rich and a poor rationality, although these have become lines of division among human beings. Reason, as the laws of thought in us, is the common ground for all who think. It is the common ground between theists and non-theists, even when different claims are being made about reason based on different views of reality and human nature. To make any claim using concepts, judgments, and arguments is to use reason. No one professes to make a claim which is both true and not true, at the same time and in the same respect. One cannot deny that reason is the common ground and yet hold that contradictory statements cannot both be true. That would be to affirm the law of non-contradiction, a law of reason, as common ground, while denying reason is the common ground.

Reason is *ontological*. It applies to being as well as to thought. There are no square-circles. This is known by reason alone. What is logically impossible is ontologically impossible.[10] There is no being from non-being; there is no uncaused event (see Chapter 4). Reason applies to all being, to the highest being, to God's being. God is not both *a* and *non-a*. God is not both eternal and non-eternal, at the same time and in the same respect. As an aspect of God's being, reason is eternal, not created. The laws of nature in theism are created; the laws of reason are not created, but that by which creation comes to be. Miracles may be acts of God which stand above, apart from, or against the laws of nature, since these are created laws, but miracles cannot be against reason. If water is changed into wine, it is not both water and not-water (that is to say, wine) at the same time. Claims made by science or by religion or by philosophy which go against reason are unwarranted and cannot stand.

---

10. Plato, *Complete Works*, ed. John M. Cooper and D.S. Hutchinson (Indianapolis, IN: Hackett Publishing Company, 1997), "Republic," 509. Here, the first principle of being, the *principium essendi*, coincides with the first principle of knowledge, the *principium cognoscendi*. This is implicit in saying thought is about being. Plato affirmed that the light which is higher than the sun (illustrated in the Allegory of the Cave) is both the source of being and the source of the intelligibility of being.

Reason is *transcendental*. It is authoritative. It stands above all thinking and makes thinking possible. It cannot be questioned for it makes questioning possible. It is self-attesting. It testifies to itself and cannot be testified to by another. It is the highest authority in the realm of human knowledge.[11] The deliverances of prophets, poets, philosophers, and physicists must be in accord with reason. Prophets must speak in the name of God, consistent with what is clear about God from creation. The poet's intuition is not infallible in a morally fallible world. Philosophers cannot deny reason and make any affirmation about being. So too, physicists cannot deny reason in affirming uncaused events in the origin of the universe or in quantum physics.

Reason is *fundamental*. It is fundamental to other aspects of human personality. Beliefs direct desires and together they both move the will. We desire what we believe is the good and act to achieve what we desire. The apparent conflict between belief and desire and belief and the will are to be explained by inconsistencies and insufficiencies in understanding, lacks which are culpable or inexcusable in light of clarity. Reason is fundamental also in that its use is the source of man's greatest happiness and its disuse is the source of man's deepest misery. By reason we understand the meaning of things. Meaning absorbs and satisfies our attention. We are willing to die to preserve what gives life meaning. The lack of meaning leaves us empty and bored. We seek to escape the emptiness and boredom through excess, which never satisfies, or through death, by suicide.

Reason, as the source of meaning, is what is most basic. There will be need to return often to what is briefly sketched here. Disputes are to be resolved by agreeing on what is more basic, and reason is most basic. Reason does not persuade and should not be expected to persuade. Reason clarifies and makes us more aware. In clarifying, it compels greater consistency; it moves us one way or the other. It is the light which shines in the darkness and which cannot be withstood by the darkness. There is a choice, in the end. The choice is between reason and no reason, between meaning and no meaning, between light and darkness, between life and death.

---

11. In the prologue to his *Gospel*, John wrote: "All things were made by him" (the Logos). He goes on to say, "In him (the Logos) was life; and the life was the light of men." Many have identified this light with reason, and as such, the highest authority, which is self-attesting.

Chapter 2

———

SOURCES OF SKEPTICISM
AND FIDEISM

E PISTEMOLOGY CONSIDERS THE QUESTION "How do I know?" It must first consider the question "Is knowledge possible?" Here we will look at and respond to the claims of skepticism and fideism. We will look at informal fallacies, which are common obstacles to engaging in argument. In Chapters 3 and 4, we will look at a commonly understood definition of knowledge and objections to it. We will sketch an outline of how we can know by reason and argument and then begin application to basic beliefs in metaphysics—What is real or eternal?

SOURCES OF SKEPTICISM

Skepticism is a form of intellectual despair.[1] There are several sources of skepticism which overlap, reinforce each other, and add up to create despair. Sources of skepticism depend on one's intellectual journey.

---

1. Alan Bailey, *Sextus Empiricus and Pyrrhonean Skepticism* (Oxford: Clarendon Press, 2002), Chapters 1, 4, and 6. Sextus Empiricus, a Greek skeptic of the third century C.E., would define a skeptic as one who goes on searching, in contrast to dogmatists who think they have found answers, and to Academics who claim it is a search for inapprehensibles. But there is no hope (hence, intellectual despair) of finding answers for then one would no longer be a skeptic but a dogmatist. The skeptic believes in advance the universal affirmative statement that "To every argument an equal argument is opposed," in consequence of which the skeptic claims to cease to dogmatize. For the skeptic then, "Some being comes from non-being" is as plausible as "No being comes from non-being." Ceasing to dogmatize means that "We do not make any positive assertion that anything we shall say is wholly as we affirm it to be." There is a "suspension of judgment" which is "a cessation of the thought process in consequence of which we neither deny or affirm anything." A cessation

They depend on one's epistemological point of departure and one's view of the goal or the good. Some are common, wide but not deep; some are philosophical, deep but not wide; and some are both wide and deep, where philosophy has influenced popular culture. Consistent skepticism denies that anything is clear. Skepticism is rooted in uncritically held assumptions.

Worldview Pluralism

There are many worldviews, and in any worldview there are many divisions. Some of these divisions are longstanding and new divisions arise. All of this is *prima facie* evidence that the truth has not been reached and not likely to be reached. Skepticism seems to be an appropriate response to the existence of many worldviews.

Other responses, however, can be considered. While there are many views there are not many basic views. With respect to what is real or eternal, there are only two basic views: "all is eternal" (in some form or other), or "only some is eternal" (that is, some is eternal and some is not eternal). These views are contradictory; both cannot be true and both cannot be false. And it should be clear to reason which of the two contradictory views lacks coherence of meaning. Furthermore, the many views are held according to differing degrees of consciousness and consistency. No one is fully conscious of and consistent in one's basic beliefs. There is an admixture of both basic beliefs in each person, with one being more basic (subjectively) than the other in each person. One's presupposition, epistemological personality (see *Reason and Personality*, Chapter 2), and cultural upbringing (background) affect the degree of consciousness and consistency in one's belief system. When conflicting beliefs within one's doxastic system surface, the belief which prevails in a person will depend on one's mood, that is, one's willingness at the moment to engage in critical thinking to consistently resolve the inconsistency.

---

of the thought process by the skeptic is a move to silence, a move required for consistency. See also: https://plato.stanford.edu/entries/skepticism-ancient

Pragmatism and Skepticism: What Matters Is What Works

Since in all cultures human beings are born, grow, reproduce, and die regardless of belief systems, these systems are thought to be not that relevant in relation to basic practical matters. It is thought that since the basic results are the same, differences in belief do not matter. The different beliefs are, pragmatically speaking, the same.

In response it can be said that we as persons do make choices about how we live, and about the worldview and values of others we associate with. It matters if we live under freedom or not, whether we are educated or not, whether we are monogamous or not. We seek more than animal survival. Belief systems shape cultural choices, and what works depends on one's view of the good, which depends on one's belief system. Pragmatism (Peirce, James, Dewey, Rorty) therefore cannot side-step metaphysical beliefs and worldviews based on these. If mere instinctive animal existence is all that matters ("Fill their bellies and empty their heads"—Lao-Tzu), then discussion is beside the point. But man does not live by bread alone; we need meaning. Rational existence goes beyond animal existence.

Truth and Power: Who Is to Say Which View Is Right?

The way things seem to work out in history is by a power play or by tradition. Truth comes out of the end of a gun, imposed on a conquered people (see Foucault). It is later internalized and transmitted as the received tradition. The invaded are colonized, mind and body. Post-colonials who claim to resist hegemony can do so only to a degree. Those at a distance look on and ask, "Who is to say which view is right?"

This version of history is overly simplistic. Ideas are never inserted by mere power. They attempt to gain footing by ideology and propaganda which rationalize the exercise of power. People who lose a grasp on reality are swayed by propaganda insofar as they do not think critically. In the *Brave New World*, unless the populace is continually drugged ("Religion is the opiate of the masses"—Marx), new ideas arise. The mere antithesis will naturally occur to some. So there are Gulags, but never enough. And the conquerors are often overtaken by the ideas of the conquered (the Goths and Vandals in Europe, and the Mongols in East and West and South Asia). In the final analysis, it is not who is to say what is right, but what is to say. Lasting authority is rational, not personal. It is based on insight, not might. Reason as the laws of thought is what is to say, and reason is common to all and in all.

Construction and Deconstruction: It Is All a Matter of Interpretation

In contrast to objectivist claims in modernist narratives of reality, grounded in the natural and social sciences, postmoderns have discerned meta-narratives at work in constructing any narrative of reality. Everywhere and always interpretation and construction are at work, in contrast to a neutral or objective point of view. Paradigms may shift in science. The current naturalistic evolutionary model replaced the theistic/creation model and may itself one day be replaced. In the reading of literature, history, and scripture, interpretation is at work. Our own life experiences, inner and outer, are constantly being interpreted and reinterpreted by us and others. We have outgrown the naïve objective neutrality of modernism and have entered the age of hermeneutics in which no grand narrative is to be privileged or valorized. Attempts to deconstruct dominant narratives are themselves merely alternative narratives told in light of meta-narratives which are current.

In response it can be said that it is a higher level of awareness to recognize interpretation and construction at work. These are two functions of reason in addition to the formative and the critical uses of reason. But philosophy does not end with noticing interpretation; rather it begins there. It recognizes that no experience is meaningful without interpretation, and that we interpret experience in light of our basic beliefs. It recognizes that we construct a coherent world and life view based on interpretation, using good and necessary consequences. The first work of philosophy then is to test basic beliefs for coherence of meaning. Some basic beliefs are seen to be incoherent upon critical examination. Interpretation grounded in an incoherent basic belief cannot be sound. One may say it is all a matter of interpretation, but not all interpretations are coherent.

Relativism and Tolerance: It Is All Relative

Tolerance is seen by many as a cardinal virtue. Absolute claims are seen as incompatible with tolerance. They are also seen as closed-minded, and, as a matter of fact, contrary to the obvious reality of cultural relativism. Relativism requires religious tolerance, and tolerance in turn presupposes relativism, which assumes an absolute skepticism regarding any absolute claim. Tolerance is a starting point of argument; it is not something to be argued for. Anyone with politically correct sensibilities would know this. Diversity is to be affirmed. The Other is not to be judged and excluded by external standards, but is to be included in a multi-cultural world.

In response it must be said that the relative tolerance of cultural relativism is not the absolute tolerance of individual liberty. Individual human rights are not guaranteed by cultural relativism which would absolutize for the individual the cultural standard of the group into which one has been born or raised. Individual human rights depend on one's view of human nature and of the good. Historically, it appeared in the *Declaration of Independence* that "all men are created equal" and that "they are endowed by their Creator with certain unalienable Rights." (Happiness, though, should not be considered the good; and without the good these rights may cause conflict and intolerance.) Diversity is not merely in gender and ethnicity, but is intellectual, in worldviews, which cuts across all other diversity. But affirming intellectual diversity would be affirming contradictory views. To include all, without freedom to discuss basic beliefs, is to exclude all from one and the same rational community, and to undo individual communities themselves. For the obvious fact of cultural relativism is that each culture expresses a worldview and that values in each are relative (or rationally related) to the basic beliefs of that worldview. Worldviews are constructed and altered to increase and preserve meaning. To flash freeze a culture by denying change through the process of a critical search for meaning is to falsely absolutize a culture and to become intolerant of the fundamental human need for meaning. In the name of openness, the mind of relativism has become closed.

Tradition and Transcendence: No View from Above

Tradition is both universal and unique. Each person has a tradition or background in which one has been brought up. Yet the background for each person is, when fully accounted for, unique. Each person grows accustomed to one's familiar surroundings; each person begins one's epistemological journey from familiar territory. What we are comfortable with becomes the norm for truth. What is given by testimony, filtered by the uniqueness of our being from our earliest and most impressionable age, is taken as truth, at least to begin with. And some have said that however far we go, we never leave home. Our destination (destiny) is said to be determined by our origin: by early childhood (Freud); by socio-economics (Marx); by the sum of pleasure/pain stimuli (Skinner); by biology (Darwin); or by geography (we were the land's before the land was ours). When tradition in the broad or narrow sense is taken as the standard of truth, and we encounter other traditions, our convictions either harden into prejudices or melt into uncertainties. We are then either estranged from others, as defined by our tradition, or from ourselves, as defined by our traditions.

Can we transcend tradition or are we always historically situated? Is every aspect of our being conditioned or only some aspects? Are basic aspects and basic beliefs conditioned? Are we first Asian or European, or are we first human? Can we communicate with others or are we locked out by alterity and incommensurability? Can we cross cultures? Can we leave ours and enter another by changing our basic beliefs and grow in our understanding of a new culture as we grew in understanding of our earlier culture? It seems that conversions are too commonplace to deny. We can transcend tradition because, while all traditions seek in common to make sense of the world, all are not formed on foundations that have been equally subjected to critical reflection. Persons, as they come to think critically about basic things, may reject or reaffirm their tradition based on what they discover by critical thinking. While the rate of growth in understanding a new culture may be slowed by what must be unlearned from the old, the critical understanding can far exceed the merely traditional process which receives testimony without understanding. Critical thinking receives testimony based on understanding insofar as the meaning of testimony is consistent with basic things that are clear to reason, which is available to all persons.

Persuasion and Proof: Pseudo-argument and Sound Argument

Given all our differences and different interests, short of the actual use of force to get our way, we seek to persuade. Yet given our differences, most of which arise from lack of critical self-examination, we do not seek to persuade through the critical use of reason. Nor are we inclined to be so persuaded. There arises then a yawning gap between persuasion and proof, between rhetoric and logic, between propaganda and dialogue, between pseudo-argument and sound argument. Appeal is made to unenlightened self-interest rather than the good. Authority is personal rather than rational. Intuition by association replaces rational inference. Meaning is casually ignored or equivocated, all for presumed self-interest rather than common interest through common understanding. Since we are regularly persuaded by pseudo-arguments (see the list of Informal Fallacies), we persuade others in the same way. When pseudo-arguments do not work, we think no argument will work and give up on argument. And when sound arguments do not persuade, we think they are without any effect and give up on argument. Instead of working to understand what went wrong, we despair and yield to skepticism.

If the good can be attained apart from understanding, why should we trouble ourselves or others with sound argument? Or, if lack of understanding has no long-term or lasting effect, why trouble ourselves or others to understand? But if the need for meaning through understanding is vital, if it makes all the difference in the world, if it is a matter of (spiritual) life and death both now and always, then seeking to understand is not seen as a burden. The characteristics of the good must be brought into view and sustained in view, deepened in understanding, integrated into one's worldview, as well as incorporated into a way of life for all and by all who see the good to be intrinsically pleasurable. All choosing and valuing is in relation to the good. The effort to understand and to not be seduced by appearances of alluring pseudo-arguments makes sense only in relation to the good. Since the good is both grounded in and required by human nature, it is not only knowable, but inescapable, and attainable by all. The siren song of intellectual despair is a lament grounded neither in our being nor in other beings, but in the non-being of pseudo-arguments.

Appearance and Reality: Common Sense and Realism

Many beliefs spontaneously occur by the constitution of our being. The existence of the external world, other minds, and memory beliefs (for example, of where we were an hour ago) are immediately given and described as properly basic (Plantinga) or as common sense (Reid). In all ages, all people act on the basis of common sense almost all the time. Common sense is the simplest form of realism. It uncritically or naively takes the world as it appears for reality. It assumes that appearance is reality. For example: the ocean is blue; the earth is flat; the sun rises in the east. These are all appearances, not reality; yet they have been believed by all at some time. These judgments take the condition of the perceiver for granted. They work for everyday practical purposes until these purposes change or until the condition of the perceiver changes.

Challenges to realism have been raised by anti-realism (see Chapter 6). Locke's representational realism distinguished primary qualities (size and shape) as real while secondary qualities (color, hardness) are mind-dependent. Berkeley showed that both are mind-dependent and Hume showed we have no sense experience of cause or of mind. Kant's critical realism distinguished the phenomenal world as mind-dependent and knowable from the noumenal world as mind-independent but unknowable. Hegel, Schopenhauer, and Bradley postulated varying degrees of idealism to fill this unknown, all very far from common sense, but no closer to knowledge of reality. Plantinga's contemporary return to Reid's common sense philosophy gains for it a place at the table by way of *prima facie* warrant; but without a principle of exclusion from the table, clarity and inexcusability become excluded. On this road to epistemological perdition where no one is lost, no one can be saved.

Intuition and Certainty: Sign and Reality

Intuition as a direct immediate awareness of reality is relied upon by many as the source of certainty. It is direct and immediate in that it moves immediately, that is, non-inferentially, from the sign perceived to the reality, or takes the sign for the reality. For example: pleasure is the sign of the good (or the effect of possessing what we believe to be the good). A smile is a sign of friendliness. Sex is the sign and seal of love and is often taken as the reality or the proof of love. A beautiful person (outwardly well-formed) is taken as a good person (inwardly well-formed). The more passionate the feeling aroused by the sign (or symbol) the greater the certainty. The particular by metaphor reveals the universal. For Keats, "truth is beauty, beauty truth—that is all you know on earth and all you need to know." Intuition (the heart, not the head) guides us into (and out of) relationships. Artists and musicians feel deeply and express that feeling by natural signs (sound, color) in-tuited. Mystics in every land and every age, in every worldview, claim to experience oneness with ultimate reality. Intuition takes itself to be infallible (in perceiving sign/reality relationships) insofar as it assumes this is a morally ideal world. For Rousseau, and for many, human be-ings are seen as naturally good, based on intuition; evil arises not from within but from outside the person (in the environment).

We do not have good reason to believe that this is a morally ideal world, that the sign is always accompanied by the reality, that evil arises only from without. A person may smile and smile and be a vil-lain (Shakespeare's Iago). Sensibility is not a better guide to relation-ships than sense (Jane Austin's *Sense and Sensibility*). Passion is not a guide for politics. Passion can be equal on both sides of a controversy and a person may switch sides with equal passion. One can have zeal without knowledge. Keats found truth is beauty only when frozen to-gether in art (*Ode to the Grecian Urn*), not elsewhere (*Lamia, La Belle Dame sans Merci, Eve of Saint Agnes*). Socrates did not find knowledge among the poets, and Plato restricted artists in the republic. Mystics, insofar as they think about their mystical experiences, interpret their experience differently (Nirvana, Brahman, Tao, God). Rousseau does not get a free pass on his claim that evil is from one's environment in light of the creation–fall–redemption worldview: out of the heart proceed evil thoughts (Jesus); the heart is deceitful above all else (Jer-emiah). Feelings may arise from several sources: one's biology, one's basic beliefs, or one's natural sensibility, all of which are variable and co-mingle, making one's feelings and intuitions less than infallible and even less than a generally reliable guide in basic matters.

Empiricism: Knowledge by Sense Experience

Empiricism is the epistemological view that all knowledge arises from sense experience. Radical empiricism goes beyond sense experience to affirm inner or religious experience grounded in intuition. Empiricism begins with common sense realism. Proof is by seeing and touching. It has been articulated and developed in the British empiricist tradition and has been assumed in much of contemporary analytical philosophy. It has been applied to meaning as well: the meaning of a statement is its method of verification. If there is no empirical way to verify the truth of a statement, that statement is considered meaningless. Empiricism has increasingly been assumed in the natural sciences and natural science is becoming the stronghold of empiricism. It professes to be the only true source of knowledge, publicly verifiable, and therefore authoritative for all. It is validated by its recurrent technological miracles and it is in turn richly endowed by public grants for research and development.

Science generally, and empiricism particularly, have shown themselves to be vulnerable in a variety of ways. Far from knowing that all knowledge is from sense experience, it may be argued that some knowledge is not from sense experience (for example: there are no square-circles) or that there is no knowledge from sense experience (pure data of sense experience is not meaningful without interpretation). We do not know the reality of an external world from sense experience (as has been observed by Berkeley), or the reality of mind and causality (argued by Hume), or the reality of substance and identity/unity (the position held by Kant). By means of the senses, we do not know there are essences, or universals, or permanence, or concepts, only particulars and momentary sense impressions. Nominalism, skepticism, and legal positivism have been recurrent in ancient, medieval, and modern philosophy when the senses have become the sole source of knowledge. The antinomy of permanence and change has recurred in the East as well, between Madhyamika Buddhism and *Advaita* Vedanta. Scientific knowledge is based on observation and limited by observation. It relies on induction to go from the observed to the unobserved. Induction assumes uniformity of nature. The past and the future are like the present. The forces now operating have always operated and in essentially the same magnitude. Extended further, how things now operate is said to explain how things originate. Observation can falsify general statements. It cannot verify them. Observation cannot disconfirm the existence of non-physical realities without assuming methodological naturalism—that all phenomena can be explained in natural terms. This in turn assumes metaphysical naturalism, that all of reality is natural, that nothing is supernatural.

Given these assumptions, all distinctions can and must be reduced to simpler, natural terms. Mind must be reduced to brain, biology to chemistry, chemistry to physics, and physics to geometry and to mathematics—Pythagoras claimed that numbers are things and things are numbers. Within reductionistic explanation, as anomalies multiply, a paradigm shift may occur but the project goes on. In reductionism, there is no logical or ontological gap between mind and brain, between non-physical mental images and physical neural impulses. There is only the project of empiricism itself, with the promissory note—someday it will be explained, naturalistically, by more observation. Science assumes induction and reduction; it assumes uniformity and naturalism, none of which are based on nor can be based on observation. By transgressing its stated boundaries, it advocates a dogmatic naturalistic interpretation of the world. With good reason, in postmodern consciousness, the world constructed by science is no longer being privileged.

Reason: Its Uses, Its Limits, and Its Limited Use

Reason itself becomes a source of skepticism when it is misused or not fully used. It is misused when used as a source of truth rather than as a test for meaning. It is not fully used when it is used to construct a worldview and not first used critically as a test for the meaning of one's own basic belief. The antinomy of trusting in reason to know the truth and not trusting in reason to know the truth is grounded in the failure to use reason critically. There are several uses of reason which are to be distinguished and used in order, proceeding from the more basic to the less basic use.

Reason has been misused as a source of truth. Certain convictions are treated as self-evident to reason, and foundational, requiring no further need for defense. Descartes' *cogito ergo sum* is said to be self-evident every time it is thought. Thomas Jefferson took it as self-evident that all men are created equal. These views may be true, but the question is, are they self-evident? Are alternative views immediately self-contradictory? Are Hindu, Buddhist, or Naturalist views of the self immediately self-contradictory? Or do they require at least a few steps in reasoning to show they are contradictory? If so, how would Descartes go about showing the steps in reasoning leading to self-contradiction? In showing one's view of the self, must the existence of God first be addressed, and does this require attention, in proper order, to the ontological, cosmological, and teleological arguments? Clarity is not incompatible with a step-by-step approach in argument and seems to require it if thinking proceeds from what is more basic to what is less basic.

Reason has not been fully used if it is not first used critically at the basic level. Reason is said to have reached it limits when more basic issues of permanence and change, unity and diversity, substance and causality, are not first settled. Reason is used to form concepts which grasp the essence of things, the set of qualities which all members have which they always have and which distinguish them, by the law of identity, from non-members. Essences can be questioned where permanence (there must be something eternal) has not been settled. To question the ontological possibility of relationship between *a* and *non-a* is to question the possibility of unity of diversity and whether anything can exist at all, a point not disputed by many. It is not to be assumed that the relationship between *a* and *non-a* is necessarily exclusionary (as being and non-being), but it may be complimentary (as wise and happy), or inclusive (as infinite and finite). Without permanence, essence, unity, and identity, concepts are empty and words become meaningless. To deny the precondition for being and thought, to deny the ontological status of reason, to deny the Logos in the world, is to leap into the abyss of personal and cultural nihilism.

Many have said reason cannot grasp reality for any number of reasons. Aquinas, going back to Aristotle's Unmoved Mover, and later, Kant encountered an antinomy regarding time and creation: the world had a beginning (in time), and, there never was a time when the world did not exist. The antinomy assumes that time itself did not begin with creation, an assumption arising from a failure to understand the nature of time as relative to change. Kant assumed reason cannot grasp the noumenal world (*a priori* categories are mind-imposed on the world as we know it). Yet to distinguish first among things-in-themselves (a chair-in-itself is not a table-in-itself) and then to make the chair-in-itself the cause of what appears, however much the mind shapes its input, is to know much about the noumenal world, making it not a totally unknown. Mahayana sutras decry the intellect as getting stuck in antinomies: "everything has a cause" and "nothing has a cause"; "everything is eternal" and "nothing is eternal." But this is merely to assume that all is one and that contraries are indeed contradictories.[2] Again, it is thought that reason cannot grasp reality. For example, categorical reason cannot grasp the being of Christ as both infinite and finite.[3] One must transcend categorical reason for a transcategorical reason, or for meditative reason, or for a higher "double-bracketed" [[reason]].[4] But this is to assume a rational opposition between the infinite and the finite, rather than saying the infinite does and must include the finite. The same is to be said of reason in relation to the Tao (Lao Tzu), or Anaximander's *apeiron*, or Shankara's Nirguna Brahman—convictions arrived at by not critically examining assumptions.

Again, it is said that reason cannot grasp reality for it cannot grasp the particular. True enough, reason does not give nor does it claim to give the fleeting particulars of sense impression, but it can grasp the abiding uniqueness of a particular—it can grasp the essence of Soc-

---

2. "All is eternal" (universal affirmative) is not contradicted by "none is eternal" (universal negative). These are contraries, which are both universals, and which may both be false at the same time. The contradiction of "all is eternal" is "some is not eternal." Opposing "all is eternal" to "none is eternal" as if those were the only possible oppositions assumes that all is of the same kind, i.e., all is one. To reject this (false) opposition as gross and crude philosophy and then reject reason as incapable of knowing, is to fail to use reason to see that the problem is the false assumption that "all is one."

3. Ashok Gangadean, *Between Worlds——The Emergence of Global Reason* (New York: Peter Lang, 1998), 179-180. "Christ-being is dialectical in the sense that if taken in essential terms as one being which is both finite and infinite at the same time (two natures) it presents itself to understanding as being contradictory . . . Christ-being may be taken of an exemplar of all beings . . . It is transcategorical, like all beings . . . It is only in this way that the Christ can be the real mediator, the savior." But if the infinite is not opposed to, but is inclusive of the finite, unlike black and non-black, why should Christ-being be considered contradictory to reason in the ordinary sense of reason? Until it is shown to be contradictory, one is not obligated to consider "global" reason.

4. Ashok Gangadean, *Meditative Reason—Toward Universal Grammar* (New York: Peter Lang, 1993), 103-118. Meditative or global reason appears to make the same move to give up "categorical" reason, and for the same reason as others in the monist "all is one" tradition.

rates which characterizes Socrates through a lifetime of development and change, provided that the categories of analysis of personhood are sufficiently in place. Or, it is said, reason cannot grasp degrees, that the law of excluded middle is insufficient for this. Bald or not-bald does not capture balding. But this is a faulty application—the categories rather should be balding or not-balding, the latter being able to include both bald and not-bald. Or, it is said, reason cannot grasp relationships—it separates into *a* and *non-a*, but not both *a* and *non-a* at the same time. Having separated mind and body into exclusive categories, there is no middle term by which to relate them, precipitating the enigma and conundrum of the mind-body problem. Reason does affirm unity of diversity without reducing one to the other. The world is neither pure unity nor pure diversity. By the law of non-contradiction, nothing is both *a* and *non-a*, at the same time and in the same respect. But every being is a unity of *a* and *non-a*. Unity of diversity, and therefore relationship, is a given in all views. Whether something more complex can be explained by lesser diversity will depend on the rational analysis of elements of diversity.

Lastly, it is said that rational coherence is insufficient for settling disputes between worldviews for there are many equally logically possible worlds or worldviews. And further, it cannot settle disputes within an inconsistent set of beliefs. Reason says both cannot be true, but it does not say which of the two is not true. These perceived limits of reason do not apply upon further analysis of what constitutes a worldview. In its essential and most basic features, there are not many possible worldviews. Either all is eternal in some form or another (material monism, spiritual monism, or dualism), or only some (God, the Creator) is eternal, and it is clear to reason whether all or only some is eternal (see arguments in *Part II: Metaphysics*—what is real/eternal?). If a worldview is incoherent in its essence, then all non-essential variations will also be incoherent. If any worldview is coherent in its essence, then non-essential differences in that world (for example: Why are there x vs. x+1 atoms or persons or units of evil in existence?) may not now be known and may remain an unknown without unsettling what is known at the more basic level.

In general, a worldview is not a set, but a system of beliefs, the less basic beliefs being built upon the more basic beliefs. When a less basic belief conflicts with a more basic belief, the less basic, in that system, must be given up. But reason, as most basic in every system, cannot be given up. There may be constructed alternative and coexisting systems of analysis beginning with different sets of axioms (several geometries, game theories, etc.) which may or may not be compatible with the actual world. In neither case is there a philosophically relevant limit on reason to settle actual disputes in this world.

Attitude: The Fundamental Source of Skepticism

Philosophy is an attitude. It is the love of wisdom. It is also an application—that of self-examination, critically examining our basic beliefs for coherence of meaning. This attitude cannot be taken for granted as it does not appear to be widespread. To seek wisdom is to seek to know the good and the means to it. If the good is clear, it would appear that human beings do not ordinarily seek the good. We pursue what we believe is the good for ourselves, as we conceive of the self. Our view of the good is based on our view of the self. That conception of self, however conflicted and incoherent, we take for granted. It is the self we love, defend, and seek to fulfill, come what may. We do not re-examine our view of our self unless it is fundamentally challenged. We neglect, avoid, resist, and deny reason unless its demands become persistent and inescapable, at which point we have entered into a life crisis. We are forced, out of need for meaning, to reconsider basic things. As we move from the darkness of meaninglessness to the light of meaning, a new self is born, a new life begins. Short of this challenge and requirement of change, we do not seek and we do not understand basic things about God and man and good and evil. Rather, we are moved in justifying our view of self in all its conflicts and incoherence, whether we are learned or unlearned, whether by skepticism or fideism. Skepticism justifies itself over and against various forms of fideism, but not against its own incoherence. Disputes between skepticism and fideism therefore are interminable, an inherent consequence of explicitly or implicitly denying that some things are clear to reason.

SOURCES OF FIDEISM

Sensus Divinitatis: Is Knowledge of God Immediate or Inferred?

All men, some have claimed, have an immediate knowledge of God. This is other than an acquired or an inferred knowledge. This is sometimes referred to as the *sensus divinitatis* (the SD view) and has been appealed to by several in the Reformed community (Calvin, Hodge, Van Til, Plantinga, Oliphint.)[5] There are differences among upholders of the SD view regarding the content of this knowledge, how it arises, and whether it is present as a propensity or an actuality.

The SD view assumes a common sense realism, which assumes that appearance is reality, and that there is an external physical world. When arguments arise against an immediately held, non-inferred belief in God or the external world, it is not evident that intuition must override reason. If this override is not evident, it is not sufficient to base the knowledge of God on an immediately held belief in the face of what seems to be rational, and therefore *prima facie,* objections to that belief.

Knowledge and Accountability

An attempt is made to establish accountability by some, though not all, holders of the SD model based on immediate knowledge. It is said by these proponents of SD that this knowledge gets through, and it is suppressed and therefore men are without excuse.

This view assumes that if one does not have knowledge, one cannot be held responsible or that one is not culpable for failure to acquire knowledge. But failure to seek and to understand describes a univer-

---

5. John Calvin, *The Institutes of the Christian Religion*, trans. and ed. Ford Lewis Battles (Grand Rapids, MI: W.B. Eerdmans, 1987), Book 1, Chapter 3; Charles Hodge, *Systematic Theology* (Peabody, MA: Hendrickson Publishers, 1999), Volume 1, 191-195; Cornelius Van Til, *The Defense of the Faith* (Phillipsburg, NJ: P&R Publishing, 1967); Alvin Plantinga, *Warranted Christian Belief* (Oxford: Oxford University Press, 2000); K. Scott Oliphant, *Reasons for Faith: Philosophy in the Service of Theology* (Phillipsburg, NJ: P&R Publishing, 2006), 134. The SD view occurs in those cited here with many variations, held more or less consciously and consistently. Worship of "wood and stone" (Calvin), or a higher power on whom we are dependent (Hodge), is taken as evidence of SD. But God as a "higher power" could be the Greek god Zeus, who is neither infinite, eternal, nor unchangeable as is the God of theism.

sal, basic, moral failure. The prayer, "Father, forgive them, for they know not what they do," assumes ignorance is culpable.

This view assumes that knowledge of the truth does not set a person free, that moral bondage is not due to a lack of knowledge. To avoid denying freedom through knowledge, a distinction has been made in kinds of knowledge. But if knowledge based on true understanding sets one free, can there be a knowledge based on misunderstanding or lack of understanding?

The idea of inexcusability and suppression of the truth has been variously understood. An account of how a belief originates is not an account of suppression and inexcusability. A belief is suppressed by (or rejected for) an alternative belief for which one presumably has reasons. If it is clear that there are no reasons in support of one's unbelief, then unbelief is inexcusable. To merely reaffirm that "everyone deep down knows God" does not show clarity by showing the inexcusability of unbelief.[6]

The Magisterial vs. the Ministerial Use of Reason

It is acknowledged by those who uphold the ministerial use of reason that reason is necessary to receive revelation (the formative use of reason). It is also acknowledged that reason is useful in giving reasons for the truth of revelation. But it must never be the magistrate over or judge of the truth of revelation. It is a maidservant, not a mistress, and the strongest condemnation is reserved for the arrogation of the role of magistrate by reason. It is of use in systematizing truth (the constructive use of reason). And it is used to interpret scripture and to support one interpretation over and against another interpretation (the interpretive use of reason). It may even be used to critically

---

6. Inexcusability has not been given much attention in the history of theism. Where it has received attention, it has often been based on a form of the SD view. St. Paul seems to have made it the starting point in establishing man's need for redemption (*Romans 1:20*), as also the *Westminster Confession of Faith (1.1)*.

   See: https://thewestminsterstandard.org/the-westminster-confession

   Anselm's famous ontological argument tried to show the foolishness of unbelief, but this and other forms of natural theology have been met with counterarguments by Hume and Kant among others. Inexcusability assumes the clarity of general revelation, which theists, who affirm the creation–fall–redemption worldview, need to show by "taking thoughts captive" raised up against the knowledge of God (*2 Corinthians 10:4*).

test alternative beliefs for coherence of meaning. But here the line is drawn by those regarding reason as servant, not judge. They claim it cannot—it shall not—be used to judge the truth of revelation. Is this line being arbitrarily drawn?

It should be granted here, over and against deists (Herbert) and dogmatic rationalists (Wolff), that special revelation is necessary and does not and cannot *originate* from reason. But since reason is necessary to receive *and to understand* revelation, revelation must necessarily pass the minimal test of intelligibility. What is contradictory and is seen as contradictory is unintelligible and cannot be thought and therefore cannot be believed. What is an actual and what is an apparent contradiction must be discerned, often with much effort, to uncover hidden assumptions. To separate the formative and interpretive uses of reason is artificial, and to apply the critical use of reason to other scriptures and not to one's own scripture is arbitrary in the extreme. As an alternative to several forms of SD—whether a vague higher being (Calvin), or basic theism (Hodge), or full theism (Oliphint), or the triune God (Van Til)—one can posit innate (non-empirical) concepts that are applied either to God or to the creation (e.g., finite or infinite, temporal or eternal, changing or unchanging). All men have these concepts. How they should be applied (whether only to God or to the creation) is clear to reason.

Ontology and Epistemology: Can Reason Grasp Ultimate Reality?

To say "reason is ontological" means that reason applies to being as well as to thought. It means that there are no square-circles, no *a* that is *non-a*. It applies to all being, the highest being, including God's being. God is not both eternal and non-eternal, at the same time and in the same respect. Miracles may transcend a created law of nature, but not a law of reason, which is uncreated.[7] There should be no grounds therefore for saying reason cannot grasp reality.

This is not to say that by reason one can have exhaustive knowledge of anything, finite or infinite. Human knowledge is finite. It may

---

7. If God in his being *cannot* be both *a* and *non-a*, then reason applies to God's being. And if God's being is eternal, then reason is eternal, and is therefore uncreated, and unlike the laws of nature which are created.

grow forever and still be finite. But we know in part, beginning with what is most basic. The less basic, which is unknown, does not set aside the more basic that is known. There is an incomprehensibility grounded in our finitude which does not negate knowing in part.

There is also an incomprehensibility that is qualitative. We can never know the infinite or the finite as God knows himself or the creation. What is known is by revelation through the acts of creation and providence, processed through a particular human mode of consciousness. All attempts to know God's being directly apart from revelation and directly as God knows himself are utterly futile. Disputes about the divine essence in itself and analogies from it are to be avoided. Kant distinguished the noumenal world (as-it-is-in-itself) from the world known by human consciousness (phenomena) and noted antinomies that the mind falls into in attempting to go beyond its limits. Yet Kant could not resist drawing unwarranted implications about the noumenal realm in distinguishing it from the phenomenal realm.

If reason is ontological, then that is common ground in all disputes between worldviews. As a precondition for intelligibility, it cannot be questioned or abandoned and yet retain intelligibility in any utterance. As a constitutive characteristic of being *per se*, the validity of reason does not need to be, nor can it be, established by appeal to God's being or will, which already presupposes reason.

Faith and Reason

It has been argued that faith is other than reason, that it goes beyond reason, and that it may even go against reason. These responses are understandable, given skeptical claims concerning the possibility of knowledge: postmoderns (all is interpretation—one cannot transcend one's historical situatedness); the probability factor in all historical argument (Schelling, Kierkegaard, William L. Craig); the puzzles that arise from confusing logical with empirical gaps (mind and brain); and explaining unity of diversity (*a* and *non-a*). What has Jerusalem to do with Athens?[8] Faith comes first, then understanding: I believe

---

8. For recent disputes among Reformed apologists on faith and reason, see Robert Charles Sproul, John H. Gerstner, and Arthur W. Lindsley, *Classical Apologetics: A Rational Defense of the Christian Faith and a Critique of Presuppositional Apologetics* (Grand Rapids, MI: Zondervan, 1984); Alvin Plantinga, and Nicholas Wolterstorff, eds., *Faith and Rationality:*

in order that I might understand (*credo ut intelligam*). Or, faith completes the natural limits of understanding as grace completes nature (Aquinas). Faith cannot be subject to the vagaries of philosophy or science, it is said. Faith must take God at his word. It believes because God said it.

Longstanding disputes require a deeper understanding. What has scripture to do with philosophy? Is scripture as redemptive revelation presupposed by, and required by, the clarity of general revelation? What has faith to do with reason? Does not truth presuppose meaning? Can a belief be held more than the understanding of its meaning content? If not, then faith *is* understanding, and I believe *in so far as* I understand (*credo inquantum intelligo*). Faith is inseparable from reason as truth is inseparable from meaning.

If one argues from the nature of things, do we not argue from necessity to actuality, rather than from possibility to probability?[9] Are there logical gaps or only empirical gaps?[10] Does unity presuppose diversity, and vice versa, does diversity presuppose unity? Is the Word of God only scripture or are the presuppositions of scripture also the Word of God? It would be premature at this point to give up hope for a deeper understanding. Faith and reason need not, and, it appears, cannot, part ways.

Reason and the *Testimonium Spiritu Sancti*

Reason, it is said, is one thing, and the work of the Holy Spirit another. What is necessary for faith is the witness of the Holy Spirit, the *testimonium Spiritu Sancti*. Man by reason cannot presume to do the

---

Reason and Belief in God (Notre Dame: University of Notre Dame Press), 1984; K. Scott Oliphint, *Reasons for Faith: Philosophy in the Service of Theology* (Phillipsburg, NJ: P&R Publishing, 2006).

9. If one argues from the probability of the resurrection to its actuality, as it is common to do, in relation to the resurrection of Jesus, the gap may be unbridgeable. But if one were to argue from the necessity of the resurrection (on a prior conception of God, creation, fall, and redemption) to the actuality of the resurrection, then the gap, if any, would be easily bridged.

10. The mind-body problem famously illustrates this: Is there a logical gap between mind and body? Is there a logical gap between the extended/physical realm and the non-extended/spiritual realm? Is a neural impulse, located in the brain, logically identifiable with a mental image which has no spatial location or size? (See the reasons for the minor premise of *The Third Argument Against Material Monism*, Chapter 5.)

work of the Holy Spirit. Salvation is by grace, not works. Man's reason, it is said, is finite and fallen. Sin has had a negative effect on the human mind (the noetic effect). Reason does not persuade; the Spirit does. The Spirit regenerates. No one else, and nothing else, can.

The work of the Spirit is not in question. But does the Spirit work by and with the Word or apart from the Word? Does the Spirit work to convince, persuade, enlighten, and illuminate the mind by and with sound argument or above or apart from sound argument? Are there independent and inherent characteristics of a sound argument or must something be supernaturally added to make it sound? Do sound arguments ever fail to accomplish their purpose—is that purpose only to persuade or is it either to compel *or* to persuade? Can it compel a person to shut one's eyes (turn off one's mind) in order to avoid the force of a sound argument? Is it reason that is finite and fallen or is it man that is finite and fallen? Is it reason that fails to understand or man who fails to seek and understand through reason? Is the use of reason opposed to or independent of grace, or is the use of reason itself a work of grace? Is the use of and proper response to sound argument a purely natural occurrence or is it itself something of a miracle?

Reason and the Particular

Reason, it is said, cannot grasp the particular, the individual, or the unique, and reality consists of particulars (Scotus, Nietzsche, Derrida). Reason grasps the universal and the abstract, not the singular, concrete which can be known only in existential encounter. Hegel and Marx got it backwards. The individual is not for the state, but the state for the individual. For Kierkegaard (and Barth) the highest stage on life's way is that of faith in which there is a teleological suspension of the rational, the universal, the ethical. How else can the act of faith, seen in Abraham the man of faith, be understood, if it is to be understood at all? How else can he obey the command of God to sacrifice his son, his only son Isaac whom he loves?

The individuality of Abraham and the nature and content of his faith are to be seen not in a fragmentary episode of his life, but in the continuity of his understanding developed and expressed in the entirety of his life. They encompass his worldview concerning man's origin and destiny, the outworking of God's purpose in world history, his understanding of sin and death, the curse and the promise, all in place before his leaving the city of man for the city of God, a city with foundations.

The necessity for the resurrection in order to inherit the promise made to him, his understanding of the significance of sacrifice, circumcision, and the manner of the birth of Isaac—all of this preceded Abraham's offering up of Isaac and was part of his understanding during the act of sacrifice, leading him to see how God himself would provide the lamb that takes away the sin of the world. He reasoned that God could and would raise Isaac from the dead to fulfill the promise God made. Abraham's faith in offering up Isaac was a deepened understanding of what he already believed when he first received the call and the promise in Ur of the Chaldees. It was anything but a leap beyond reason, and his uniqueness is comprehensible only in understanding all the particulars of his life story in its entirety.

Reason and Rationalism

Exalted claims have been made in the name of reason, provoked in part by internecine wars, abuses, and superstitions in the name of religion. The Enlightenment affirmed the sufficiency of reason and experience to guide all human affairs. God's supernatural actions in the world were removed from providence first by deists—Hume (*On Miracles*),[11] and then by Kant (*Religion within the Bounds of Reason Alone*), and later from creation by Darwin's theory of evolution and by

---

11. David Hume, *Enquiries Concerning Human Understanding*, 3rd ed. (New York: Oxford University Press, 1975), 127. (See Section X, "Of Miracles.") "Upon the whole, then, it appears that no testimony for any kind of miracle has ever amounted to a probability, much less to a proof; and that, even supposing it amounted to a proof, it would be opposed by another proof, derived from the very nature of the fact, which it would endeavor to establish. It is experience only which gives authority to human testimony; and it is the same experience which assures us of the laws of nature. When, therefore, these two kinds of experience are contrary, we have nothing to do but to substract the one from the other, and embrace an opinion, either on one side or the other, with that assurance which arises from the remainder. But according to the principle here explained, this substraction, with regard to all popular religions, amounts to an entire annihilation; and therefore we may establish as a maxim, that no human testimony can have such force as to prove a miracle, and make it a just foundation for any such system of religion." Hume's criticism of course would not hold if miracles were not the *foundation*, but played a different role in one's system.

contemporary naturalistic cosmologies. As the naturalist worldview unfolded, its excesses and superstitions were seen, and its pretensions to neutrality and morality were exposed. It appeared too that claims made in the name of reason had their dehumanizing limitations. The idol of reason was then dethroned, and became subject to abuse and degradation. Over and against contemporary malaise, directionlessness, and nihilism, there is a resurgence of religion, and with it a recurrence of conflicts and wars in the name of religion. Are we forever to be caught in this bi-polar mindset, between faith and reason, between fideism and skepticism, between the right and the left?

There is a common failure to use reason on both sides of the dispute—one in the name of reason, the other in the name of God. Both rationalists and fideists failed to address the origin and significance of natural evil in light of the clarity of general revelation. In addition, fideists failed to address the nature and relation of moral and natural evil from special revelation. Given this common failure as human beings, it is ironic how each side has opposed the other, except that fideists had more opportunity to understand moral and natural evil based on scripture. Neither side can speak to the other of this common failure, so the opposition goes on. But no one is obligated to take sides in this futile dispute. No one is obligated to choose between reason without God or God without reason. A deeper sense of reason as the Logos in human nature, and a deeper use of reason in light of clarity, would shatter the pretensions on both sides and get us past the dangers of competing idolatries.

Reason and Hermeneutics

As rationalism failed to use reason in understanding general revelation, fideism failed to use reason in interpreting special revelation. The principle of *Sola Scriptura* has been understood and applied variously. The more strictly the principle of *Sola Scriptura* has been applied, the more literalist it has become. It has excluded the use of external and internal contexts in interpretation. The less it has used good and necessary consequences in interpretation, the more explicitly literal it claims to be, to the point of denying the presence of interpretation altogether. As in science, some claims are made as unquestionable facts rather than data interpreted in light of certain assumptions. Those dissatisfied with literalist meaning have countered with claims of a deeper meaning. As with literalists who are not bound by context and reason, spiritualists also are free to roam allegorically in the field of imagination. Literal and allegorical interpretive frameworks become antinomies opposing each other throughout history, while sharing common hermeneutical assumptions.

A proper view of *Sola Scriptura* is that it is a principle of authority set against all other claims based on special revelation. It is not set against reason and the clarity of general revelation, but presupposes them as its most basic context.[12] As the Genesis account is to be understood in light of what is clear from general revelation, a second layer of context is added from which to interpret subsequent scriptures, using good and necessary consequences. Heaven and hell become understood in light of the more basic notions of good and evil and life and death. Good and evil are understood in light of creation as revelation and in light of clarity and inexcusability. Eschatology becomes understood in light of man's chief end (the good) and in light of how evil is made to serve the good. A presuppositional hermeneutic understands what is less basic in light of what is more basic. It seeks to become more conscious and consistent in understanding assumptions used in interpretation.

Piety and Intellect

Piety is seen by many as a simple devotion, unencumbered by intellectual concerns. The heart is seen as independent of the head and the head as antithetical to the heart ("The heart has reasons that reason cannot know"—Pascal). This has been fertile ground for fideism. There are warnings cited from scripture against vain philosophy, and against being puffed up by knowledge. There are exhortations to become like little children and to not lean on one's own understanding. God is said

---

12. The opening words of *Genesis* "In the beginning God created . . . ." presupposes the existence of God, a belief in the existence of God and divine revelation, including the context and purpose of revelation, and an understanding of what "God" means. This in turn presupposes an understanding of Spirit, infinite, eternal, and unchangeable. These presuppose an understanding of being, qualities, essence etc. Later statements in the earliest chapters presuppose an understanding of good and evil and of life and death. Understanding *Genesis 1–3* in this way then becomes the basis of understanding all that comes later in *Genesis* and throughout the scriptures, to the last book.

to hide truths from the wise but reveal them to babes. Not many wise are called by God to faith. God uses the weak and foolish things to confound the strong and the wise. Intellect is dismissed as being of the soul, not of the spirit, by which one communes with God. And finally, piety is said to be rewarded by seeing God in heaven face-to-face in a beatific vision. Even notable thinkers like Aquinas and Al-Ghazali are said to have reached crises of intellect, gone through a dark night of the soul, and then entered into a mystical communion with God.

Aside from the question of contextual interpretation for each fragment of scripture cited, and the need for critical awareness in interpreting intuitive experience, there are weighty and pressing reasons not to accommodate an anti-intellectual split in the human personality or in piety. One is called to love God with the whole heart, the mind included, beginning with the understanding. One is called to go on to maturity from infancy in understanding in order to attain to the fullness of God. One is warned against zeal without knowledge and called to piety (holiness or sanctification), which comes from knowing the truth. One is reminded that all suffer under natural evil as a call to seek God, that no one seeks and no one understands, and that all are constantly called to stop and think, to earnestly seek to understand. The wisdom literature in scripture exalts understanding and warns against the folly of fools and the complacency of the simple. And finally, the outcome sought is not an individualistic beatific vision, but the earth being filled with the knowledge of God through a corporate, cumulative, work of mankind in history.[13]

---

13. For the problem of anti-intellectualism in American life, see Richard Hofstadter, *Anti-Intellectualism in American Life* (New York: Knopf Publishing Group, 1966). For the problem in the Church, see Mark A. Noll, *The Scandal of the Evangelical Mind* (Grand Rapids, MI: William B. Eerdmans Publishing, 1995), and James W. Sire, *Habits of the Mind* (Downers Grove, Illinois: InterVarsity Press, 2000). The problem is not limited to some segments of mankind or of the Church; it is as broad and as deep as the misconceptions regarding good and evil. While the intellectual life may have been encouraged at times by some, its necessity has not been adequately secured. Referring to intellectual notables in recent evangelical history, Noll, *Scandal*, 4, says, "None of them believed that intellectual activity was the only way to glorify God, or even the highest way, but they all believed in the life of the mind, and they believed it *because* they were evangelical Christians." If there are other and higher ways to glorify God, then the intellectual life is not necessary for all. More would be needed to secure it for all, specifically in regard to understanding good and evil. Evil for all has not been seen as the failure to seek and to understand what is clear to reason in general revelation; and the good for all has not been seen as the knowledge of God filling the earth through the work of dominion. The popular view of heaven as

Reason and the Mysteries of the Faith

Mysteries are things formerly hidden and now revealed. They are not given in general revelation, but only in special revelation. They did not and could not originate in human understanding. Mysteries are supremely objects of faith. They are said to be beyond reason and appear to be against reason. They are sometimes said to be paradoxes. The deepest mysteries have been the occasion of the deepest consternation of the mind and the source of deepest division. Although not linked to any particular faith, they have been particularly present in the Christian faith. Doctrines of the Trinity and the Incarnation are said to be marks of orthodoxy. The doctrine of freedom and predestination has divided the faith. The problem of evil troubles all who think about their faith. Besides these, there are other teachings put forward as dogma that are equally or more perplexing. How can it be known what is to be believed within a religion or between religions if reason is to be suspended in matters of faith?

History shows that these doctrines do not simply fall out of the sky. They arise first from the reading of scripture, which itself unfolds organically, and are expressed initially in the Church's liturgy. Given admixtures of understanding within the community of faith, differences are expressed and questions arise. Discussion occurs and reaffirmations are made based on good and necessary consequences of scripture. New implications are drawn, raising new questions and new challenges, all of which are a natural part of becoming intellectually more conscious and consistent. After much discussion by leaders and teachers meeting in councils (at times prolonged over decades because of circumstance and politics), a consensus is reached. Faulty and contradictory misunderstandings of doctrine are removed and the theologically more precise and nuanced confession of faith is attained. Those in subsequent generations, without knowledge of the Confession or the clarifications made through discussion, often repeat old questions and old errors.

Much of what has been clarified during the discussions are misunderstandings rooted in deeply embedded assumptions from general

---

complete blessedness in the next life, through a direct vision of God, makes knowledge of God through the work of dominion in this life unnecessary (See application of *Moral Law 4*, on false hope). What is regarded as unnecessary is, in time, naturally disregarded.

revelation, which are being used to understand special revelation. In these discussions, analyses and distinctions need to be made concerning temporal and logical relations, concerning individuals and essences, concerning the nature of unity and diversity, concerning the logical relationship of finite and infinite, concerning the nature of freedom and causality, and concerning first and second causes. In the course of progressing in understanding, what appeared to be against reason (paradox) is seen to be not against reason, but in accord with reason, and eventually it may be seen to be what reason should expect. At the same time, those paradoxical claims which are in fact actual contradictions are exposed as such, despite the theological hair splitting undertaken in their defense. There is often resistance to reason in defense of dogma. This resistance, however, is not restricted to theological dogma, but is present wherever deep commitments are implicated, beginning with the discussion of uncaused events and being from non-being.

Reason and Personality

There are many kinds and levels of diversity in human nature, each capable of occasioning tensions within a person and between persons, when what is more basic is not in place.[14] One strand of diversity having an epistemological lifestyle implication is that of personality inclination. Some are inclined to the life of thought, some to feeling, and some to action. No one is exclusively one or the other, but one or the other is dominant in each person. There are philosophers and artists and businessmen. In the modern West there was an age of Rationalism, Romanticism, and Pragmatism or Realism.[15] In the ancient

---

14. There is a *broader* aspect of human nature which all humans share, consisting (in part) of the *formal capacity* for basic belief and the conception of justice. There is a *narrower* aspect consisting of the *content* of basic belief and belief about human nature and about justice. There is a diversity of personality characteristics—whether one's focus is upon thought, or feeling, or upon the practical (in biblical context, the prophetic, priestly, or kingly focus). There is a body/soul diversity in human nature, as well as a male/female diversity. In addition, there is a diversity of cultural/educational backgrounds for all persons, as well as an individual uniqueness characterizing each person.

15. Romanticism in European culture in the 19th century focused upon feeling and was a reaction to the excesses and sterility of Rationalism; it was not a correction based on the critical analysis of the inadequate use of reason at the basic level. So too, Pragmatism-Realism was a reaction to the excesses of Romanticism. Without adequate critical analysis to establish philosophical foundations, cultures are caught in a cycle of reactions until they end in cultural exhaustion and collapse.

East there was the yoga of knowledge (*jnana*), of love (*bhakti*), and of action (*karma*). The Hebrews recognized the functions of the prophet, priest, and king. Some rely on reason, some on intuition, and some on sense experience as a primary source of knowledge.

Some are not inclined to philosophize about their epistemological lifestyle, but there are philosophies advocating each (reason or intuition or the senses) as the primary source of knowledge. Plato, in Raphael's *School of Athens*, points upward to the One known through reason; Aristotle points downward to the many known through the five senses. The Buddha is often depicted sitting on the lotus, eyes half closed, seeking intuitive awareness. The many, not inclined to philosophize, hold to basic belief fideistically, whatever that belief may be. Divisions along these lines are recurrent in every group throughout history. Is there hope for unity?

There is a real diversity among persons, but the diversity properly understood is the basis of unity, not disunity. There is a natural unity and a natural order for unity in each person. Unity among persons begins with unity in a person. The split in a person is not between the functions of intellect, emotions, and will, but within each function, beginning with the intellect.[16] And here the need for meaning as intelligibility precedes the need for meaning as significance and meaning as purpose (as in attaining the good). One's view of the good, which is the source of unity, is based on one's view of human nature, which is based on one's view of what is real. What is real is known by reason. Reason then, as the source of the knowledge of the good, is the primary source of unity.

Knowledge of the good is necessary to attain unity—through which unity the good is realized. Knowledge can be cultivated through an appropriate process of education. The attainment of some measure of

---

16. A dramatic example of the split occurring in the understanding can be seen in Peter's denial of Christ. He had confessed that Jesus was the Christ, but failed to understand that Christ must suffer. When Jesus was arrested and taken into trial, Peter's world(view) fell apart due to the manifestation of a hidden contradiction in his understanding, which he soon realized, and he was later willing to die for the one he had earlier denied. It was not due to *akrasia*, a weakness of the will, nor was his denial due to any supposed conflict between thought and feeling. Examples can be multiplied, and analysis can reveal lack of understanding or contradictions in the understanding. Other ways of affirming the priority of the intellect in a person are to say that knowing the truth makes a person free, or, a person is transformed by a renewing of the mind, or, a person is sanctified by knowing the truth.

the good requires self-discipline undertaken under wise guidance. The attainment of the full measure of the good requires the deliberately coordinated effort of very many people over a long period of time. It is a task for all of mankind. Only a common understanding of the good, attainable by all, can bring about the good, to be enjoyed by all.

INFORMAL FALLACIES

How do we know when we have been presented with a proof? Is proof necessary and sufficient for knowledge? And how do we identify a basic belief? What makes a belief basic? Before engaging these questions, it would be helpful to recognize what is not a proof—what are some of the common pitfalls of pseudo-arguments. Agreeing that these are pitfalls before we fall into them will help us to avoid them, and, if we do fall, to recover from our error rather than compound it by excusing ourselves.

The following is a list of a dozen of the most common pseudo-arguments, called informal fallacies. These are the names usually given to each, although the examples used to illustrate them vary greatly.

Appeal to Fear. This is the use of threat to persuade to action. In a case of censorship by the state, Socrates was threatened with death in order to get him to stop raising questions which undermined the existing authorities. It did not succeed with Socrates because it did not show that physical life (a secondary good) was better than intellectual life (the primary good). Socrates chose to die physically rather than die spiritually by giving up what gives life meaning. Socrates feared what should be feared. "What shall it profit a man if he should gain the whole world, and lose his own soul?" Jesus asked.

Appeal to Pity. This is an appeal to the compassion of the hearer to persuade to action. It succeeds where the good of the recipient is not kept clearly in mind. It manipulates the idea of love by separating it from the good and the need for discipline in order to achieve the good. In literature and politics, people are often presented as victims, needing compassion, rather than as rational beings responsible for knowing what is clear. Appeal to fear and pity is often used and often succeeds because we are not concerned to think critically about the good.

Straw Man. This is an argument against a misrepresentation of a position rather than the real position. Care and honesty are needed to avoid a straw man. Sometimes passionate advocates of a position do not themselves represent it accurately. Sometimes we are willing to argue against the weakest representation of a position rather than the strongest, simply because it is easy and popular to do so. Popular views in religion are not as well considered as the historical view, agreed upon after much discussion, or as the critical thinking of philosophical reflection which responds to challenges not yet addressed by the historical view. We should be willing to address the most thought-out position.

Ad Hominem. This is a statement against the credibility of a person rather than against what the person said. Discrediting a person by questioning their motives or background or attitude is used as an excuse to avoid addressing what the person said. The position must be addressed in any case and should be addressed first. *Ad hominem* is not to be confused with a statement against another person's position. A statement against a person's position is not to be taken as a personal attack. Objections should be directed to what is more basic.

Appeal to Authority. This is an appeal to a person or a document as an authority to settle a dispute, where that person or document is not an authority. This is often done where there is insufficient respect for the authority of reason as self-attesting. Appeal is sometimes made to scripture or to science to settle disputes about origin when these are not relevant authorities because of their assumptions for which no proof is offered.

Ad Populum. This is an appeal to the current widespread acceptance of a view as a reason for its truth. It asks: How could any slightly reasonable person not believe what is now commonly believed by all the prestigious journals, by the most influential people in society, and by all of one's associates? But all the worldviews cannot be right. At most only one view is right, so numbers alone cannot decide. Present popularity does not pass the test of what is accepted by thoughtful persons over a long time. Some views are intellectually fashionable, and fashions change. It is possible to fool a majority of the people some of the time.

Begging the Question. This is an argument which expects the hearer to assume what the argument should be proving. It occurs where one is not aware of one's assumptions. We believe A, because of B, because of C, because of A. It is arguing in a circle. The smaller the circle the more vicious is the circle. It has been suggested that all arguments are ultimately circular, that we argue *from* our presupposition *to* our presupposition. This would be true if reason were not natural, ontological, and transcendental.

Red Herring. This is arguing beside the point rather than to the point. It is a distraction from the argument under consideration by bringing in something that appears associated, but which is irrelevant. It appeals to exceptions as counting against the rule rather than an exception which assumes the rule. A brain-damaged person does not disprove that all humans are rational, but that the capacity for rationality in some has been impaired. When context of discussion is ignored, we lose focus on what is relevant, follow a stream of consciousness, and end up chasing rabbits.

Appeal to the Unknown. This is an appeal to an unknown in order to avoid having one's position disproven. Key terms which are commonly understood at the beginning of an argument are ambiguated and emptied of meaning at the end. Any position is compatible with an unknown.[17] Sophistical obfuscations, making distinctions without differences, are standard ways to appeal to unknowns. It is also done by shifting the burden of proof (I believe *p* until you show otherwise), or by pounding the table, that is, insisting one knows without offering any proof of knowing.

Post Hoc. This is faulty causal reasoning based on insufficient observation. Fully stated, it is *post hoc ergo propter hoc* (after this therefore

---

17. The unknown must be distinguished from the unknowable as well as from the known. An unknown at a less basic level does not affect what is known at a more basic level. In this sense, we know in part. An unknown at a more basic level undermines all that comes after it. An unknown or an unknowable at the most basic level makes all knowledge impossible.

because of this). This is often manifest in superstitions (walking under a ladder, a black cat crossing one's path, going through rituals for good luck) and pseudo-science (astrology, divination, and magic). It may also occur in learned discussions where actual non-natural causes are discounted *a priori* and natural causes must therefore be sought.

Hasty Generalization. This is making a statement about an entire group based on a very limited observation, perhaps only one case. Statements about persons as members of a group defined by gender, personality, ethnicity, religious belief, or occupation are at times based on only one or two encounters. One feels depersonalized by being categorized and this is often resisted as stereotyping. But a generalization is not hasty if it does not apply to every member of a class, yet is true of a significant majority. It is not unreasonable to say that this is what one can ordinarily expect from those who consistently hold to a particular worldview. There is a natural connection between belief and conduct in all human beings.

Complex Question. This is a question that assumes more than the listener is ready to assent to. It is also known as a loaded question, since it is loaded with a questionable assumption. A complex question can be deceptively simple ("What is eternal?" rather than "Is there something eternal?"), but it puts the respondent in a dilemma, since any answer to the unacceptable assumption is inappropriate to the one answering. A complex question will distort or end conversation unless the questioner is willing to examine the assumption of the question and to split the question into parts and ask the more basic part first. A related fallacy is the *complex assertion*. It is an assertion, the meaning of which when applied to itself, or to the premises on which it rests, defeats itself. It is true and therefore false at the same time. Like the complex question, it cannot be engaged with meaningfully. This is just one set in the class of self-refuting statements. If "knowledge is not possible" is true, then it can never be known or asserted and is therefore a false assertion. And if I claim I know that knowledge is not possible, then there is one thing I know, which makes my claim false.

Chapter 3

KNOWLEDGE, ARGUMENT, AND PRESUPPOSITION

KNOWLEDGE

TO BELIEVE THE CONCLUSION of a sound argument because the argument is seen as sound is to possess knowledge. This is stated more formally by saying:

A person S knows a proposition p if and only if:
  i. p is true
  ii. S believes p
  iii. S is justified in believing that p

These three conditions are said to be necessary and sufficient for knowledge.[1] These conditions have been challenged as being neither necessary nor sufficient for knowledge, but the challenge is plausible only until an ambiguity in understanding the third condition of justification is clarified, and only by focusing on secondary rather than primary beliefs.

Edmund Gettier has argued that these conditions are not sufficient,[2] and Alvin Plantinga has argued that these conditions are not necessary.[3] Both have argued in ways that have caught the attention of

---

1. Plato, *Complete Works*. This seems to be the working definition in *Theaetetus*, 201, and in *Meno*, 98. Pure experience, devoid of all interpretation, is not yet knowledge.

2. Edmund Gettier, "Is Justified True Belief Knowledge?" *Analysis* 23 (1963), 121-123.

3. Alvin Plantinga, *Warrant: The Current Debate* (Oxford: Oxford University Press, 1993). Also, *The Analytic Theist: An Alvin Plantinga Reader*, James F. Sennett ed. (Grand Rapids,

academic philosophers. Gettier has argued using peculiar counter-examples and Plantinga by appealing to properly basic beliefs. But if one distinguishes a *prima facie* (weak) and an *ultima facie* (strong) sense of justification it can be seen that neither Gettier nor Plantinga is arguing against justification in the strong sense of the term. Weak justification does not guarantee knowledge, whereas strong justification does.

Gettier's counterexamples rest on two peculiarities. *First,* there is an ambiguity based on the collapse of sense and reference in the statement "The man who will get the job has 10 coins in his pocket." The description fits two persons in the example, yet the sense in the mind of the speaker fits only one person. The truth of the conclusion trades on this ambiguity. *Second,* one is justified only in a weak sense in believing what the boss says regarding who will get the job, without knowing the reliability of the boss in keeping his word. The ambiguity of sense and reference and the reliability of testimony can be handled with the present definition of knowledge as justified, true belief.

Plantinga's objection rests on two factors: *first,* a theory that justifying one's belief can be undermined by improperly functioning faculties, and *second,* that belief in God is properly basic, occurring spontaneously and requiring no justification, for a person under certain circumstances.[4] Regarding proper function, the faculty of reason, used critically at the basic level, is not like the faculty of sense perception. The former may be used or not used, by choice; the latter may dysfunction in use due to organic brain conditions beyond one's choice. Dysfunction is not disuse. Introspection helps in the former, not in the latter. Regarding what is basic, what is properly basic is not the same as what is logically basic. The former can be objected to, the latter cannot be objected to. "God created all things" has been objected to, and so is not initially strongly justified. "Being cannot come from non-being" has no defeaters.

MI.: Wm. B. Eerdmans, 1998), 162-163.

4. Alvin Plantinga, *Warrant and Proper Function* (Oxford: Oxford University Press, 1993), 4-11. A belief is properly basic for Plantinga which spontaneously arises under certain circumstances. Belief in the external world, other minds, and memory beliefs are said to be properly basic. Belief in God is also considered properly basic by Plantinga. Those lacking this belief either are not in the right circumstances or do not have properly functioning cognitive faculties. A belief warranted at one time may not be warranted later upon facing defeaters.

KNOWLEDGE BY REASON AND ARGUMENT

We know by reason and argument. The pseudo-arguments are used as substitutes for argument and preclude the use of arguments. Because of the use of pseudo-arguments, we seldom get to engage in genuine arguments. They must therefore be watched for and guarded against constantly. But how do we know by reason and argument? Knowing is a category of thought; it is not a category of being. Being and thought are distinct, though related. The epistemological is not to be confused with the ontological. Thought is thought about being. Being is ontologically prior to thought, both as the object of thought (what is thought about), and as the subject of thought (the being of the person doing the thinking). But what is first in the order of thought is not what is first in the order of being. Reason, the laws of thought, is first in the order of thought. What is eternal (God or matter) is first in the order of being. We know being through thought and we may recursively interpret thought, not in light of being itself, but in light of our thought or belief or view of being. Our first thought about being, any being, is that reason is not only epistemological, but that reason is ontological as well; reason applies to being as well as to thought. In looking at knowledge of being therefore, we must look at reason in its first use—reason as formative.

Concept

Reason as formative is used to form concepts, judgments, and arguments—the forms of all thought. Concept is the first act of reason. In a concept the mind grasps the essential nature of (a class of) beings or aspect (quality, state, relation, or activity) of beings. The essence of a being or aspect of a being is the set of qualities that all members and only members always have. A concept is expressed by a term (a word or group of words). We have the concept of pen, rock, horse, man, finite, angel, happy, on the table, running. A concept is universal in two senses: it applies equally to all members of a class, and it is the same in all thinkers who think about the class of things, such as horse, man, angel, etc. A concept is not an image, which is given through the senses, and which is always particular to the object perceived, and to the perceiver. A concept is not a sensation (pleasure or pain), nor the association of an image and sensation, nor orderly behavior. Sounds and behavior can express sensation, but these are not terms expressing concepts. If animals could think, they would have concepts which were universal to all thinkers, and we would be able to communicate with them as with other human beings. The difference would be one of language which could be learned, as any human language, apart from training and conditioned response.

Concepts are formed by and express the law of identity: *a* is *a*. Pen is pen, horse is horse, man is man, man is not non-man (that is, rabbit, rock, angel, star, etc.). In forming concepts, we classify and we identify by distinguishing *a* from *non-a*. Concepts are naturally paired as complimentary, as *a* and *non-a*. All humans have the qualities of rationality and animality. We have these and related qualities such as wisdom, power, and goodness, in a finite, temporal, and changeable way. So concepts assume being and essence. But concepts are logically ordered so that a less basic concept "man" becomes imbedded in and affected by more basic concepts like "matter," and this in turn by still more basic concepts like "eternal." Humans differ in making judgments about basic concepts such as whether matter is eternal and whether all being is material. We therefore disagree on the concept of man. Is man as a body/soul unity the image of God, or is man as a being which is entirely material the image of the animal? The term "man" therefore is philosophically ambiguous among different users of the term, even while it is denotatively, as far as its members, not ambiguous.

Because the concept "man" differs philosophically among different users of the term, this is not to deny that concepts grasp essences. Different conceptions of essence are not the denial of essences as such. In the process of being formed, and in being connected with more basic concepts, concepts may be well formed or not well formed, coherent or incoherent. Unknown aspects do not invalidate aspects that are known. Disputes about what is eternal do not overturn what it means to be eternal, although they affect what it means to be human, in part. If basic things are clear, then what is eternal is clear. If these things are not clear, then nothing is clear, and we are left with skepticism or fideism. Skepticism and fideism are just what are being objected to in this work and will be addressed as we go further.

Some further clarification about concepts and words is in order. Words are used ambiguously not only by different schools of philosophy; they are ambiguous to all users of a language in a conventional sense. A term can be equivocal (different unrelated meanings), analogous (different related meanings), or univocal (only one meaning) in its conventional use. Dictionaries take note of this form of ambiguity, but not of philosophical ambiguity. And there are different meanings of words when language is used for different purposes, for example, in poetry, in advertising, in work, in worship, in ceremony, etc. Here meaning is taken as use in a particular form of life.[5]

Because words are signs of thought and meaning, which are as broad and full as life itself, and because we are ever increasing in our exploration of meaning, the adaptation to relatively few words to express this range of meaning is a sign of human genius, not a sign that words signify nothing except other signifiers. Postmodernists reject essences *per se* as part of their anti-realist view of knowledge.[6] Words do not express concepts which grasp essences; the meaning of words is learned in a linguistic community and words refer only to other words as taught in that community. Meaning of words may be extended and transformed by a linguistic community, apart from reference to their being and essence, through the use of metaphor and word association in the use of pun, but the extension and transformation of meaning are still rule-governed and grounded in the relation of concept to being and essence, and will be analyzed accordingly when used as support for skepticism. Here we merely anticipate, we do not engage,

---

5. Ludwig Wittgenstein, and G.E.M. Anscombe, *Philosophical Investigations* (Ames, IA: Blackwell Publishing, 2003). He maintains there are many different uses of words and sentences, that language is learned in a form of life, that every belief is part of a system of beliefs. Therefore, while context determines meaning and accounts for ambiguity of words, this does not address concepts which are expressed by words and are grasped, not learned. Words are ambiguous, concepts are not. See also: Ludwig Wittgenstein, G.E.M. Anscombe, and G.H. von Wright, eds., *On Certainty* (New York: Harper & Row, 1972), 61-65, 100.

6. Friedrich Nietzsche, *The Portable Nietzsche*. Translated by Walter Kaufmann. (New York: Penguin Group, 1977), 483. Nietzsche, to whom postmodernists trace their near intellectual ancestry, could not avoid the connection between word and reason and concept and essence: "'Reason' in language—oh, what an old deceptive female she is! I am afraid we are not rid of God because we still have faith in grammar." The word of man (grammar) is grounded in the Word of God (Logos).

the claims made by postmodernism about meaning and reference in language in support of a skeptical outcome.

Judgment

Thinking begins with concept, but does not end there. The next natural step is the formation of judgment, a mental act, which is expressed verbally in a statement. In a judgment the mind relates two concepts by affirmation or negation. A predicate "red" is affirmed (or denied) of a subject "apple." "Some apples are red." This is a distinct level of thought, having different properties and relations than concepts. Simple judgments are either true or false. They differ in quantity and quality according as the subject is understood as "all" or "some," and the copula (is/is not) is affirmative or negative. There are four forms of the simple judgment.

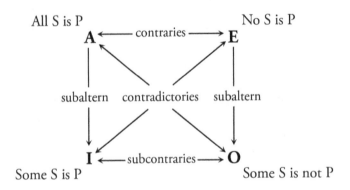

Applied to basic concepts such as "being" and "eternal" we have four statements: "all (being) is eternal" (universal affirmative, or A for short); "none is eternal" (universal negative/E); "some is eternal" (particular affirmative/I); "some is not eternal" (particular negative/O). These four forms of judgment are related in a variety of ways, two of which are particularly important for explaining knowledge by reason and argument.

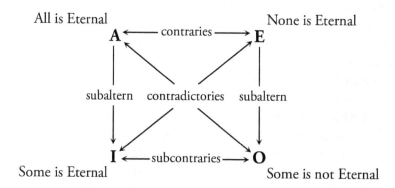

When an assertion is made as true and there is objection, the opposite or contradiction is being asserted. "None is eternal" is contradicted by "some is eternal," and "all is eternal" is contradicted by "some is not eternal." Contradictory statements, by the law of non-contradiction, cannot both be true and cannot both be false. One must be true and the other false. Contradictories differ in two ways, by quantity and quality (A/O and E/I). The contradiction of "none is eternal" is not "all is eternal" (E/A), since both cannot be true, but both can be false. These are contraries, not contradictories. Contraries share a common assumption (all are in the same class). Many disputes argue for contraries, where both are wrong because of a common assumption. This opposition is sometimes called an antinomy. A statement can be disproved by proving its contradiction is true, or it can be proven by disproving its contradiction, by showing the contradiction lacks meaning. Proof of a statement by showing its contradiction cannot be true because it is meaningless is called proof by *reductio ad absurdum*. Proof by *reductio* is used often in philosophy.

Argument

An argument is the third and final or complete act of reason. It follows naturally from judgment, as judgment follows naturally from concept. When someone makes an assertion which is not self-evident and is not ordinarily something to be believed by testimony, we need reasons for believing what is said. When a speaker gives reasons (premises) for what we are expected to believe (the conclusion), we are given an argument. To give an argument for what we say is to treat our hearers with the dignity of being rational beings. The expectation in return is that the hearer will believe the conclusion of the argument if the argument is sound, or, will object to the conclusion because the argument is unsound, and will be ready to show how the argument is unsound. An argument is sound if its premises are true and it is valid. An argument is valid if the premises logically support the conclusion. The rules of validity from premises which are either simple or compound statements are commonly accepted and are not a matter of dispute. Not to believe the conclusion of a sound argument is to disqualify oneself as a person committed to the use of reason, and thereby no longer qualified to participate in dialogue with those who are committed to reason.

We can affirm then that we know by reason and argument. Argument is one use of reason and assumes reason. There is no argument for reason itself, and none is needed. Reason is transcendental or self-attesting; it makes thinking possible. As the laws of thought, it is common ground for all thinkers. Whether thought and the true/false distinction can be accounted for consistently within one's worldview, is not to call reason into question, but one's worldview. If reason is given up, there is an end to all thought. Nothing remains but silence and the question of integrity. What applies to reason applies as well to other basic concepts like being, substance, essence, change, and causality, which have been common ground in disputes in the past. The denial of these concepts makes thought impossible.

PRESUPPOSITION

Most Basic Concept

We know the basic things by reason and argument. Basic beliefs are about basic things and basic beliefs are about basic concepts. We can identify basic beliefs and their different worldviews by identifying the basic concepts. The most basic concept is about existence, whether something is or is not. "It is blue," "It is long," "It is used for writing," assume "It is." "It is" assumes the distinction of now and not now, whether past or future. Past and future are further distinguished by always and not always. What has always existed in the past and will always exist in the future is eternal. What has not always existed is not eternal; it is temporal. So there are two kinds of existence, temporal and eternal. Of these two, eternal is more basic than temporal, for two reasons. Logically, the mind cannot stop with temporal. It asks, "Where did it come from?" Logically, the mind must stop with the eternal. It cannot ask, "Where did the eternal come from?" Ontologically, what is eternal would be the source of what is temporal. So, an eternal being is logically and ontologically more basic than a temporal being. Our most basic concept of being is "eternal" and the most basic belief is an answer to the question "What is real or eternal?"

In philosophy, after epistemology, the question of metaphysics (What is real?) is most basic. The distinctions in epistemology, as we saw, were between those who say basic things are not clear (skepticism and fideism) and those who say knowledge is possible, either by reason (rationalism), or by experience (empiricism), or by rational presuppositionalism (reason is the test of the meaning of basic beliefs). In metaphysics, the distinction is between those who say "all is eternal" (in some form or other) and those who say "only some is eternal." "None is eternal" is logically self-contradictory and therefore meaningless, and cannot be true, as we will soon see. We will further subdivide these two basic views and identify the historical manifestations of these views. Before doing so, we should clarify a bit further the meaning of "eternal."

That which is eternal has always existed and will always exist. It did not come into being. It is independent of other beings for its existence for it is self-existing, not having come into being. Whatever comes into being is dependent and likewise finite and changeable. What is eternal does not depend on another for its continued existence; it is self-maintaining. And what happens in it is to be explained from within itself. It is self-explaining. If anything lacks the qualities of being independent, self-existing, self-maintaining, and self-explaining it cannot be eternal. We should also distinguish what is eternal *in time* (that is, what is aeveternal) from what is eternal *outside time*, where time is an aspect of things created. What is everlasting, continuing on forever, could have had a beginning and need not be eternal, that is, without beginning. The status of a timeless eternity applied to God has been questioned by, for example, Open Theists.[7] The status of an eternal being in time has raised the question whether time can be infinite and whether the infinite is divisible, as in the *kalam* cosmological argument. The *kalam* cosmological argument was developed in medieval Islamic scholasticism. It shows the necessity of a First Cause based on the impossibility of an infinite, temporal regress of past events. These questions will require clarification of the nature of time, but do not, for now, obscure the distinction between what is with beginning and what is without beginning.

Most Basic Belief

The basic beliefs about what is eternal are "all is eternal" and "only some is eternal." Since these are contradictories, only one can and must be true. Under "all is eternal" are included material monism (all is matter and matter is eternal), spiritual monism (all is spirit and spirit is eternal), and dualism (both matter and spirit exist and both are eternal). For logical completeness, we can add the category of logically possible worlds to include logical possibilities imaginable, which are neither monist nor dualist. Under "only some is eternal" are included all beliefs in God the Creator (Judaism, Christianity, Islam, Deism), where what is eternal would have brought into existence or created what is not eternal.

These general beliefs of material monism, spiritual monism, dualism, and theism have been the basis of the worldviews which have come to expression in cultures and civilizations in world history. These views have been held more or less consciously and more or less consistently. History is an outworking of the challenges of reason to the coherence and meaning in a worldview. These challenges have come to individuals and to cultures as a whole; they have come from within a culture and from the outside; they have come at the basic level and at secondary levels. Worldviews, when challenged, may collapse, precipitating a crisis of faith. One may recover coherence by deeper insight, or one may change one's basic belief about reality, or one may become skeptical about any answer to basic questions. Authorities may seek to protect the prevailing worldview from challenge by re-

---

7. Richard Rice, and John Sanders, *The Openness of God: A Biblical Challenge to the Traditional Understanding of God*, ed. Clark H. Pinnock (Downers Grove, IL: InterVarsity Press, 1994).

stricting freedom of speech. But this is short-sighted and suggests that one's view cannot withstand a challenge. Since the need for meaning is fundamental and more basic than the need for power or prestige, and since challenges arise from within each person as self-consciousness increases, challenges are both natural and inevitable and should not be avoided.

Chapter 4

———

ON ETERNALITY
AND CAUSALITY

THERE MUST BE SOMETHING ETERNAL

W E WILL BEGIN TO ANALYZE basic beliefs for meaning. Before looking at various answers to the question "What is eternal?" we must ask, "Must there be something eternal?" The answer to this will begin to show how basic things are clear to reason. The following is offered as proof that there must be something eternal:

1. Contradictory statements cannot both be true and cannot both be false (at the same time and in the same respect).
2. The contradiction of "some is eternal" is "none is eternal."
3. If "none is eternal" then:

   All is temporal.

   All had a beginning.

   All came into being.
4. If all came into being, then being came into existence from non-being.
5. Being from non-being is not possible.
6. Therefore, the original "none is eternal" is not possible.
7. Therefore, its contradiction "some is eternal" must be true.

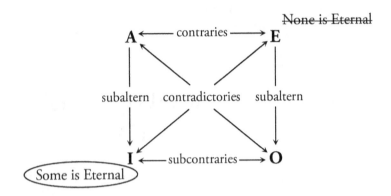

"None is eternal" applies to all being whatsoever. It applies to particular beings as well as the substance out of which being is formed. It applies to material being as well as to non-material being (spirit), to visible being as well as invisible being. It applies against an infinite series of momentary beings. Atoms do not create other atoms *ex nihilo*, nor does a temporal spirit have the power to create other spirits or atoms *ex nihilo*. Being comes from being alone. Non-being is the absence of being and of the power to cause to be.

If being could come from non-being, then there would be no distinction between being and non-being (*a* could then be *non-a*). If being could come from non-being, then there could be uncaused events. There would be no way to distinguish a caused from an uncaused event. When basic distinctions collapse, all distinctions resting on them become meaningless. It is clear, therefore, through the use of reason, that something must be eternal. For a skeptic to doubt this is to give up reason. To give up reason is to give up meaning. "There must be something eternal" is maximally clear since the opposite is not logically possible. If it is not clear to reason that being cannot come from non-being, then nothing can be clear. To assert "being from non-being" at the micro level in quantum physics, or at the macro level in an inflationary theory of the origin of the universe, is to give up reason. To assert uncaused events in support of a contra-causal freedom is to give up reason. To assert "some is eternal" is to deny at least some interpretations of the first noble truth of Buddhism, that all is dukkha/impermanent/lacking self-existence/dependently co-arising. It is to deny at least some interpretations of Heraclitus, that all is fire or flux or becoming or change, without any permanence whatsoever.

A closer and somewhat extended look at causality and uncaused events is appropriate here in light of objections which might be raised against this first and most basic argument to show there must be something eternal. If there is agreement on what is more basic, there can be agreement on what is less basic.

ON CAUSALITY AND UNCAUSED EVENTS

The argument against "nothing is eternal" is a *reductio ad absurdum* argument. That is to say, it is absurd or rationally unintelligible to think being came into existence from non-being. To assert "being from non-being" is to assert uncaused events. Some analysis may help clarify matters further.

The Epistemological Status of Belief in Causality

Belief in causality is not an empirical claim. Causality, or its absence, cannot be known by observation. There is not any indicator, and there can be no indicator, of causality or the lack of causality. Belief in causality is transcendental. It is a necessary condition for the intelligibility of the world and of thought.

1. If there can be one uncaused event, there can be more than one uncaused event. Any or many or all events may be uncaused. There is no non-arbitrary rational way to limit the number of uncaused events.

2. If one uncaused event is logically possible, then all events can be uncaused, and then nothing would be logically impossible.

3. If uncaused events were possible, it would be possible for there to be no causal connections whatsoever between a thought or a sense impression and a cause in either the external world or in my mind. There could be no causal connection between what one person said and what the other person heard, or between one thought and another (premise and conclusion) in anyone's mind, or between intention

and act in any person. As a matter of integrity, belief in causality is a necessary condition for belief in thinking and for dialogue.

Being from Non-Being and Uncaused Events

1. Being from non-being is not creation *ex nihilo*. In creation *ex nihilo*, God exists eternally (in contrast to nothing is eternal), and God acts to bring the world into existence. The world coming into existence by a divine act of creation is not an uncaused event.

2. Being from non-being is not coming into existence by an unknown or unknowable cause (as in quantum physics). An unknown or unknowable cause is still a cause; it is not non-being.

3. Being from non-being is not causation by an invisible being, material or spiritual. Appeal to a singularity to explain the origin of the universe is not an uncaused event, since there are no uncaused events.

4. An uncaused event is not the same as an uncaused being. An uncaused being is an eternal being. An event is not a being.

5. Being from non-being is like an atom or a sub-atomic particle or a person coming into existence from absolute non-being, without any cause whatsoever.

6. Being from non-being is not to be understood as being caused to be by nothing or non-being as the cause. Nothing or non-being is not a cause. Caused by nothing is equivalent by obversion to not caused by anything. Not caused by anything is an uncaused event.

Is Being from Non-Being a Contradiction?

1. Being from non-being is said to be like *a* from *non-a*. Since *a* from *non-a* is not a contradiction (like matter from spirit or a chicken from an egg), then being from non-being is not a contradiction.

Response: Being from non-being is not like *a* from *non-a*. *Non-a* is still in the category of being, not non-being. Being from non-being is like *a* from neither *a* nor *non-a*, if *a* and *non-a* can be considered to encompass all categories of being. It would be like matter from neither matter nor spirit, or, a chicken from neither chicken nor egg.

2. Since being from non-being is not a contradiction like a square-circle, it is said to be not a contradiction (even if it is thought to be false and unbelievable).

Response: Being from non-being is not a formal contradiction stated in this form, but it implies a formal contradiction. If being from non-being were possibly true, then being would be no different from non-being. If being is no different from non-being, then being is non-being, which is a contradiction. It violates the law of identity and the law of non-contradiction: something is both *a* and *non-a*, at the same time and in the same respect.

Is Being from Non-Being Clearly False or Does It Require Proof by What Is More Basic?

Does this proof depend on the Principle of Sufficient Reason (PSR), that there is a sufficient reason for everything that comes to pass?

1. There is more than one form of the PSR. Which form might be appealed to as more basic?[1]

2. Is the PSR any different in meaning from no uncaused events or no being from non-being?

3. Is there any persuasive difference between the two—would those who affirm uncaused events be any more likely to affirm PSR?

---

1. G.W. Leibniz, George R. Montgomery, and Albert R. Chandler, *Discourse on Metaphysics and the Monadology* (Mineola, NY: Dover Publications, 2005). Leibniz wrote, "No fact can be real or existent, no statement true, unless there is a sufficient reason why it is so and not otherwise." And elsewhere (in his essay, "The Principles of Nature and of Grace, Based on Reason"): "The first question which should rightly be asked is this: "Why should there be something rather than nothing?" The Principle of Sufficient Reason can be understood differently and applied with different results to the existence of God, to the creation of particular beings, and to providential acts regarding those beings. That something exists is common ground to all in the history of philosophy. Here we are examining PSR in relation to being a support for, or more basic than, "no being from non-being."

Permanence, Change, and Causality

The classic metaphysical antinomy between change (all is flux, change, *dukkha*) and permanence (the world of plurality and change is an illusion, maya, unreal) either affirms uncaused events or denies change and causality altogether. If there is no permanence of being continuing from one moment to another, then each moment of being is wholly independent in arising and does not and cannot dependently co-arise. Momentariness, over and against any possible form of permanence, is a mere succession of being from non-being. If one instance of being from non-being is unintelligible, an infinite series of being from non-being would be infinitely unintelligible. On the other hand, denying all causality, by denying all change, will be seen to be equally unintelligible.

Is Freedom Incompatible with Causality?

The classic antinomy between freedom and determinism rests on an incompatibilist notion of freedom in relation to causality. Since *ought* implies *can* (the ability to do otherwise), and, an effect necessarily follows from a cause (it could not be otherwise), causality is often denied in order to preserve freedom (Kant and William James). Libertarians affirm uncaused events in order to preserve moral intelligibility in the universe. But moral intelligibility cannot be sealed off from the loss of metaphysical intelligibility through uncaused events. If there are uncaused events, an "act" can be uncaused by an intention to act or not to act. On the other hand, if "can implies want" (I can use my reason if I want to), then freedom, defined as doing what I want, is not incompatible with causation. The choice here is not between determinism (all events are caused) and indeterminism (some events are uncaused), but between an intelligible and an ultimately unintelligible definition of freedom.

Skepticism and Causality

Fully consistent skepticism (Sextus Empiricus) must ground itself in the logical possibility of an uncaused event. If all things are possible, and if every view is equally opposed to its contradiction, then "all came into being from non-being" would be possible and "nothing came into being from non-being" would be equally as possible as "something came into being from non-being," that is, by an uncaused event. But to allow the logical possibility of uncaused events is to allow the possibility that *a* is *non-a*, which denies reason and the intelligibility of all thought. If "all views are possible," then equally "no view is possible." This is the end of all views and is not itself a view. The alternative to "all views are possible" is that "all logically possible views are ontologically possible." This alternative does not add much to our understanding, but it does invite us to explore which views are logically possible.

The argument to show there must be something eternal is about our most basic belief. To avoid it, one must avoid the distinction between being and non-being, and between temporal and eternal. Everyone who professes to make meaningful statements can and should be asked to respond to this argument, or to show how any of their other utterances can be meaningful without making these distinctions. This argument is the cornerstone belief of any worldview. If we cannot know this, we cannot know anything else. It would be futile to go any further in discussion without agreement on this basic belief. We are therefore not obliged to consider the views of anyone who neglects or avoids this argument. On the other hand, if we know by reason and argument that there must be something eternal, we can agree on much more. Basic things are clear. If we agree on what is more basic, we can agree on what is less basic.

To assert "some is eternal" does not prove that this "some" is God. It means *at least some* is eternal, not, *only some* is eternal. Perhaps all is eternal. Further argument would be needed to show that only some is eternal. In the argument to show "some is eternal" we have used a *reductio* argument. We have also used a form of the ontological argument, which argues that what cannot be conceived cannot exist. An eternal being is a being than which nothing greater can be conceived. Since there must be something eternal, an eternal being is also a being which necessarily exists, a being which cannot be conceived not to exist. (To say at least some is eternal does not mean only one is eternal. Whether it is possible for there to be more than one being that is eternal will be examined later. This is prior to considering whether a second eternal being must necessarily exist, or only one must necessarily exist.) It is not being argued that having existence as a predicate is to be greater than what lacks that predicate. It is not being argued that we know something exists by reason. That something exists is not being argued for since it is common ground. No one has ventured past solipsism. It would be self-refuting to say that nothing exists. To assert an eternal being must exist is to assert the greatest possible being must exist. Nothing (temporal) is as great as or greater than an eternal being. And there would be no way to say one eternal being is greater than or better than another eternal being. By aiming at less with this form of the ontological argument, we can avoid many of the historical objections raised against Anselm's version.[2]

---

2. John H Hick, and Arthur C. McGill, eds., *The Many-Faced Argument* (New York: Macmillan, 1967). Norman Malcolm's article discusses the merit of Anselm's argument in connection with the assumption that existence (outside the understanding) is a perfection. The argument offered here is i) that *eternal* existence (or aseity, that is, self-existence) is a perfection, so that two eternal beings would be equally perfect, and the highest conceivable beings, and ii) that an eternal being exists outside the understanding because the alternative "none is eternal" is inconceivable (contradictory). At this point, the eternal being could be matter, or matter and spirit (dualism), or spirit only (spiritual monism).

—

PART II

METAPHYSICS

—

Chapter 5

MATERIAL MONISM

GENERAL BACKGROUND

IF THERE MUST BE SOMETHING ETERNAL, if "nothing is eternal" cannot be true, then what is eternal? Material monists claim that all is one substance—monism—and that this substance is matter. Hence, matter or the material universe is eternal. In Carl Sagan's words, "The cosmos is all that is, ever was, or ever will be."[1] It denies the existence of all non-physical being, in contrast to spiritual monism, dualism, and theism. There is no God, no soul, and no afterlife. Everything in the universe can, in principle, be explained in purely natural terms. For this reason, material monism is also called naturalism, or materialism.

Naturalism is currently the dominant view in the academic world and has permeated all areas of the professional world and popular culture. It is the assumption on which science today operates. It is not restricted to any social or economic group or to any particular lifestyle—intellectual, mystical, or practical. The materialist is most readily identified by the belief that there is no afterlife ("When you're dead, you're dead."), and that there is no God. Materialism first appeared at the beginning of Greek philosophy. In contrast to explanation in terms of the all-too-human gods of Homer, Thales taught that all explanation is in terms of impersonal laws of nature consisting of one substance—water. This was a fundamental shift, for understandable reasons, but problematic in its own way. Revisions occurred through the Pre-Socratic philosophers until dualism was put forward

---

1. Carl Sagan began his famous television series *Cosmos: A Personal Journey* (PBS, 1978-79) with these words. See also: Carl Sagan, *Cosmos* (New York: Random House, 1980).

by Socrates, developed by Plato, and revised by Aristotle and applied as a worldview. Greek dualism was challenged in part and absorbed in part by Christian theism. The highest good for Christianity, influenced by dualism, became the beatific vision of God. The soul freed from the body directly contemplates God. Medieval Christianity rested upon a dualist synthesis of nature and grace, and reason and faith. The view of good and evil derived from this synthesis allowed for teachings about saints and merit and purgatory and indulgences, along with superstitions and moral laxity.

The Renaissance sought relief from the insufficiencies of medievalism in returning to the classical world. The Reformation challenged the medieval view of God's grace and of its administration. The divisions of faith had political implications and wars racked Europe for over 100 years. Some thinkers sought a new common authority, apart from faith, in reason alone. The Enlightenment challenged faith: "Dare to reason."[2] The god of "reason alone" displaced the God of scripture in public life. The realm of natural explanations expanded. Today, a consistent naturalism must disallow any non-natural explanation from every aspect of the world. Essential problems, present from its beginning, remain in the materialist view. But there are new challenges now, given the cultural authority of science today, and the ongoing problem theism has in working out the relation of faith and reason. Today, dogmatic theism is being opposed to by an equally dogmatic naturalism.

Naturalism is now a developed worldview which aggressively works out its implications in culture. What qualifies for research funding, what articles get published in journals, what can be taught in textbooks and in the classroom, must conform to naturalistic paradigms. What counts as freedom and equality in determining human rights must be consistent with the prevailing views about the possibility of moral knowledge and human responsibility. What constitutes sex and love and family must respect human authenticity and autonomy as

---

2. Immanuel Kant, "Answer to the Question: What is Enlightenment?" 1784. "Enlightenment is man's emergence from his self-incurred immaturity. Immaturity is the inability to use one's own understanding without the guidance of another. This immaturity is self-incurred if its cause is not lack of understanding, but lack of resolution and courage to use it without the guidance of another. The motto of enlightenment is therefore: *Sapere aude!* Have courage to use your own understanding!"
https://www3.nd.edu/~afreddos/courses/439/what-is-enlightenment.htm

conceived by those who shape public opinion. Culture wars are the tip of the iceberg in worldview conflict. A whole way of life is at stake in arguing for or against a basic belief. More pointedly, the meaning of our existence is at stake in arguing about what is eternal. Everyone stands to gain the highest good by honest and diligent participation.

THE FIRST ARGUMENT AGAINST MATERIALISM: THE MATERIAL WORLD IS NOT ETERNAL

Is matter eternal? Is matter all that exists? Is this something which is clear to reason? The argument begins with assuming that the material world exists and with the reality of change in this material world. Can change be explained in material terms alone? Is the material world self-explaining? Is change a unique process which comes to an end, or is the material world self-maintaining? The first argument against materialism argues that the material world is not eternal, because it is not self-maintaining.

The argument, formally stated, is as follows:

Major premise: If the material world were eternal, it would be self-maintaining.

Minor premise: The material world is not self-maintaining.

Conclusion: Therefore, the material world is not eternal.

Is this argument sound? First, is it valid? Do the premises logically support the conclusion? There is no disagreement about this. By the formal rules of logic (*modus tollens*) it is valid. Second, are the premises true? The major (first) premise is true analytically, that is, true by analyzing the meaning of "eternal." What is eternal is independent, self-existing, self-maintaining, and self-explaining. The relevant kind of self-maintaining is dynamic rather than static, since the universe is highly differentiated and changing. What about the minor (second) premise? This is not self-evidently true; it requires reasons to be given in support of it. It requires an argument. There are three reasons given in support of saying the material world is not self-maintaining: the first, about the material world in general; the second, about the major parts of the material world (about the sun and stars); and the third, about the material universe as a whole. Let us look at each.

In general, the material world is highly differentiated. There is hot and cold, dry and wet, hard and soft, rock and sand, building and soil. These differences interact with each other. The interaction continues until sameness is reached. The condition of sameness remains the same when left to itself. This process is explained in physics by the 2nd Law of Thermodynamics (entropy): There is increasing randomness and sameness in the physical universe. A cup of coffee on a table will interact with the room temperature until both come to the same temperature, and then, left to itself, will remain the same temperature. A building left to itself will eventually decay, crumble, and become undifferentiated from the ground on which it is built. In all our ordinary experience, entropy is universal. In general, therefore, there is no reason to believe that the material world is self-maintaining. There is every reason to believe that the material world, governed by the law of entropy, is not self-maintaining.

In its major parts, the material world is not self-maintaining. We can know the sun will burn out without learning this from science. The sun is finite in size, and so are the stars. This is obvious to any casual observer. Anyone who wants to can see this. Even an uneducated, abused, child in Ubangi Bangi can see this. The sun is giving off heat. Again, this requires no argument. Anyone with ordinary sense experience can see this. If the sun is limited in size and is giving off its heat, it cannot do so forever. The sun will cease giving off its heat. It will burn out. And when it does, left to itself, it will remain burnt out. The sun therefore could not have been burning forever. The sun, in itself, although it is the most lasting thing in our experience, is not self-maintaining. It is not eternal. In the ancient world, in Egypt, India, Greece, and Persia, the sun was worshiped as a god. If God is the highest being, that is, eternal, then the sun is not to be worshiped as god. Some further explanation, if any were possible, would be necessary to justify this practice. When challenged by reason in history, the practice of worshiping the sun was abandoned as incoherent.

That leaves the universe as a whole as the last possible ground on which to hope to show it is self-maintaining. The argument from Aristotle, used to affirm a first cause, has been opposed by appeal to an infinite regress. This has in turn been objected to by the logical impossibility of an infinite regress in time (the *kalam* argument[3]). Nietzsche appealed to an eternal recurrence, exactly repeating itself, and tried to find some way to maintain human significance in a never-ending cycle. The current view in physics affirms a beginning of the universe, expanding from one place and time, in an explosion called the Big Bang. To maintain eternality with change, the universe is said to have gone through the Big Bang event innumerable times. For there can be no unique or one-time event for a reality which is eternal in time. This view is called the Big Bang Oscillating Universe Theory. The claim that there is an eternal cycle meets several objections.

First, on empirical grounds, given current understanding of the cosmos, there is not enough mass in the known physical universe to allow gravity to pull the expanding universe back, in order for the Big Bang to occur again. This is the problem of the missing mass or dark matter, which has been proposed to be present and yet has not been detected. Ten times as much mass as is currently known to exist is needed for gravity to do its work.[4] This is not a small amount. Occasional reports suggest rogue planets at the fringes of galaxies or an abundance of ghost-like particles called neutrinos are candidates to account for the missing mass. No proposal has received general acceptance and the problem persists. On the face of it, there is no warrant, except the requirement of assumption, for saying the Big Bang will be repeated. Left to itself, the universe will come to sameness and die a heat death. It is not self-maintaining. But claims regarding missing mass, like all empirical claims, are technically falsifiable. There is warrant for saying the physical universe as a whole is not self-maintaining. But this warrant, based on missing mass, falls short of proof. Suppose the missing mass were found, and in just the right amounts, there would be a *second* problem of a different kind, which logically encounters the problem of entropy. Since the force pulling the universe in is said to generate the force that will push the universe out

---

3. The *kalam* argument is one form of the cosmological argument, developed in medieval Islamic scholasticism, to show the universe began to exist based on the impossibility of an infinite regress of time. For an extended discussion on the cosmological argument, see William L. Craig, and Quentin Smith, *Theism, Atheism, and Big Bang Cosmology* (Oxford: Oxford University Press, 1995).
   See also: https://plato.stanford.edu/entries/cosmological-argument/#4.3

4. Robert Jastrow, *God and the Astronomers* (New York: W.W. Norton & Co, 2000), 131.

again, rather than the universe ending as a black hole, at some point the force pulling in would have to equal the force pushing out. At that point, equilibrium would be reached and the process of expansion and contraction would come to an end. The universe would reach sameness in entropy. It would not be self-maintaining and therefore it could not be eternal.

At this point, we are beyond empirical claims, on either side of the issue. As with early Greek philosophy, cosmology is a branch of metaphysics, subject to logical rather than empirical scrutiny. Logical objections to non-empirical claims must be logically met. Tentativeness and pragmatism cannot be used to forego philosophical criticism. Changing the definition of matter is an option, as long as it is not an appeal to an unknown. But this is not easily done, as Thales saw when he claimed all is water and all is full of soul—that nature is alive. Hylozoism was rejected by materialists and non-materialists alike in history.

The problem with the model of self-maintaining by oscillation has been seen by some[5] and another model has been proposed. It is the inflationary theory of the Big Bang proposed by several cosmologists in the 1980's, including Andrei Linde and Stephen Hawking.[6] Alan Guth is its current spokesman. According to this view,[7] there are two kinds of vacuum, a true vacuum and a false vacuum. The true vacuum is empty of matter and empty of energy. The false vacuum is empty of matter but not of energy. At one time all of space was a true vacuum. Nothing in nature remains quiet. Everything, including the true vacuum, is subject to fluctuation. This fluctuation of the energy field which is "absent in the true vacuum but not entirely," "would happen very rarely, but could not be ruled out." This fluctuation brought about the energy of the false vacuum, which expanded rapidly. This is the Big Bang. It would appear that Guth is claiming that being (energy) came from non-being (the true vacuum). Guth certainly continues to give this appearance. The cover of *Discover* magazine, April, 2002, represents his view to be saying, "The universe burst into something

---

5. Paul Davies, *The Mind of God* (New York: Simon & Schuster, 1992), 50-54.

6. See the latest expression of Andrei Linde's view at: https://web.stanford.edu/~alinde/

7. The vacuum fluctuation, or true vacuum to false vacuum view, of the Big Bang has been presented widely to thoughtful readers by Victor Weisskopf, "The Origin of the Universe," *The New York Review* Vol. 36, Number 2, February 16, 1989.

out of absolutely nothing—zero, nada."[8] The inflationary theory has ballooned to include countless universes all continually being born of nothing. And so it is. But can a rational person believe such a thing? No, not now, nor in the past.

These three reasons—not enough mass, force in would equal force out, and true vacuum to false vacuum as being from non-being—refute the claim that as a whole the physical universe is self-maintaining. Neither in general, nor in its parts, nor as a whole, is it self-maintaining. Therefore, we conclude that the minor premise—that the universe is not self-maintaining—is true and that the argument is sound. And it is clear. One has to give up reason to believe that being can come from non-being in the inflationary view of the Big Bang.

The appeal to uncaused events is not new in the history of materialism, in its attempt to avoid entropy. Epicurus long ago appealed to uncaused events (the atomic swerve theory/*clinamen*) to account for change in sameness.[9] In his view, all atoms were moving in the same direction at the same speed (sameness). Then one atom swerved (uncaused event), colliding with others and producing the differentiated condition we now see. Thales' inability to account for change and dryness (different from the wetness of water) led Anaximander to appeal to an unknown—the *Aperion*, the Indeterminate—to account for change. Anaximenes suggested Air, which was close to, but not entirely, an unknown. Then four elements were used to explain change (Empedocles), followed by an indefinite, innumerable number (Anaxagoras).[10]

Plato and Aristotle broke with materialism and used dualism in order to explain change by efficient, formal, and final causes. Dirac in

---

8. One suspects that Guth does not literally hold that view, but that there is some form of energy from which the universe arose. The critical point for the naturalist position must be to represent this view so as to rule out the clear possibility that this energy is from God. This position may be obscured in its representation to avoid God as the source of the universe, and will require scrutiny to discern what is in fact being said, if it is contrary to popular representations. To search this out, see Alan Guth, *The Inflationary Universe: The Quest for a New Theory of Cosmic Origins* (New York: Helix Books, 1997).

See also his web page at: https://physics.mit.edu/faculty/alan-guth/

9. For Epicurus' Atomic Swerve (*clinamen*) Theory, see Titus Lucretius Carus, *On the Nature of Things*, trans. Martin Ferguson Smith (Indianapolis, IN: Hackett Publishing, 2001), 2.216-93.

10. Philip Wheelwright, ed., *The Presocratics* (New York: Odyssey Press, 1966).

the 1930's spoke of an evenly-heated vacuum everywhere. Then something happened (uncaused event) and the diversity of the universe became manifest.[11] Fred Hoyle's Steady State Theory[12] had hydrogen atoms continually appearing from nowhere, to account for the present preponderance of hydrogen atoms in a world in which atoms naturally combine to form heavier elements. Bertrand Russell, well-known in the mid-twentieth century, affirmed naturalism while maintaining that the probability that the universe will die a heat death is so great that the alternative is not worth considering.[13] More recently, as we have seen, forms of the Big Bang theory have attempted to account for cosmic change in purely natural terms.

Stephen Hawking attempted to explain change in natural terms alone. He thinks that a black hole becomes a singularity when it "sinks to zero in size so that the density of matter and the curvature of space-time become infinite."[14] One must ask, how is a singularity which is

---

11. Paul Dirac, *Principles of Quantum Mechanics* (Oxford: Oxford University Press, 1982). (See what has come to be called the Dirac Sea and vacuum polarization for Dirac's concept that all of space was an evenly heated vacuum.) Here the concern is how change occurs from an original sameness (an evenly heated vacuum or entropic state) to the highly differentiated universe.

12. Fred Hoyle, *The Nature of the Universe*, 2nd ed. (Oxford: Basil Blackwell, 1952).

13. Robert E Egner, and Lester E Denonn, eds. "A Free Man's Worship," *The Basic Writings of Bertrand Russell* (New York: Simon & Schuster, 1961), 67.
See also: https://www3.nd.edu/~afreddos/courses/264/fmw.htm

14. Stephen W. Hawking, *A Brief History of Time* (New York: Bantam Books, 1988). Although his earlier work focused on singularities (when the universe was at zero size), Hawking later offered a "proposal," a mathematical model, that seeks to avoid the notion of a singularity in which time would begin by creation. Creation by God is seen by Hawking as incompatible with understanding: "God may know how the universe began, but we cannot give any particular reason for thinking it began one way rather than another," 136. "But if the universe is really completely self-contained, having no boundary or edge, it would have neither beginning nor end; it would simply be. What place, then, for a creator?" 141. "Only if we could picture the universe in terms of imaginary time *[p]* would there be no singularities *[q]*," 138. In the picture he offers of moving from the North Pole to the South Pole in imaginary time (figure 8.1), he claims that "Even though the universe would have zero size at the North and South Poles these points would not be singularities . . . ." It is hard to see why not. The analogy does not transport from a point on the whole (points of North and South Poles on the earth) to the whole as a point—the universe at zero size. The distinction itself between real and imaginary time is collapsed, or inverted: "So maybe what we call imaginary time is really more basic, and what we call real is just an idea that we invented to help us describe what we think the universe is like," 139. Earlier it was said that "only if *p* then *q*." A necessary distinction earlier between real and imaginary time now becomes meaningless in order to avoid singularities and a beginning to the universe.

"zero in size" different from non-being? And how is it still material if it has no size? If it is not non-being and not material, how is this source of the universe different from spirit? Hawking thinks that the singularity of the universe as a whole implies a time when the laws of the universe did not exist. How then can the set of laws described by the unified theory be a scientific equivalent to the Creator? He thinks that the need for a beginning is done away with by appeal to "imaginary time" in which "the distinction between time and space disappears completely." But what is the distinction, if any, between imaginary time and what we might call real time? If the distinction is that real time has a beginning, but imaginary time has no beginning or end, how is this distinction different from the distinction of time and timeless eternity? Here we have Hawking's appeal to matter without size, a Creator with a beginning, and no beginning in imaginary time, in order to avoid incoherence in the current naturalist view of origins. But these distinctions introduce new sets of problems which may be worse than the first. Reason seeking clarification of meaning compels us to move from incoherence. But a move to silence, or a move to an unknown, by making distinctions without specifiable differences, is not an improvement.

What might a materialist say in response to a non-materialist who says, "Appeal to an uncaused event is not rational"?

Materialist: Why should reason be an absolute? Reason is an aspect of human consciousness, which has evolved and is still evolving.

Non-Materialist: If reason is not an absolute, then contradictory statements can both be true. "All is matter" is not rationally true if "some is not matter" can also be true at the same time.

Materialist: "All is matter" is pragmatically true; it works for me.

Non-materialist: A statement about what works or satisfies is a statement about oneself and not about the world or about what is real.

Materialist: About what is real I make no statement.

Non-Materialist: As rational beings, we cannot give up reason and thought and the need for meaning; we can only give up our integrity, our concern for consistency.

At this point, the Materialist is moved to silence and there is nothing more to be said.

THE SECOND ARGUMENT AGAINST MATERIALISM: THINKING IS NOT A MOTION OF ATOMS

The second argument against materialism shows that thought cannot be explained in material terms. It argues against reductive materialism which would reduce thought to some material category.

The second argument, formally stated, is as follows:

Major premise: If all is matter, then thinking must be motion of atoms in the brain.

Minor premise: Thinking is not motion of atoms in the brain.

Conclusion: Therefore, it is not the case that all is matter.

Is the argument sound? It is valid by *modus tollens*. Are the premises true? The first premise requires some clarification. It is not saying that thinking is "caused by" motion of atoms in the brain. It is saying that thinking is identical with motion of atoms in the brain. Neither side disputes that the brain is involved in thinking, or that there can be brain activity without thinking. The question is whether thinking is entirely a brain or a physical activity. The question is not whether new properties emerge from new relations of physical things, but whether the new properties are physical properties. Fire is a new property emerging from new physical relations of fuel, oxygen, and a flame, but fire is not thought to be a new non-physical property. So, if all is matter, then thinking is a physical property, a new physical relation of physical parts. It would be motion of atoms in the brain, whatever new form that motion would take.

The second premise likewise requires explanation. Two things are said to be identical if they have the same set of qualities. Thinking has the qualities of true and false. Motion of atoms has the qualities of up and down, fast and slow, straight and curved, etc. True and false cannot be identified with any pair of, or combination of pairs of, up/down, fast/slow, and straight/curved. Fast/slow admits of degrees whereas true/false does not. Up and down differ, without one being preferable; in true and false there is difference and preference, etc. Fast and straight differ, but both are seen as physical properties. True and fast differ, but they are not both seen as physical properties. True has no spatial quality as fast does. To place the predicate "true" within the category of the physical is a category mistake. Therefore, thinking is not motion of any kind.

The argument is sound since it is valid in its reasoning and its premises are true. Reductionism of any kind has been found problematic. Qualitative differences cannot be reduced one to the other. Geometry (space) has a mathematical aspect, but it is not reducible to math. Space is continuous, but numbers are discrete. Not to recognize this leads to Zeno's paradoxes of motion, in which motion is explained mathematically.[15] Attempts have been made to reduce chemistry to physics, biology to chemistry, psychology to biology, and faith to psychology. In each case, the distinctiveness of each aspect has asserted itself and freed itself from reduction. A being is a unity of diversity. There is diversity within categories (blue and red) as well as between categories (living and non-living). These diversities differ in kind.

Diversities may be ordered, one presupposing another, but that does not make one kind reducible to another. Reducing all reality to matter requires the naturalistic thinker to seek some kind of natural explanation for thought. Marx, Freud, and Skinner did so. For Marx, religion is the opiate of the masses.[16] Religious belief is reduced to economic categories of rich and poor. How is true and false to be derived

---

15. When space and time are reduced to numbers, then every segment of space and time becomes infinitely divisible. Since an infinite series cannot be crossed in finite time, the crossing of the stadium (an infinite series in space in actual finite time) cannot be explained "rationally". Achilles cannot overtake the tortoise in a foot race if the tortoise has a head start. At every moment in time, the arrow is at rest at some point in space, so motion is not explicable. Parmenides had denied the rationality and therefore the reality of change. Zeno, his disciple, developed these paradoxes in support of Parmenides' thesis. The irrationality of motion depends on the Pythagorean assumption that all is (reducible to) number. But the area of a circle, which is definite, and the length of the hypotenuse of a right-angle triangle, cannot be represented definitely since pi and some square roots cannot be represented by a definite number.

16. "Religion is the sigh of the oppressed creature, the heart of a heartless world, just as it is the spirit of a spiritless situation. It is the opium of the people." Karl Marx, *Critique of Hegel's "Philosophy of Right,"* ed. Joseph O'Malley, trans. Annette Jolin and Joseph O'Malley (Cambridge: Cambridge University Press, 1970).

from rich and poor? Applied to Marx himself, is his view determined by his economic condition? If so, then all views merely differ. Then Marx's view would be neither true nor false, contrary to what he is asserting to be true. His assertion is a complex assertion, which is self-refuting. The same is true of Freud, who would reduce belief to repression of sexual instinct, connected with early childhood training. Likewise, this is true of Skinner, who reduces thinking to conditioned response. In each case, reducing the rational to the non-rational does away with a meaningful distinction between true and false. Materialists cannot explain the reality of thought in natural terms. Since any assertion is a form of thought, the materialist must choose between retaining thought and giving up materialism or trying to keep materialism while giving up thought. The choice to be made is obvious.

THE THIRD ARGUMENT AGAINST MATERIALISM: THE MIND IS NOT THE BRAIN

The third argument against materialism shows that some non-material thing exists. It shows that the soul exists by showing that the mind is not the brain. As the second argument shows that thought cannot be accounted for as brain activity, the third argument shows that perception, and self-consciousness which accompanies it, cannot be accounted for by brain activity alone. We do not hesitate to say we have a brain. We also say we have a mind. But we are puzzled when asked if we think with our mind or our brain. We are unsure if the mind is the brain or if the mind is the soul. Yet the mind is such that if we had a mind, we would surely know it. We would not need to seek special psychic phenomena or out-of-body or near-death experiences to know this. What we are looking for would be so obvious that we would be inclined to overlook it. The third argument begins with our claim about knowing most certainly that the physical world exists, and by analysis goes on to show that what we know most certainly is not that the material world exists, but that the mind exists, and that this mind is not the brain.

The third argument against materialism, stated formally, is as follows:

Major premise: The most immediately known is the most certainly known.

Minor premise: The self is the most immediately known.

Conclusion: Therefore, the self is the most certainly known.

Again, we ask, is this argument sound? It is a valid form of the categorical syllogism. If A is B, and C is A, then C is B. This is the same form as the well-known syllogism: if all men are mortal, and Socrates is a man, then Socrates is mortal. Is the first premise true? By common consent, it is. I say I know there is a table before me because it is immediately present to me in time and space. Is the second premise true? We can see it is true by analysis of what is meant by "most immediately known" in relation to time and space.

The table that I see, or, more properly in material terms, the cause of the table that I see, is said to be several feet in front of me. And it is also said that I see the table with my eyes and my brain. I see the table through a process of light waves coming to my eyes, neural impulses firing in my brain, and presumably more. The analysis of what is most immediately known proceeds as follows:

First: There is a cause of the table that I see several feet away from me.

Second: The light waves coming from the table to my eyes are more immediate than the table. Yet the light waves are not themselves seen, nor are they conceived to be shaped like the table. Another step is needed to get to the table that I see.

Third: Neural impulses form in my optic nerves, and in the process of perception, are more immediate than the light waves. But the neural impulses are not seen and they are not conceived to be shaped like a table. Furthermore, the neural impulse is the last brain activity. Another step is needed to get to the table that I see. It must go beyond the neural impulse, the last brain activity; therefore, it must go beyond the brain.

Fourth: The next step is the table that I see. The table that I see is not a physical table anywhere in my brain, nor is it identical with the cause of the table that I see, which is outside my brain. But if the table I see is not in space at all, either inside or outside my brain, neither is it nothing at all. The table I see must be a non-physical, that is, mental image representing the neural impulse. This mental image is more immediate to the perceiver than the neural impulse. Unlike the neural impulse, (the content of) the mental image *is* seen, and it *is* shaped like a table. Furthermore, the mental image does not perceive itself, but I am aware of myself as the perceiver.

Fifth: The self is more immediately known than the mental image; it is the perceiver of the table; and I am aware of the self as having no size but having consciousness. Furthermore, there is nothing of which I can be more immediately aware than myself.

This self, which is most immediately known, and which is characterized by having consciousness and having no size, is the same in characterization as the mind, the soul, and spirit. They are one and the same, since each is said to be conscious, and there is only one center of consciousness. If the analysis of "most immediately known" in steps 1-5 above is correct, then the minor premise "the self is most immediately known" is true. Since the argument is valid and the premises are true, the argument is sound. The clarity of this argument rests on three points: i) I see the table through my eyes and brain process, ii) A neural impulse is not a mental image, and iii) I (the self) am the perceiver of the table, different from the table perceived.

   Attempts have been made to refute the conclusion by objecting to steps in the analysis. *First*, the self is identified with the bundle of mental images (Hume).[17] *Second*, talk about mental images and states can be avoided by talking about behavior (analytical behaviorism). *Third*, the physical nerve fiber and the non-physical mental state can be identified indirectly (the neutral identity thesis). We will look at each of these.

---

17. David Hume, *A Treatise on Human Nature*, L.A. Selby Bigge edition (Oxford: Clarendon Press, 1888), 252.

Hume assumes and develops the empiricism of Locke and Berkeley. Apart from analytically true statements (2+2 = 4), all knowledge comes to us through our senses. I would know the self only through the senses, on Hume's assumption. But, he said, "When I enter most intimately into what I call *myself*, I always stumble on some particular perception or other, of heat or cold, light or shade, love or hatred, pain or pleasure. I never can catch *myself* at any time without a perception, and never can observe anything but the perception. I do not see any self among the sense impressions. If there is a self it can only be the bundle of mental images."[18] Hume is restrained by his empiricist assumption from seeing the obvious. What is the "I" that is doing the looking in the first place? It is distinct from each and every image, even as it is obvious that the images do not perceive themselves. The self therefore cannot be reduced to "a bundle of mental images," and this is clear from the very expression used by Hume to speak about "seeing mental images."

The second objection maintains that we can avoid talk about mental images and states and so avoid language which would seduce us into thinking there is a non-physical reality. We can just as well talk about behavior rather than mental states. What is meant by a mental state term is just a statement about behavior. "X is in pain" is analyzed to mean "X is exhibiting pain behavior." This is called analytical behaviorism. It has been applied to animal behavior, and to artificial intelligence, and has called into question any essential difference between animals, humans, and computers. As Gilbert Ryle famously said, with deliberate abusiveness, there is no "ghost in the machine."[19]

Analytical behaviorism is to be rejected as a satisfactory way to explain mental state terms. A person may exhibit pain behavior without having any pain. Actors do this, and sometimes unconscious persons have motor reflex responses without feeling pain. Furthermore, one may feel pain and not exhibit pain behavior. We all sometimes do so. Even in extreme pain, one may not show pain behavior, as in the case of self-immolation in fire by Buddhist monks in the Vietnam War. Programmed pain behavior, without any feeling of pain, can be man-

---

18. Hume, *Treatise*, 252.

19. Gilbert Ryle, *The Concept of Mind* (New York: Barnes and Noble, 1949), 15.

ifested in artificial intelligences, as well as under varied mental states such as hypnosis and under physical states such as local anesthetics.

The neutral identity thesis seeks to avoid what is taken to be limitations of language in identifying the non-physical with the physical. Pain and nerve fiber appear to belong to different categories, but by inventing a new neutral entity—call it "fibain"—we can identify the two so that it can be said, without contradiction, that the very same entity which is conducting nerve impulses (a nerve fiber) is aching unbearably (pain). This linguistic maneuver is insufficient because it does not pay attention to the essential properties of pain and fiber. When essential properties of each are considered, the contradiction is obvious. "The very same thing that has no size (pain) has size (fiber)."

The minor premise "the self is most immediately known" stands. There is every reason to believe it and no reason to doubt it. The self is the perceiver of mental images; it is not a bundle of images. Pain is not pain behavior. What has no size is not the same as what has size. In each case, the law of identity must be denied in order to avoid what is clear. The third argument against materialism is sound. It must be concluded that the mind (soul or consciousness) is not the brain. Therefore, it must be concluded that it is not the case that all is matter.

Taken together, the first, second, and third arguments against material monism show that it is clear that all is not matter and that matter is not eternal. The initial assumption itself, that matter exists, is called into question by the third argument. For if all that I am aware of is my mind and its ideas, an argument would be needed to show that the cause of what I see is something physical, rather than my mind or some other mind. Idealism cannot be dismissed by waving one's hand, or by kicking a rock, or by appeal to common sense, or by appeal to properly functioning faculties operating under appropriate circumstances.

THE FOURTH ARGUMENT AGAINST MATERIALISM: NATURALISM IS NOT BASED ON SCIENCE

Before leaving material monism to examine spiritual monism, the case for naturalism based on science must be considered. Science has enormous prestige, based in large part on its practical accomplishments. People believe in science because of its "miracles." It claims to be publicly verifiable through experiments which can be repeated. It commits itself to finding natural explanations for what it observes. It employs methodological naturalism in its search for knowledge. It rules out supernatural or non-physical explanations in principle. It therefore has assumed metaphysical naturalism (all is matter and matter is eternal). If the material world were self-explaining, it would be unnecessary to bring in God in order to explain its order or design. To be self-explaining would refute any argument from design. The naturalist worldview has clashed with the worldview of historic Christian theism. Two very different creation accounts arise from naturalism and theism.

There are three issues involved in this controversy. *First*, by what method is the dispute to be settled—by appeal to science, or to scripture, or to the critical use of reason in philosophy? *Second*, if differing assumptions are being used to interpret what is observed, which assumption, given the existing common ground, best interprets the data? And *third*, is there a compromise position (theistic evolution) which would be acceptable to both sides?

Issue 1: By What Method Can Origins Be Known: Science or Scripture or Philosophy?

There has been long and heated controversy between science and religion without resolution. This is an indication that there are different assumptions in the dispute which are not being addressed. Science assumes that all is matter, and that only natural forces operate; it has not attempted to prove this. Christian theism assumes the existence of God the Creator; it does not attempt to prove that God the Creator exists. No resolution can be expected until there is agreement on what is more basic. Without proof of one's assumption, dogmatic naturalism (antitheism) is being opposed to dogmatic theism. And neither science nor religion is willing to offer proof of its first principles. The question of proof of first principles belongs to the realm of philosophy. If the issue is to be settled it is therefore to be settled by philosophy.

There are objections to philosophy from several directions, so further explanation is needed. *First*, philosophy isn't trusted by either scientists or theologians. Its record has not been that good; in fact, it falls a little short of abysmal. After 2,500 years of waiting, hope for an answer now seems absurd. *Second,* some scientists say science can correct itself even if the question of God the Creator remains unanswered. Intelligent design can be discerned apart from any worldview on strictly scientific grounds, so philosophical argument is not needed. *Third,* some theologians will say that neither intelligent design in science nor philosophy will go far enough. Perhaps they may get as far as theistic evolution, which is itself disputed, so only appeal to revelation will suffice.

A brief apology for philosophy may be permitted here. *First,* ironically, the abysmal record of philosophy is not a total failure. To agree that we have not come up with a satisfactory answer is a significant agreement. We agree on what does not work, even if we have not come up with a satisfactory answer. *Second,* no one else is willing to try to prove first principles. *Third,* the question of what is real in any case belongs in principle to philosophy. *Fourth,* the question is unavoidable. It must be answered and any answer will be a philosophical answer, however uncritically held. *Fifth,* the critical process of history is not over. As humans, we can become more critically aware of our assumptions, even though it may be slow. *Sixth,* for the theological reader, one need not rule out divine grace working in philosophy. *Seventh,* the critical use of reason can expose assumptions and compel change thereby, whatever the direction of change.

The penetrating presence of assumption in science can be seen in what is presented as "a fact of the age of a fossil that every reasonable person must accept." The carbon dating method requires three pieces of information: the present amount of C_{14} in the fossil bone, the half-life rate of decay of C_{14}, and the original amount of C_{14} present at the death of the animal. Generally, the first two points have been agreed upon. How is the original amount determined? Obviously, it cannot be by observation. Here an assumption is made. If an animal of the sort being examined were to die today, how much C_{14} would be in the bone? The amount of C_{14} observed to be present at the death of an animal today is assumed to be the same amount at the death of an animal of the same kind at an unobserved time long ago. This is to assume uniformitarianism, a principle put forward by Charles Lyell in his book *Principles of Geology,* published in 1832 and read and adopted by Charles Darwin on his voyage on the *Beagle.*

Uniformitarianism holds that the present is like the past, that the forces now operating in nature have always operated, and in essentially the same magnitude. Since only natural forces are now operating, uniformitarianism assumes naturalism, that only natural forces have operated, which assumes material monism, to the exclusion of theism. Uniformitarianism also excludes non-uniformitarianism or catastrophism, whether caused by natural or supernatural forces.[20] The "fact" of the age of the fossil is an interpretation of data in light of a basic belief, and is warranted only as much as the assumption is warranted. Philosophy is the discipline which deals with the question of the assumption whether all is matter.

Issue 2: By What Assumption Is the Data to Be Explained: Uniformity or Non-uniformity?

The second issue is: Which assumption (uniformity or non-uniformity) best explains the data of geology, biology, and astronomy? The geological data to be explained are fossil beds, coal beds, sedimentary strata, mountain ranges, volcanic plateaus, ocean depths, and meteorological changes. In biology, the stages of macro-evolution needing to be explained are: from non-life to life; from life to more complex life; from more complex life to hominids; and from hominids to humans. In astronomy, fine-tuning and the age of the universe need to be explained. In all of these, uniformity, based on naturalism, is not the assumption which best explains the data. We will look at each of these in basic ways, sufficient to show that scientific naturalism does not explain the data and that science cannot be used to support naturalism.

---

20. John C. Whitcomb Jr., and Henry M. Morris, *Genesis Flood: The Biblical Record and its Scientific Implications* (Phillipsburg, NJ: P&R Publishing, 1961). This is an attempt to interpret geological data in light of pre-Lyellian, biblical catastrophism. Naturalistic sources of catastrophism can also be offered, such as, for example, by Velikovsky. The main dispute here is between gradualism/uniformitarianism/non-catastrophism on the one hand and non-gradualism/non-uniformitarianism/catastrophism on the other hand. The problem occurs in gradualist interpretation of the Noahic flood and also in biology, in saltation theories of specie origination (Gould) and lucky-monster theories of mutations (Goldschmidt) vs. orthodox gradualist theories, with naturalists on both sides of the issue in biology. The issue is not first between natural and supernatural explanations, or between theistic and non-theistic explanations. The more basic must be settled first if there is to be progress in settling the dispute.

1. Geological Data

The geological data is not best explained by uniformity rather than non-uniformity. Fossils are not formed by the present processes seen today. Bones of dead animals ordinarily decay, decompose, and disappear. Fossil beds, containing large numbers of bones of many different kinds of animals, do not form by any process known to man in the past few thousand years. Coal is not being formed by any present process. Coal beds containing tree trunks, some buried in vertical positions, could not have happened gradually over long ages by present forces operating at the present magnitude. When trees die and fall to the ground by present processes, they decay on the surface of the ground within a few decades. They do not change into coal. Sedimentary strata, found abundantly all over the earth, were laid down by water. Was it gradual, over millions of years? Lack of erosion and refilling between contiguous layers indicate rapid occurrence, which is inconsistent with uniformity. Mountain ranges show simultaneous folding activity over hundreds of miles, which is not explainable by shifting of fault lines in earthquakes over time. Widespread simultaneous volcanic activity, necessary to create volcanic plateaus, has not occurred at that magnitude in human history. Underwater canyons two miles deep indicate the sea level once rose quite rapidly. Animals frozen quickly and buried in the arctic region shows a rapid meteorological change over a very large region, change unknown under present conditions. Some form of non-uniformitarianism or catastrophism must be used to explain the geological data.

2. Biological Data

In explaining the origin of various life forms, macro-evolution (changes between kinds, for example, from amoeba to man) is not to be confused with micro-evolution (changes within a species, for example, the beaks of finches). Macro-evolution is said to occur by random mutation in genetic material combined with natural selection (survival of the fittest). A combination of impersonal law and chance, forces continuing to operate today, is said to be sufficient to explain every step in the process of macro-evolution. We will look at some of the basic difficulties at each stage.

a. From Non-life to Life

i. Probability in General

Order or information patterns do not occur by forces operating randomly. The simplest life form is highly complex. There is an irreducible complexity that cannot be gradually approximated. Words in a meaningful sentence, if each reduced to its simplest parts—its letters—would, if ordered by a random process, be unintelligible to an extremely high probability. In a fair coin toss, to get heads 30 times in a row is extremely improbable (one in 2^{30}). To get a meaningful sentence (equivalent to DNA information) containing 80 letters by a random process (a monkey at a typewriter) is even less probable (one in 27^{80}), too improbable to comprehend.

ii. Probability and Rationality

It is not rational to bet on what is improbable. It is less rational to bet on what is less probable. It is most irrational to bet on what is most improbable. To bet the meaning of one's life on one in 10^{100} is most irrational. Yet many naturalists have made this bet regarding the origin of human life, and therefore the meaning of life.

iii. Probability and Consistency

The argument from design is not used consistently by the naturalist. If an arrowhead, which is relatively simple, requires an intelligent designer, and a watch, which is more complex, more strongly requires an intelligent designer, then a living organism, which is still more complex, all the more requires an intelligent designer. The naturalist is unwilling to make this move.

iv. Probability and Possibility

Natural processes break down order. Complex amino acids necessary for building life would oxidize in earth's present oxygen-rich environment and be rendered useless for building life. The earth's early environment at the inception of life must therefore have been without oxygen for life to have begun randomly.[21] Yet as soon as life begins, life requires the presence of oxygen.[22] This would require an instant change in the earth's environment for life to begin and to survive. This is naturally not possible. Suggestion is made that life can come from outer space. But this is to transfer the problem elsewhere, not to solve it.

b. From Life to More Complex Life

The next step in macro-evolutionary process requires increased complexity in an already living being by random change, that is, by the forces now operating.

i. Change and Complexity

Mere change does not increase complexity. A change within a strand of DNA does not increase the number of strands in the DNA, which is needed for increased complexity.

ii. Variation and Complexity

Variation is not a sign of increasing complexity. It could be a sign of an already existing complexity, some characteristics of which become dominant or recessive at different times.

iii. Random Changes and Complexity

Micro-mutation is not an instrument of increasing complexity. Micro-mutations are random changes in the genetic code. Any random change is mostly harmful (over 99%) and breaks down order and complexity. To explain ever-increasing complexity from random change, which ever decreases complexity, is not plausible.

---

21. Jonathan Wells, *Icons of Evolution: Science or Myth?* (Washington, DC: Regnery Publishing, 2000). See Research Notes on the Miller-Urey experiment, 263-269.

22. Anaerobic (non-oxygen using) forms of life have no continuity with life-forms which use oxygen.

iv. Fitness and Complexity

Fitness is not connected to complexity. Natural selection through competition and survival of the fittest is supposed to bring about increasingly complex life forms. If fitness were measured by numbers of living offspring, then lower life forms, bacteria for example, would be fittest, not the more complex life forms. If fitness were measured by survival, then natural selection would be the survival of those that survive. In either case, natural selection and fitness do not imply more complex life.

c. From More Complex Life to Hominid

There is supposed to be a fossil record in the geological column which shows the process of gradual evolution proceeding from one era to another, up to the present. The geological column does not support the gradualism of uniformitarianism over long ages.

i. Anomalies in the Geological Column

There are anomalies in the geological column. Major divisions (phyla and class) of animal life forms appear suddenly and early in the column, without precursor, in what is called the early Cambrian explosion.[23] This is the reverse of what is to be expected in Darwin's descent from a single ancestor. There are creatures living today that are supposed to have been extinct long ago, according to the column (see for example the coelacanth).[24] There is evidence of human-like creatures in the column living long before they were supposed to have first appeared. And there are human artifacts in what are supposed to be very old (pre-human) layers in the column.[25] There are recent creatures in old layers and old creatures in recent layers. These anomalies

---

23. Jeffrey Levinton, "The Big Bang of Animal Evolution," *Scientific American* (November, 1992): 267.

24. The coelacanth is of interest in the controversy for two reasons: i) it was originally thought to be extinct due to its position in the geological column; now it is said to have persisted without change for long geological ages (30 million generations); ii) it was said to have been the transition (missing link) between fish and amphibian; now it no longer is regarded as a possible missing link. Jacques Millot, "The Coelacanth," *Scientific American* (December 1955): 37.

25. Robin Dennell, "The World's Oldest Spears," *Nature* 385, no. 27 (February 1997): 767-768.

put pressure on the idea of a geological column formed gradually over a long period of time. It is circular reasoning to determine the age of a layer by its fossils and then to determine the age of a fossil by its layer.

ii. Missing Links and the Geological Column

If gradualism is true, there should be innumerable links in the geological column which fill the gap between the major classes of living things. However, these links have not been found and are presumed missing because of incompleteness in the fossil record itself, or because of incompleteness of our knowledge of the fossil records. Nothing can be pointed to unequivocally as a transitional form. Archaeopteryx, once the nearest thing to a missing link between reptile and bird, is no longer considered such. Modern bird fossils have been found earlier than archaeopteryx.[26] Shift from a Linnean to a Darwinian cladistic classification of life forms[27] has altered the ancestor-descendant relationship and the time frame in which a fossil must appear in order to be a missing link.[28]

iii. Homologies and Common Ancestry

Are similarities in living things from common plan or common ancestry? It has been an axiom of Darwinian gradualism that closeness in structure (morphological or molecular) implies closeness in origin. Are morphological homologies independent *evidence for* common ancestry, or are they *defined on the basis of* common ancestry? Molecular analysis does not resolve ancestry because different protein and DNA sequences yield multiple ancestries. The same gene has produced non-homologous limbs in different phyla, and homologous structures have been arrived at by different development pathways.[29] If the axiom of homology and common ancestry is not warranted by the evidence, then homology must be from a common plan. If there is not descent from one common ancestor, the alternative explanation

---

26. Tim Beardsley, "Fossil Bird Shakes Evolutionary Hypotheses," *Nature* 322, no. 21 (August 1986): 677.

27. Cladistic classification is based on homology defined as similarity based on common ancestry.

28. Wells, *Icons*, 135.

29. Wells, *Icons*, 73.

is that descent is from a common plan. A plan implies that there is intelligent design and that there is not a family tree of life to be traced from simple to more complex life forms.

iv. Punctuated Equilibrium

The pressure against uniformity and gradualism in biological origins has produced non-gradualist explanations. Punctuated equilibrium (PE), advocated by Stephen Jay Gould, reckons with sudden appearances, with no change after first appearance, and with lack of missing links.[30] According to PE, massive genetic changes occurring rapidly (the lucky monster theory of Goldschmidt) account for origins better than gradualism. Yet the account for origin by special creation is more plausible than PE. But a creation account is not permitted by the assumption of methodological naturalism.

d. From Hominids to Humans

i. The Path of Ascent

There is no path of ascent from hominid to human that is agreed upon among anthropologists. Opinions fluctuate on what is and what is not human (and therefore what the path might be) and are sometimes misled by hoaxes.[31]

ii. The Problem of Reconstructions

The fluctuation regarding path of ascent reflects problems of recovering fossils that fit time and place requirement of the path of ascent. Fluctuations also reflect the considerable use of imagination and assumption in reconstruction from small fragments, sometimes from a single bone.[32]

---

30. Nyles Eldridge, "Punctuated Equilibria: An Alternative to Phyletic Gradualism," in *Time Frames: The Rethinking of Darwinian Evolution* (Princeton: Princeton University Press, 1985).

31. Piltdown man turned out to be a hoax; Nebraska man was based on a pig's tooth; *Ramapithecus*, Java man, *homo erectus*, and *homo habilis* were errors of classification. The status of *Lucy* the Australopithecine and Neanderthals are not fixed, or have been changed from their original classifications.

32. Marvin Lubenow, *Bones of Contention: A Creationist Assessment of Human Fossils*, Rev. ed. (Grand Rapids, MI: Baker Books, 2004).

iii. Human Rationality

There are differences in kind between rational and non-rational communication. Humans have both kinds, but have not crossed the rational communication barrier with animals. Programmed intelligence is not rationality, nor is association of images, sensations, and behavior the same as concept and thought.

iv. Mind and Brain

The mind is not the brain. Human thought and consciousness cannot be explained by natural forces now operating. The gap is ontological, and cannot be filled by unlimited exploration of natural processes in the brain or in quantum physics.

3. Astronomical Data

a. Fine-Tuning of the Cosmos

Recent discoveries in astronomy have revealed how finely tuned the forces of the cosmos must be in order for there to be a universe at all, and furthermore to have one that can make life possible. Changes of one part in 10^{40} in electromagnetism or gravitation would make the formation of the sun impossible (Paul Davies).[33] The ratio of speed of expansion to total density at the beginning of expansion of the universe is such that a change in one part in a million million would make the difference between re-collapse and everlasting expansion (Stephen Hawking).[34] Initial state low entropy condition arising by chance is calculated to be one part in $10^{10(123)}$ (Roger Penrose).[35] Scores of instances of fine-tuning have been identified and summarized.[36] Appeal

---

33. Paul Davies, *Superforce: The Search for a Grand Unified Theory of Nature* (New York: Simon & Schuster, 1984), 242.

34. Hawking, *Brief History*, 121-122. "If the rate of expansion one second after the Big Bang had been smaller by even one part in a hundred thousand million million, the universe would have recollapsed before it ever reached its present state." Likewise, slight changes for "aesthetic or metaphysical reasons" (136), in any theorist who sees this degree of precision, can make a difference between belief in God or recollapse into unbelief.

35. Roger Penrose, C.J. Isham, and D.W. Sciama, eds., "Time-Asymmetry and Quantum Gravity," in *Quantum Gravity*, 2nd ed. (Oxford: Clarendon, 1981), 249.

36. John D. Barrow, and Frank J. Tipler, *The Anthropic Cosmological Principle* (Oxford: Clarendon Press, 1987), 601-627; Hugh Ross, *The Creator and the Cosmos: How the Greatest*

to necessity and chance to explain the origin of the universe itself in natural terms alone, apart from intelligent design, is to shift from calculating probabilities within the actual world to calculating probabilities between logically possible worlds. What is meant by a world and whether it makes sense to speak about logically possible worlds will be examined later.

b. Age of the Cosmos

Apart from the nature of time itself and the relation of time and eternity, there are uniformitarian assumptions in thinking about the age of the universe that are not warranted in light of current views about the expanding universe. This is more than whether the speed of light has changed. Uniformity assumes that the age of the universe is the same everywhere. Given two commonly held views, a third is warranted. *First*, the universe expanded. This is the commonly accepted Big Bang cosmology. It has also been referred to as the white hole cosmology, the reverse of a black hole, since matter expands out from the white hole. *Second*, time is affected by gravity. *Third*, by inference, the event horizon, which is determined by the field of gravity surrounding the white hole, has shifted. As the universe expanded, with less mass at the center, the event horizon grew smaller. The greater part of the universe exists outside the event horizon, compared to what is at or near the center of expansion. Gravity affects clocks outside of the event horizon differently than clocks within the event horizon. So, the age of the universe, relative to the event horizon, is not uniform.[37]

In all three areas of geology, biology, and astronomy, uniformity based on naturalism is not required to explain what is observed, nor is it the best explanation of the data when we go beyond what is observable. The case for naturalism, based on science, cannot be made, since science, in explaining the past, is based on naturalism.

Scientific Discoveries of the Century Reveal God (London, Ontario: NavPress Publishing Group, 2004), 105-121.

37. D. Russell Humphreys, and Ken Ham, *Starlight and Time: Solving the Puzzle of Distant Starlight in a Young Universe* (Green Forest, AR: Master Books, 1996).

Issue 3: Theistic Evolution: Is a Compromise Position Possible?

Is a compromise position in the evolution/creation controversy possible? Some theists and some evolutionists believe a person can hold to both.[38] Others believe that theistic evolution compromises both science and theism, that one can hold to both only if one is unaware of what consistency requires or is not concerned about consistency. There are four points which are at issue: the concept of man as a body/soul unity, the concept of human equality, the concept of divine goodness, and the concept of science and divine intervention.

1. Man Is a Body/Soul Unity

Naturalism (N) maintains that there is no soul which exists apart from the body. Historic theism (HT) affirms that man is a body/soul unity and the soul survives the death of the body. Theistic evolution (TE), like HT, maintains that man has a soul which survives the death of the body and, in addition, incorporates evolution by saying that a hominid became human when God infused a soul into it. TE's view of the infusion of a soul requires saying that the life and the soul are not the same. But since the soul is the center of awareness, and since the hominid, without a soul, already had some form of perceptual awareness, having both life and soul would produce two centers of awareness, which is contrary to the unity of one conscious self. This would also permit the soul to leave the body and for the being to continue to be alive. Neither N nor HT would find this compromise possible or plausible.

2. Concept of Human Equality

Both N and TE would claim evolution is continuing, even in man, and therefore some humans are naturally more fitted to survive than others. The ideology of a superior group or race would be hard to resist by a consistent N or TE, even when they would find it hard to

---

38. Theistic evolution, or evolutionary creationism, is widely held in many religious circles: popular writer and apologist C.S. Lewis, *The Problem of Pain* (New York: Macmillan, 1974); John Polkinghorne, physicist and Anglican theologian; Howard Van Til (Dutch Reformed); Pierre Teillard de Chardin (Roman Catholic); Dobzansky (Russian Orthodox biologist).

accept. HT would reject this ideology and affirm that all men are created equal, in the image of God, and that creation has ended.

3. The Divine Goodness

N and TE would affirm that the struggle to survive and physical death are natural. TE would further affirm that these are compatible with divine goodness. HT would affirm the original creation was very good, that animals devouring each other in nature, and old age, sickness, and death in human beings, are incompatible with the divine power and goodness manifested in the original creation. HT affirms that natural evil (the curse) was imposed in connection with moral evil (the Fall). Darwin attempted to reconcile his 19th century deistic conception of God with waste and pain in nature by distancing God from the creation by the long process of evolution.[39]

4. Science and Divine Intervention

N finds any introduction of God to fill the gaps in explanation in the natural world as unnecessary (god of the gaps) and a source of illimitable arbitrariness. TE must introduce God to infuse a soul into the body and to guide the process of micro-mutations which would, in most cases, be harmful to an organism's improvement in evolution. HT holds that God is necessary to create each kind, to sustain the creation, and to rule the creation in order to restrain and remove moral evil. The acts of God in creating and sustaining the universe are necessary for, and supportive of, scientific investigation. Divine intervention (miracles), understood in light of creation, fall, and redemption, are not arbitrary and do not undermine rational understanding of the world.

For the reasons stated above, a compromise position TE is not acceptable to consistent naturalism and to consistent theism. Since naturalism has been objected to on the basis of the three arguments against materialism, the alternatives to naturalism remain to be critically examined. The most prominent alternative to naturalism in the West today is historic theism. But there are other alternatives besides

---

39. Cornelius Hunter, *Darwin's God: Evolution and the Problem of Evil* (Grand Rapids, MI: Brazos Press, 2002).

theism. Spiritual monism, dualism, and logically possible worlds, which share the assumption of naturalism that "all is eternal," must next be examined critically, as naturalism was, before considering the view of theism that "only some is eternal."

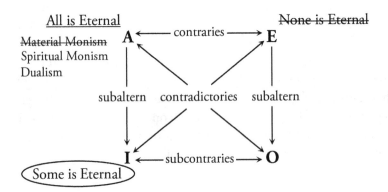

Chapter 6

_____

SPIRITUAL MONISM
AND ANTI-REALISM

INTRODUCTION

A NATURAL ALTERNATIVE TO THE material monism of the modern West is the spiritual monism of the ancient East. As Western naturalism attempts to explain mind in terms of matter alone, so Eastern idealism attempts to explain matter in terms of mind alone. Both affirm all is eternal in some form or other; both deny dualism, and both deny theism. Matter only appears to exist and the self only appears to be distinct from God. From the enlightened point of view, these appearances cease to exist.

There are many points of contact with this seemingly strange view. Transcendental Meditation (TM)[1] and the Hare Krishna[2] movement have their roots in classical Indian philosophy and religion. Belief in reincarnation, New Age, and current interest in spirituality have roots in Eastern mysticism. Yoga and meditation are presented as means

_____

1. Transcendental Meditation (TM), taught by Maharishi Mahesh Yogi, introduced a form of Indian meditation to the West in the 1960's and subsequently. It is a popularization of Eastern spirituality based on the teaching of Shankara, an 8th century Indian philosopher and theologian, who taught an absolute non-dual interpretation of the *Upanishads* (the last part of Vedic scripture known as Vedanta), which views ultimate reality as impersonal.

2. The *Hare Krishna* movement is a popular form of Eastern spirituality in Vaishnava (Vishnu/Krishna) tradition which was introduced to the West by the Indian monk A. C. Bhaktivedanta in the 1960's. It is based upon the teachings of Ramanuja, a 12th century Indian philosopher and theologian, who, in contrast to Shankara, interpreted the *Upanishads* (Vedanta) as teaching a qualified non-dual or personal view of reality. It is one of the major schools of Indian religious thought. What is of interest here is that Eastern spirituality and philosophy have a significant appeal in the West, even at a popular level.

of preparing for and achieving realization of the true self. Spiritual monism in one form or another is the basic belief of the Hindu worldview. Some forms of "meditation Buddhism" are indistinguishable from philosophical Hinduism. Theosophical and religious metaphysical teachings syncretize all religions as different paths to the one ultimate reality.

Spiritual masters, gurus, and swamis have come from the East to teach this ancient wisdom to the West. It has penetrated popular culture in talk shows and cinema. It reflects growing dissatisfaction with both the barrenness of a mechanistic view of life given by science and the banality of popular religion and culture. Knowledge is sought through mystical experience attainable by all who follow a spiritual path. What sense experience is to material monism, mystical experience is to spiritual monism. Appeal to experience, any experience, outward or inward, encounters the same problems of interpretation, as we shall see.

Belief in reincarnation is a core belief in spiritual monism, affirmed by both the less thoughtful and more thoughtful, and by all the pathways to enlightenment in this worldview. This belief asserts that the soul existed before this life and will continue to exist in another life form (human or otherwise) after this life, unless one has obtained *moksha* or enlightenment. Ordinarily, the soul is thought to have always existed and to have gone through innumerable cycles of birth, old age, sickness, and death. Release from rebirth is the desire of the devout. Classical Indian civilization is ordered to achieving this goal through life stages and caste duties. A spiritual evolution occurs through the cycles of rebirth until one is finally released from reincarnation by realizing the true nature of the self and reality.

What are the reasons given for the belief in reincarnation if it is to avoid dogmatism, and does belief in reincarnation, upon critical analysis, retain meaning? There are appeals to special experiences like déjà vu, recalling past lives, and having extraordinary powers. A strong feeling of remembering a person or place, but not from this life, is explained as remembrance from a past life. But the phenomenon of remembering can be explained by subtle changes in brain chemistry or by double neuron firings. Recollection of past lives is notoriously problematic. More people last year than in previous years recalled being Napoleon in a previous life. And having a language without having learned it can be accounted for naturally by electromagnetic communication signals in the airways, or supernaturally by activity of communication with spirits as in the channeling of mediums.

REASONS FOR AND AGAINST REINCARNATION

There are philosophical reasons for belief in *reincarnation*. It is an alternative to the emptiness of belief that all ends with death. It explains events in this life which are hard to explain by the effects of karma from previous lives. It is hopeful in that one has many lives to obtain enlightenment. It is fair in that one suffers for one's own karma only, not for another's. And lastly, reincarnation and release is at least a logically possible worldview.

1. It Is an Alternative to No Afterlife

One's view of the afterlife is a core belief. It is universal in every worldview and significant in terms of one's view of the purpose of life. Belief that there is no afterlife has a dampening effect on this life. It is a necessary condition for rationally justifying human significance. If we are like the beasts that perish, what is the point of striving other than for mere survival? Reincarnation seems to alleviate this burden, but not sufficiently. It offers immortality of a sort, but not personal immortality. The soul is stripped of memories which are part of personal identity, as it goes from one human life to another. Since the soul reincarnates into animal form, the distinction between human and animal with respect to the soul is lost. In the final state, whatever the soul is, it is not recognizably personal. Other alternatives to reincarnation which preserve personal identity are available in other worldviews, unless one is prepared to say that finite personal existence is inherently suffering and is therefore not to be preserved.

2. It Explains Why Things Happen

Why an American actress should be strangely attracted to a British ambassador so as to have an affair with him is explained as having been married to him in a past life (a spouse could suggest that they wait for a future life). Why a doctor who has adopted medical practices based on the unconscious deliverances of a clairvoyant should continually have difficult cases in her practice is explained by not yet having learned from failures in past lives. Why someone should win a big lottery is good karma. Why that person should then become indolent and drunk is bad karma. Why he should then go through recovery and there meet the love of his life is good karma. And why she should subsequently divorce him and leave with all his money is bad karma. And why he should be then inquiring about the truth of karma, is, well, no longer a matter of karma, but a very natural question. Since karma can explain everything—but only after the fact, and that in contradictory ways—it is no explanation at all.

3. It Is Hopeful

To have another chance to achieve enlightenment seems hopeful at least. But if one considers that this is the umpteenth (life)time, the zest of hope diminishes. And if one has had an infinite number of previous lives, for a thoughtful person, hope ceases.

4. It Is Fair

Granted one is supposed to suffer for one's own karma, why does one have to go through so many lives to learn what one should? Is it fair to suffer through many lives to learn what is not clear? Does karma apply where what one is to learn is not objectively clear? And if it is clear, why is there a need for many lives to learn what is clear? If it is not clear, it is not fair to suffer through many lives, and if it is clear, one life should suffice.

5. It Is Possible

If the soul is eternal, then it has had an infinite number of lives to achieve its goal. If the goal were reachable in time, it would have been reached already. In fact, it would have been reached innumerable times, so that there would be no unique once-and-forever release from the cycle of reincarnation. There is no unique event for any being which is eternal in time. Release from reincarnation is not possible.

An eternal soul in an endless cycle makes striving for release mean-ingless. The incoherence of this has been seen and acknowledged by thoughtful believers in reincarnation. Seeing the incoherence has compelled a change in how to view reincarnation. The world of rein-carnation (*samsara*) is seen as phenomenal existence, which is unreal from the ultimate (enlightened) point of view or state of awareness. Reality is dependent on one's state of consciousness or is a construct of consciousness. Hence, the claim of spiritual monism that reality is mind and its ideas.

IDEALISM: SPIRITUAL MONISM AND ANTI-REALISM— IS REALITY MIND-DEPENDENT?

Spiritual monism can be understood as a well-developed form of ide-alist philosophy. Idealism in its many forms is set over and against realism in its many forms. Realism affirms a mind-independent real-ity. Idealism affirms that what we call the world is mind-dependent. Berkeley's analysis of Locke's empiricism and representational realism led to his view that reality is what we perceive (*esse est percipi*).[3] Kant, responding to Hume's skepticism, attempted a Copernican revolution in epistemology, making the mind central and active in the process of knowing.[4] The categories of reality are imposed on the world by the categories of the intellect. Causality is not in the real or noumenal world, but it is necessary in the phenomenal world. Hegel saw the noumenal world as Spirit realizing itself in the process of world histo-

---

3. George B. Berkeley, *Berkeley's Three Dialogues between Hylas and Philonous*, ed. Colin M. Turbayne (New York: The Liberal Arts Press, 1954). If all knowledge is from the senses, according to Locke, and sense impressions are immediately perceived, then since intense heat immediately perceived is pain according to Berkeley, and pain is in the mind, then heat (and all other sensible qualities, primary and secondary) is in the mind. From this, Berkeley drew the conclusion: *esse est percipi*—to be is to be perceived.

4. Whereas the empiricism of Locke, developed by Berkeley and Hume, viewed the mind as passive in the knowing process, Kant made the mind active and controlling, in forming sensory input through the forms of outer intuition (space) and inner intuition (time), and through the categories of the intellect—causality, substance, identity, etc. The change from passive to active role is likened to Copernicus's view of the sun, rather than the earth, at the center of things. What is contributed by the mind is part of the phenomenal world of appearance, not part of the noumenal world—the world as it is in itself.

ry,[5] akin to the qualified non-dualist interpretation of the Upanishads by Ramanuja.[6] Unlike Hegel, F.H. Bradley assigned all relations, which are contradictory in his analysis, to the realm of appearance.[7] Reality is absolute, beyond distinctions of relations, and grasped only in the experience of its totality all at once. Bradley's absolute idealism is more like Shankara's absolute non-dual interpretation of Vedanta.

It would be appropriate to engage the range of idealist and anti-realist positions at this point, in trying to show that basic things are clear. The range of philosophical idealism is sufficiently seen in the following instances: i) the brain in the vat problem, ii) Berkeley's idealism, iii) Kant's view of causality, iv) absolute non-dualism (Shankara), v) qualified non-dualism (Ramanuja), vi) Nagarjuna's middle way, vii) Pragmatism (William James/Dewey/Rorty), viii) constructive idealism of postmodernism (Nietzsche/Derrida), ix) existentialism and the limits of reason (Kierkegaard). By looking at what is basic in each instance, we can avoid squandering efforts on secondary issues, and by looking at several issues cumulatively, we can achieve a more satisfactory response to multi-faceted idealism. The goal is to avoid skepticism and dogmatism by seeing what is clear, and the method is the critical use of reason to analyze assumptions for meaning.

Forms of Idealism

1. The Brain in the Vat[8]

This is a bone tossed to graduate students in philosophy to chew on. It is like the problem of persons in the movie *The Matrix*, or like the problem of Descartes' deceiving demon. How do I know that my sensory awareness is not being caused by another through the direct stimulation of the brain? This world is not like the world of *maya* (illusion)

5. Georg Wilhelm Friedrich Hegel, *Lectures on the Philosophy of World History*, trans. H.B. Nisbet (Cambridge: Cambridge University Press, 1975). This is the traditional interpretation of Hegel's phenomenology of Spirit, the view of Reason realizing itself in World History. An alternative view can be found at: https://plato.stanford.edu/entries/hegel/#PheSpi

6. C.J. Bartley, *The Theology of Ramanuja: Realism and Religion* (London: Routledge Curzon, 2002).

7. F.H. Bradley, *Appearance and Reality* (Oxford: Clarendon Press, 1930).

8. Hilary Putnam, *Reason, Truth and History* (Cambridge: Cambridge University Press, 1982), 1-21.

in absolute non-dual Vedanta. Here the material world exists (at least as the brain in the vat) and the self as aware and capable of thought exists, and this self is capable of critical thought in considering the question "How do I know I'm not a brain in a vat?" Presumably it can conceive of the alternative "not a brain in a vat" and can conceive of causality. Just to consider the question meaningfully presupposes previous knowledge of "the world." This "brain" (not a liver in a vat) could know that there must be something eternal, and that thought is not motion of atoms, that the thinker is finite and not infinite, and is in time and not eternal. This would be sufficient to know some basic things that are clear, enough to avoid skepticism. The content of this knowledge will be added to in the next step.

2. Esse Est Percipi

Berkeley's analysis of perception led him to affirm the existence of the mind and its ideas. He postulated God, not an external physical world, as the cause of what he saw. Unlike the brain in a vat, the existence of the material world is denied, and unlike absolute non-dualism, the existence of the self is affirmed. Can it be known whether or not the physical world exists?[9] Assuming, with Berkeley, both causality and the self, it can be asked, "What is the cause of what I see?" Berkeley thought the cause was another mind, in this case God. It could have been an evil spirit (Descartes), or a mad scientist, or a hypnotist. Could it not be one's own mind? The cause of what I see could then be my mind (mm), some other mind (om), or outside of all minds (oam).

If the cause of what I see were my mind (assuming no physical reality whatsoever), then it would be a case of imagination (not dream-

---

9. G.E. Moore, *Selected Writings*, ed. Thomas Baldwin (London: Routledge, 1993). G.E. Moore argued in defense of common sense and against skepticism and idealism in his 1925 essay, "A Defense of Common Sense." In his 1939 essay, "Proof of an External World," Moore gave a common sense argument against skepticism by raising his right hand and saying "*here is a hand.*" Moore here made appeal to a Moorean fact. According to Keith DeRose, a Moorean fact is something we (claim to) know better than the premises of any philosophical argument to the contrary. Norman Malcolm, among others, found Moore's "*here is a hand*" argument against skepticism lacking and ineffective. It seems that Moore and other common sense philosophers who think no more is needed confuse *prima facie* warrant with *ultima facie* warrant. Something more *is* needed.

ing or hallucinating, which assumes bodily existence). Imagination assumes the self and intentionality. If the cause were my mind (my imagination), I would have total control (tc) over what is imagined. As it is, I do not have total control over what is present to my mind. Therefore, the cause of what I see is not my mind. If the cause were another mind, then I would have no control ($\sim$ c) over what I see (as in images passing on a movie screen). It is not the case that I have no control ($\sim \sim$ c). By intending, I can direct my attention to the floor next, or to the wall next, etc. Therefore, the cause of what I see is not another mind. If the cause is not my mind or another mind, then the cause is outside of all minds. What is outside of all minds is the physical world. Therefore, contrary to Berkeley's scenario, the physical world must exist.

The argument may be summed up here:

1. mm ∨ om ∨ oam
2. mm ⊃ tc
3. ~ tc
4. ∴ ~ mm   (from 2 and 3)
5. om ⊃ ~ c
6. ~ ~ c
7. ∴ ~ om   (from 5 and 6)
8. ∴ oam   (from 1, 4, and 7)

If the objection is raised that my intentions are caused by another mind, then are all or only some intentions caused? If all intentions are caused, then an essential aspect of the self as able to intend is denied, which is contrary to the initial assumption of the self, which by nature is able to intend. But if only some intentions are caused, then can the difference between an apparent and a real intention be known? If they are indistinguishable, then the distinction is without a difference and is meaningless. It is an appeal to an unknown. Furthermore, intentions are immediately known in the act of intending and are therefore incorrigibly known. I cannot be mistaken about knowing that I intend.[10]

3. Kant on Causality and the Real World

Kant said he was awakened from his dogmatic slumber in Wolffian rationalism by the skepticism of Hume, which denied any knowledge of necessity in cause-and-effect relations based on experience. This denial made the certainty of scientific knowledge of cause-and-effect relation in the world impossible. But the necessity of cause and effect in the world made human freedom impossible (as Kant understood freedom), and with the denial of freedom, the denial of responsibility, which is at the heart of meaningful moral experience. Kant solved his dilemma by attributing the necessity of causal relations in human experience as a category of the intellect, imposed by the mind upon what is given through the forms of intuition of space and time. The world of human experience is governed by causality, which makes science possible, but the world in itself is without causality, which makes freedom and morality possible.

There are two difficulties with the removal of causality from the noumenal world. Since there is a relationship between the noumenal and the phenomenal world, Kant speaks of things in themselves and things as I know them. There is a chair in itself and the chair that I see. It is appropriate to ask, "What is the cause of the chair that I see?" It would not be my mind, however much the data of intuition is formed by my mind. And it would not be, for Kant, another mind. The cause must be the chair in itself. But this would establish a causal connection between the noumenal and the phenomenal world, which could not be allowed on Kant's analysis of reality. Furthermore, if I am free in the noumenal world, I am not free to act so as to cause change, since causal actions are not possible in the noumenal realm. I cannot, by rational reflection, cause any change in my conduct, if cause is

---

10. One may doubt the existence of the individual self as in *Advaita* Vedanta, and so doubt the reality of one's intentions, but the problem then is the existence of the self, and not the intentions of the self. One may also wonder if God is systematically deceiving a person regarding the reality of one's intention, but the problem then is the existence of God and the nature of God as good, not the reality of one's intention. These problems have been dealt with under spiritual monism and theism.

not possible in the noumenal realm. Nor can I bring about rational reflection in myself. So moral life is not possible without causality and causal agency in the real world, that is, in the world as it is in itself.

4. Shankara's *Advaita* Vedanta

Shankara (788-820 C.E.) understands the Upanishads (the last part of the Vedas, called Vedanta) to teach that ultimate reality is Brahman, which is pure existence, consciousness, and bliss (*sat chit ananda*), and that the true self of a person, atman, is Brahman.[11] *Tat tvam asi* (that thou art). The world of ordinary consciousness, *samsara*, is *maya* (illusion) and *avidya* (based on ignorance). Ultimate reality is absolute non-dual, one without parts. This is the teaching of Transcendental Meditation (TM). That atman is Brahman is realized only by a special experience of awakening, or enlightenment, called *moksha*.

The analogy of a dream is used to explain *Advaita*. As in a dream, a common view of reality held by many is not a guarantee of truth. As in a dream, because you take yourself to be real does not mean that you are real. As in a dream, there is one self behind the many apparently real selves. As in a dream, the only way to realize it is a dream is by a special (that is, an outside-the-dream) experience of awakening.

An appeal to a special or a mystical experience is often made to confirm truth claims of basic beliefs about reality. These experiences are regarded as self-attesting: "If you had the experience, you would know." Zen enlightenment, being born again, being spoken to by God, speaking in tongues, being one with everything, are examples of internal awareness. Publicly observable miracles are also appealed to as foolproof reasons for the basic belief that God exists, rather than partial proof of secondary belief (e.g., God was with Moses, seen by the miracles he performed), which presupposes the basic belief that God exists.

Appeal to the experience of awakening has several objections. *First,* no experience is meaningful without interpretation. *Second,* the experience of pure consciousness in awakening has been interpreted in several ways (dualist, non-dualist—both absolute and qualified—the-

---

11. Shankara, *The Vedanta Sutras of Badarayana with the Commentary by Shankara* (New York: Dover Publication, 1962).

ist, naturalist, and Buddhist). *Third*, a valid interpretation must be logically coherent. And *fourth*, the interpretation of *Advaita* (absolute non-dual) is incoherent in several ways.

These incoherencies have been pointed out by the followers of Ramanuja, who reject absolute non-dualism (one without parts) for qualified non-dualism (one with parts).[12] An incoherence is contrary to reason and can be seen by anyone willing to use reason.

Objections to Shankara's Absolute Non-Dualism

1. Since the *advaitin* maintains absolute non-dualism and that the world is *maya* (illusion), the question arises: Where does the illusion (*maya*) reside? It cannot be in Brahman, since what is in Brahman is pure consciousness (without modification of thought). Furthermore, it would be unthinkable to think the highest reality is in a state of illusion. But neither can the illusion be in the individual soul, since the individuality of the soul is the product of the illusion, not its cause. Since there is no other possible locus for the illusion, if it exists anywhere, it exists only in the mind of the *advaitin* who has imagined this pseudo-concept, this logical myth.

2. How can *avidya* (ignorance) conceal Brahman? Brahman cannot be concealed from itself, since Brahman is self-conscious and self-luminous subject. Darkness cannot cover light; ignorance cannot veil what is pure knowledge. It is as absurd to think that the self can be concealed from itself, as it is absurd to think one can play hide-and-go-seek with oneself.

3. How can the world (*maya*) be neither positive (a thing) nor negative (a thought)? If the world were a thing, the non-dualism of *Advaita* would break down. But if it were merely a thought, without a thing present, then how could the illusion be accounted for? A thing (for example, a rope) is needed to account for the illusion (snake). A pure illusion, without any object, does not exist.

---

12. Chandradhar Sharma, *A Critical Survey of Indian Philosophy* (Delhi, India: Motilal Banarsidass Publishers, 1991), 358-361.

4. How can the world be described as indescribable? The *advaitin* says it cannot be described as either real or unreal. The world is not real (eternal), since this would be dualism (not non-dualism). And the world is not unreal (non-existent), for it cannot be accounted for as illusion. It cannot be both real and unreal; and it cannot be neither real nor unreal, since there is no third possibility if all is one.

Shankara must say that the world is either real or unreal, given that there must be something eternal and given his assumption that all is one. Reason requires this of him in order to be consistent with his assumption. It is possible to say what his own analysis has required him to say, that the world is neither real (eternal), nor unreal (non-existent). It is possible to say that the world is temporal (not eternal and not non-existent). To say the world is temporal is to say that only some is eternal, that the world is created by God. This would require Shankara to give up his assumption that all is one. Faced with the alternatives of giving up his assumption or giving up reason, Shankara chose to give up reason. Reason, he said, cannot grasp ultimate reality. He moved to silence.[13]

Some things are clear. The basic things are clear. It is clear to reason that all is not one, that only some is eternal. One has to deny reason to avoid what is clear. But one cannot deny reason and hold to any belief; one must move to silence if one gives up reason. Yet as rational beings we cannot give up thought and the need for meaning. We cannot give up reason. It shines in the darkness. We can only give up concern for consistency, that is, our integrity.

5. Ramanuja's Qualified Non-Dual Vedanta

Ramanuja (1017-1137 C.E.) came two centuries after Shankara and differed with his view of absolute non-dual Brahman. The world and individual existence are real and are part of the one ultimate reality.

---

13. The *advaitin's* response to the challenge of giving up reason can be fourfold: i) Appeal to higher consciousness, while admitting the contradictory nature of assertions about ultimate reality from ordinary consciousness. But this begs the question of making any assertion interpreting one's experience. ii) Assert that "absolutely real" and "absolutely unreal" are not contradictories, but contraries which can both be false. But this is not an option for the *advaitin* if all is one: contraries here are contradictories. iii) Give up reason and move to silence. iv) Keep reason and give up spiritual monism.

There is duality (*dvaita*) in the underlying oneness. Theistic language is used in the context of pantheism. The term "God" may be applied to one part of the whole or to the whole itself. The world of matter and souls is seen as the body of God. Individuals are seen as water drops which return to the ocean of divine being. A strong personal and devotional element is central. For Ramanuja, unlike Shankara, the absolute is personal, not impersonal. This teaching has come to the West in the Hare Krishna movement.

Ramanuja asserts that ultimate reality is neither pure identity nor pure difference, nor is it identity and difference, but identity in and through difference. The soul and body are seen as attributes of a substance, God. Yet the soul and body are substances themselves, having attributes, and can be further distinguished as particular, individual beings. How is the soul as an attribute of God distinct from wisdom as an attribute of God? If the soul as an individual being is distinct from other souls, how can it be a substance which is shared in common by many souls?

Let us say that attribute, substance, and a being or an individual are not being clearly distinguished here. Let us say that in philosophical discussion the soul is ordinarily regarded as an individual being of a spiritual substance, having certain attributes or qualities as spirit, and other qualities which identify it as a particular spirit. Let us say that the qualities of eternal or temporal, and infinite or finite, are basic qualities of every being and are qualities of qualities—for example, finite and temporal in being, wisdom, power, etc. Now, certain critical questions can be asked of Ramanuja's view that we are all part of God.

Are all the parts the same in essence or attribute, or are they different? If they are all the same, are all the parts finite or infinite, temporal or eternal? If they are not all the same, are some parts finite and others infinite? Are some parts temporal and other parts eternal? By getting to what is basic in concept, namely being and aspect of being, and by getting to the most basic attribute of a being, namely temporal or eternal, and finite or infinite, we can see what is clear in basic beliefs about reality.

Objections to Ramanuja's Qualified Non-Dualism

1. All the parts are the same: finite and eternal. If all the parts are finite, then the whole (God) cannot be infinite. The sum total of finite wisdom does not equal infinite wisdom. Further, what is finite can grow in wisdom, but what grows in wisdom goes through a unique process of growing in wisdom. Two problems arise here. If we continue to grow, then we (individually or collectively) cannot be infinite, since the infinite cannot increase. And if we were eternal (in time), having had infinite time already (allowing for a moment the possibility of an eternal in time), then why have we not achieved this unique stage of knowledge before? Allowing for even an extremely slow rate of progress, given our forgetfulness, in infinite time any goal can and would have been achieved by now, and would have been endlessly repeated, making our striving meaningless. It would follow then that all the parts are not finite, and, they are not finite and eternal.

2. All the parts are the same: infinite and eternal. We have seen above that since we grow in knowledge, we are not infinite, and therefore also not infinite and eternal. Further, if a being were infinite, it would be complete in itself and not stand in need of any other as a part. To be a part is to be incomplete in itself. It is therefore not possible to be an infinite part. One cannot be complete and not complete, at the same time and in the same respect. Since infinite and eternal are inseparable qualities, and apply to all qualities of a being (one is not infinite in power and finite in wisdom), one cannot be complete and incomplete, at the same time but in different respects. It follows then that all the parts are not infinite and eternal.

3. All the parts are not the same: some are finite and temporal and some are infinite and eternal. If this were the case, they would not have a part/whole relation, for what is infinite is complete in itself and does not stand in need of any other being. And if some are finite and temporal (necessarily so, as we saw above), then they came into being. They would not have come into being from non-being, but would have been brought into existence (that is, created) by what is infinite and eternal. But this would be creation, not qualified non-dualism, in which matter and souls are part of God.

It is clear then, that neither Shankara nor Ramanuja can sustain their view that all is one, whether with parts or without parts. Critical analysis of what each asserts leads to the view that all is not one, that only some is eternal. Spiritual monism therefore does not stand.

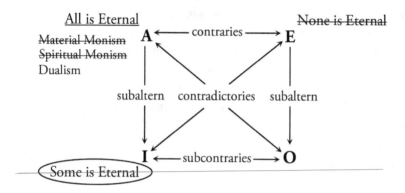

6. Nagarjuna's Middle Way

Nagarjuna, an early second century Buddhist philosopher, has given a more sophisticated interpretation of the Buddhist teaching that "all is *dukkha*," which has gained attention historically and currently in the West through the writings of D.T. Suzuki. The middle path (*Madhyamika*) is understood metaphysically: all of reality is *shunya*, empty, lacking self-existence (*swabhava*), dependently co-arising (*pratityasamutpada*). All of reality is *dukkha*, impermanent, becoming, neither eternalism nor momentariness. There is no eternal Creator. Nagarjuna is said to have thundered: "Never and nowhere can anything be produced."[14] The effect is in the cause. The universe is self-generating. The jewel is in the lotus. *Om mani padme hum.*

The Middle Path is also understood epistemologically: No object of intellect can resist scrutiny. Identity breaks down into difference upon analysis. The chariot, a thing, is a relation of its parts, and relations dependently co-arise. Reason, it is said, fixes things in identity. A new consciousness, or the recognition of a more primal consciousness,

---

14. Sharma, *A Critical Survey of Indian Philosophy*, 90. Sharma said of Nagarjuna that he begins his work by boldly proclaiming the doctrine of No-origination.

said to be presently overlaid and falsified by rational consciousness, is needed to grasp reality in relation. History is seen as a long strife-filled process toward this awakening. It is said we are now on the verge of a new age in which global consciousness, a higher or true rationality, will prevail, or should prevail, or could prevail, short of which we are headed for global disaster. The infinite reality, *logos* (word), it is said, must be recognized as inclusive of both the finite and the fallenness of the finite. It is inclusive of finite, contradictory consciousness. The unity of being-in-relation is grasped through meditative reason (see notes 3–4 in Chapter 2). All beings manifest this unity of contradictions it is said, including human beings (a unity of body and soul or non-body) and Christ's being (the infinite and the non-infinite or finite).

It remains to be seen whether a unity of diversity (body and soul) is a unity of contradiction, in the ordinary sense of reason. It seems rather to be an example of the insufficient use of critical reason and the subsequent debunking of reason's ability to grasp the real, also seen in nominalism, existentialism, pragmatism, and postmodernism. Those caught in the meshes of intellect are said to be worse than dogs.[15] They are like elephants stuck in deep mud. They can never know the real. They are incorrigible, hopeless, and destined to doom. "Everything is eternal, nothing is eternal; everything has a cause, nothing has a cause; everything is unity, everything is plurality," is said to be gross and crude philosophy. One has to go beyond the intellect to get to reality. Reality is above refutation, it is said. Reality "isn't is, it isn't isn't, it isn't both, and it isn't neither."[16] Reality is beyond all categories. Truth is not fixed, for getting hold of by analysis, the Buddha taught. It is pragmatic. It is like a raft, not to be carried but for carrying, to cross over this life which is suffering (*dukkha*). The Buddha, toward the end of his life, became uninclined toward teaching. He sermonized by silence, holding up a flower. The highest philosophy is silence.

We have encountered before this move from reason to silence. Is it necessary? Does reason lead to contradiction? Or is it the failure to use reason critically that leads to contradiction? Nagarjuna argues against antinomies—contrary statements both of which are universal—not

---

15. Sharma, *A Critical Survey of Indian Philosophy*, 89.

16. Sharma, *A Critical Survey of Indian Philosophy*, 92.

contradictories. "Everything is eternal" and "nothing is eternal." He does not look at the true contradiction to each of the above, which is "some is not eternal," and "some is eternal." He is working from the uncritically held assumption that all is one, so for him only contraries are possible, and neither is acceptable. Production, causation, or origination, in this world, is not creation *ex nihilo*. Change from milk to curds is transformation, not creation. Exemplifying the doctrine of no-origination by looking at some examples in the world does not address other examples that are closer, by analogy, to creation *ex nihilo*, nor does it address creation *ex nihilo* itself. Body and soul are different; they are not opposites, exclusive of each other. A being that is body and soul is not *a* and *non-a*, at the same time and in the same respect. *a* and *non-a* are not contradictory; *a* and *non-a* at the same time and in the same respect is contradictory. Unity of diversity can and does exist. Unity of contradiction cannot exist, either in finite being or in infinite being. The way to unity is not to harmonize contradictions through the use of a "higher" reason, or to move to silence, but to use "ordinary" reason more fully.

7. Pragmatism and the Enterprise of Knowing

We have seen several forms of the claim that human thought is a construct, that we cannot know reality, that there is no object which corresponds to human thought in the real world. This skeptical, idealist, anti-realist position is accepted by many who respond to skepticism by pragmatism. Pragmatism has always been the flip side of the coin of skepticism, but it has developed into a distinct anti-metaphysical stance in American philosophy through William James, C.S. Peirce, John Dewey, and currently Richard Rorty. It is both a theory of meaning and a theory of truth, advanced in place of the futility of traditional metaphysics, seen mostly as a quibble about words. The real meaning of a belief is seen in the action (*pragma*) or conduct it is fitted to produce. A belief is true, therefore, if the conduct has satisfactory consequences—that is, if it works.

As a procedure for settling metaphysical disputes, it is less than adequate. It assumes that what satisfies one will satisfy all. It also assumes that what satisfies a person is a construct, independent of one's belief about the good. It assumes, further, that our deepest need is not for meaning, that a meaningful view of the good is not grounded in one's view of the real. In short, it denies that reason and thought are fundamental to other aspects of human personality. It argues that the moral or practical is independent of the intellectual, and may be used to settle intellectual disputes about what is real. Pragmatism thus begs the question about how to settle metaphysical disputes, since what satisfies, or works, depends on one's metaphysical view.

Pragmatism has a mistaken or low view of human nature. It believes that man can live on bread alone, supplemented with a few "just so" stories, whether on the order of Plato's myths for the masses, or Rorty's aesthetic sensibility, satisfied through literature apart from the question of truth. On this view, Homer's stories about the gods should have satisfied. They didn't then and they won't now, even in the contemporary form of MTV. Adding soma to the mix (*Brave New World*) could not prevent the questioning "Savage" from appearing on the scene. There is always a milkmaid to hurl her milking stool at human folly, always a Luther to nail *The 95 Theses*, always a Neo who threatens *The Matrix*, always "a Voice of One Crying in the Wilderness." Bread is no substitute for truth. Pragmatism is not true because it does not work.

8. Deconstructing Postmodernism

According to the postmodern narrative, all truth is constructed. There's a constructive use of reason which constructs a worldview by interpreting experience in light of basic belief. Interpretation and worldview are inescapable. In the postmodern view, all is interpretation. Philosophy is thought to end here rather than to begin here. Contrary to the naïve realist view of modern science, postmodernism gives no privileged position to science, which is subject to paradigm shifts. Postmodernism does not purport to present any positive view of the world, but only to uncover all views as human constructs. Its agenda is to delegitimize authority based on objective knowledge claims and to allow suppressed views their day in the sun.

The attack is primarily against reason. Reason does not get to reality; it deals with concepts which are universal, and not with the particular (Nietzsche). Reality is said to be constituted of unique particulars, not universals. The uniqueness and otherness of the particular is crushed in the name of the universal. Thus, reason is not life-affirming. But life affirms itself against reason and what comes in the name of reason. Traditional religion and metaphysics and science have lost their hold on man. God is dead, and man must affirm life and meaning without God, in creative acts of will to power.

What began with Nietzsche is continued by Derrida. The history of metaphysics is built upon the polarities of reason: *a* and *non-a*, good and evil, true and false, being and non-being. These polarities are justified by the presence of God, in whom being and knowledge coincide, a presence which is not available to finite intellects. We have only a variety of socially-constructed views derived from one's linguistic community, which can never be transcended so as to be evaluated objectively, or be compared to other views. "Meaning is use" and there are many usages/diversities. There are no philosophical conflicts to be settled, only a beetle in a bottle (Wittgenstein). The attempt to establish one's own view as the truth, in light of which other views are understood, is a perpetual problem of being reason-centered, i.e., logocentrism (Derrida). Deconstruction, it is said, recognizes the limits of constructions of reason, the alterity of the other, and the incommensurability of worldviews.

In response, what is common to all worldviews is the formal structure of a worldview. In any worldview, what can be distinguished in the process of construction are: i) basic belief about what is real, ii) experience, and iii) reason used to interpret experience in light of basic belief. Not just anything can be said in a worldview. There are rules of consistency governing what can and cannot be said in a worldview, given its starting point. There is considerable agreement among members of a belief community concerning what makes sense (a faith or belief community can extend to a billion people, over several thousand years, across geographic, economic, educational, language, ethnic, and gender differences). The basic belief is not itself interpreted, but is that in light of which interpretation occurs. While experience is interpreted with varying degrees of critical awareness, at times almost unconsciously, it is still possible to distinguish the experience and the interpretation. It is also possible to have one's interpretation challenged and corrected for consistency in the set of beliefs constituting one's worldview. And lastly, the laws of reason are the same in all worldviews. Contradictions can be recognized in all worldviews.

Truth claims are made in all worldviews. And in no worldview are contradictory statements both true. Alterity does not override the formal features common to all human beings and worldviews.

If alterity were more fundamental than what is common—in this case, reason—then there would be incommensurability between worldviews. It would be impossible to communicate between worlds. But we do communicate all the time, make attempts to correct misunderstanding, and seek to persuade others to our point of view. We can understand the other, even when we don't agree. We can be challenged by those outside our community (as well as those inside) who see inconsistencies in our thinking. If nowhere else, at least at the most basic level of what is eternal—whether all or only some is eternal—there is universality of meaning and contradiction between worlds. Often enough, conversions occur and persons are able to think about what life was like before and after conversion. None of this would be possible if worldviews were incommensurable. Lack of understanding of the other occurs where we fail to recognize our own assumptions and thereby fail to recognize the assumptions of the other, in light of which they seek to make sense of the world. Since lack of awareness of one's assumptions occurs often enough, incommensurability between worlds occurs as often.

As a cultural critic of late nineteenth century Europe, Nietzsche observed that "God is dead," and "we have killed him." By pious, self-centered misconceptions, by the "wise" and the simple, the living God, The Lord of Hosts who calls each star by its name, became an idol, transmogrified into the image of man. The death of God brought the death of man, against which Nietzsche rebelled. Against this idolatry, the prophets spoke through history, calling mankind back. Nietzsche did not call men back. As a son of the spirit of the age, he accepted the death of God and prepared a way of life without God. The highest expression of human creativity by an autonomous will to power was, inevitably, an eternal reoccurrence. Without God the Creator, reason requires an eternal cycle, as it did in material and spiritual monism. Eternal reoccurrence crushes individuality and the human spirit twice as much as what it set out to remedy. Will to power cannot transcend meaninglessness by becoming a hero of the absurd.

Derrida is dismissive of reason itself because of its binary (*a* and *non-a*) structure of reality. He thinks that without knowledge of God, inaccessible to finite intellects, we must defer judgments. Deconstruction achieves deference by word play, since words refer only to other words by construction of the community. Ambiguities are brought out, or rather created, forming "difference." But deferring all judgment is not possible, even for the deconstructionist. Fundamentally, modernism is rejected over and against postmodernism. The inescapability of reason as the laws of thought, as common ground, as ontological, transcendental, and fundamental, is revealed here. Can Derrida deny the binary pair of true and false, and basic and non-basic, and still utter anything meaningful? Does he not affirm reason in seeking justification for distinction in the knowledge of God? If he is saying the being of God is necessary to justify reason, then is the being of God beyond reason (beyond both *a* and *non-a*)? If the being of God is beyond reason, how can it justify reason? And how, prior to having reason, can we speak of the need to justify reason? Isn't justification itself a rational category? In the order of knowledge, reason as the laws of thought is self-attesting and does not require justification. If Derrida is saying we cannot know that God exists, or that we cannot know anything without knowing everything (i.e., having the omniscience of God), is this mere dogmatic assertion, or does he offer proof? Can he show being comes from non-being, or does he at least believe this is possible? If even this basic belief is being deferred, along with all other judgments, how is deference different from silence?

9. Existentialism and the Leap of Faith

Existentialism affirms that existence precedes essence. It affirms the existence of the particular, the individual, over and against essence as a construct of reason. Existentialism is nominalistic in epistemology. Concepts grasp essences, which are universal; reason cannot grasp the particular. Further, we find ourselves flung into existence and must begin with our existence before determining our essence. Existentialism is nominalistic also in ontology. Only particulars exist in reality; universals do not. Further, there is no human essence *per se*; there is no Platonic form or idea in the mind of God, according to which human beings are fashioned. Existentialism is voluntaristic in ethics. Something is right because God wills it, not because of the nature of God or man. In atheistic existentialism, since there is no God to give commandments or to determine human nature, it is man who determines good and evil by choice. Authentic existence recognizes human freedom and takes full responsibility for what we become by our choice (Sartre). In theistic existentialism, the individual stands alone before the God who commands and must respond by the choice of faith, not by requirement of reason (Kierkegaard vs. Kant, and Hegel).

There are three issues to be distinguished in understanding the relation of existence and essence in existentialism: i) Does existentialism deny the existence of essence *per se*, or only the sufficiency of essence to attain to the particular? ii) Does it deny individual essences or reason's ability to grasp individual essences? To say essences do not exist is to say there is not a set of qualities (for example, animality and rationality) which exists in all members of a class (human beings). These qualities exist only in the mind, not in beings. The term "man" does not refer to anything in the world, but "Bill" and "Mary" do. But this is just to say essence refers to qualities, not beings. But this allows that beings may have real qualities. iii) If essences do not exist, is this to say qualities do not exist, or is it to say there are beings devoid of all qualities, or any fixed quality, or any general or specific quality? But if there were no fixed qualities, there could be no identity of a being through time, and therefore we could not speak of an individual being, the prize sought after in existentialism.

Concepts grasp essences. Concepts grasp only those qualities that all members of a class have. Concepts are class-relative. There is the class of pens and the class of blue-ink pens; there is the class of blue-ink pens using nibs and blue-ink pens with nibs and red exterior, etc. As the number in the set of qualities increases, the class sizes decrease down to a class with one member. This does not show the insufficiency of reason to grasp essences, but the use and usefulness of language. We can speak, as the poet Hopkins does, of "morning's minion, kingdom of daylight's dauphin, dappled-dawn-drawn-Falcon . . . ."[17] But only sometimes do we prefer poetry to prose. To be brief, we say "this bird" or "that pen," which, in context, picks out individuals.

---

17. Gerard Manley Hopkins, *Poems and Prose of Gerard Manly Hopkins* (Baltimore, MD: Penguin Books Inc., 1953), 30. See "The Windhover: to Christ our Lord." By buckling descriptors in this poem, the nominalist in Hopkins achieved the reality of Scotian particularity.

For existentialism, the concern is with human existence in the individual, as in Socrates, or in Abraham. Can reason grasp the particular? Is there an individual essence that distinguishes one individual from all others? What is the essence, if any exists, of Socrates or of Abraham? Is it the sum total of all of Socrates' qualities, or is it the set of qualities that Socrates always has from youth to old age by which we can identify Socrates and say Socrates has not changed? We do identify Socrates this way, although Socratesness is ineluctable and his uniqueness can only be identified by a proper name. The uniqueness of a person, for those who are attentive, can begin to manifest itself in earliest infancy.

It is in the realm of choice that existential anguish is most manifest, precisely because reason is seen to be of no assistance. For Kierkegaard, this is seen in the account of Abraham, who is called by God to offer up his son Isaac as a burnt offering to God. Kierkegaard sees reason as the obstacle for Abraham to overcome in order to have faith and obey God's command. In *Fear and Trembling*, he identifies stages in life's way, from the passion of the aesthetic, to the rational duty of the ethical, to the faith of the individual, standing immediately and alone before God. Individuality comes to expression only in choice by faith, by which we go beyond the universal of the rational, ethical stage. Kierkegaard asks, "Is there a teleological suspension of the ethical?" Are there times when we must go against reason in the name of faith, when we must believe over and against reason, when we must believe the promise of God and obey God by reason of the absurd? Since it is common to think that faith stands over and against reason, the example of faith in Abraham's life will be examined here at some length.

Abraham, Kierkegaard points out, is not a knight of infinite resignation. He is not willing merely to give up Isaac to God because God has commanded it. Any rational person would do so because reason commands us to do our duty, whatever the price. Abraham has a promise from God that he will be the father of a great nation, and that the promise will be fulfilled through Isaac, not any other. Abraham has to believe that the promise will be fulfilled though Isaac is destroyed. This appears to contradict reason. Further, Abraham is called to slay his son, his own son whom he loves. To kill his son is murder, which is forbidden by the command of God and by reason. Since Abraham is the father of the faithful, and the offering up of

Isaac is his supreme act of faith, this act of Abraham reveals the nature of faith, in Kierkegaard's view, as transcending reason and standing over and against reason.

Looked at in isolation from the rest of Abraham's life, Kierkegaard's account of faith is plausible. But abstracting the event from the concrete particularities of Abraham's entire life is a failure to treat Abraham as the individual that he is. While exalting Abraham's individuality, the abstracted account, which isolates the sacrifice from the particulars of Abraham's past, denies his individuality. A different picture of the mind of Abraham and of the relation of faith and reason emerges as we are immersed in the world and life of Abraham. Here are eight significant points to be considered.

Faith and Reason in Abraham

a. Abraham's Worldview

Abraham lived in Ur of the Chaldees and by his belief in God the Creator, stood in contrast to his culture and his father's house. He saw apostasy all around him. He had some sense of history, of earlier apostasy in the human race, and of divine judgment on the race. The origin of the curse and the promise from Adam would have been known to him, as well as the destruction of mankind in the flood for its apostasy. Shem, his ancestor who came through the flood, was still alive when Abraham left Ur. Abraham had some view of good and evil and man's purpose on earth, and the meaning of the Sabbath, which he held deeply enough to sustain his faith against the apostasy all around him.

b. Promise to Abraham

Abraham's worldview enabled him to understand God's promise and to make the daring step of leaving everything for the promise. Abraham was to leave his homeland for a promised land; he was to leave his clan to become the father of a great nation; he was to leave his father's household and in him all the families of the earth would be blessed. The implications were staggering, yet utterly consistent with and to be expected from his worldview. All families were now in apostasy and in need of blessing, which comes from faith in God. Blessing wouldn't come through Ur, probably the center of world civilization in its day. Ur was doomed to destruction for its apostasy. He was to leave Ur, not hope to find the fulfillment there.

The promise was connected to the land and to a people, not apart from the earth and the human family. It was not simply what comes after death in a disembodied existence, apart from what must occur on earth through history. It would reach far beyond his lifetime, first to his descendants becoming a great nation, and then to the entire world. How was he to partake of the promise on the earth in the future after he died? Since the curse, including physical death, came through sin, would not death be removed with the removal of sin, by the coming of the blessing? He had hope in the promise, for himself and all mankind. It would be difficult to believe he left everything for the promise without understanding what it meant, and that he had hope in the promise without belief in the resurrection from the dead.

Abraham had to depend on God for the fulfillment of the promise. Leaving the security of his clan, being a stranger in the Promised Land occupied by others, how could he become possessor of the land? How might he survive among strangers without protection by kin? He was now sixty years old and Sarah his wife was barren. How could he become father of a nation without even being the father of at least one? God spoke to him, not to his wife. Would Sarah obey him and leave everything to go with him into an unknown?

c. Abraham's Sacrifice

Abraham observed sacrifice, an ordinance instituted by God for the forgiveness of sin, and handed down from the day God covered Adam's and Eve's nakedness with coats of skin, signifying a covering for sin through the death of another. It was observed by Abel and Noah and Shem, down to Abraham. Abraham observed sacrifice for sin throughout his life. It was in this context that he heard God's command to sacrifice his son Isaac. There was no acceptance by God without sacrifice for sin. It was also clear that the animal sacrifice itself could not take away sin; that another human representative in the place of Adam must come to undo Adam's sin, and to do what he as the first representative head failed to do.

d. Circumcision

When Abraham was ninety-nine years old, after many years in the land, he received the sign of circumcision. He was to be reminded perpetually in his body of what it signified, in the need for a new heart to be in covenant relationship with God. The sign was applied to all males in his household, including male infants, showing the reality of sin, even in a newborn, and their need for a new heart through regeneration, which is brought about by an act of God's grace. He saw the need for regeneration of the human heart when he saw the degeneration and destruction of Sodom and Gomorrah without it.

e. Birth of Isaac

God promised Abraham at this time, long after Sarah was past childbearing, that she would bear him a son through which the promise would be fulfilled. Sarah heard and laughed, and caught in her laughter of unbelief, the child was to be named Isaac, meaning laughter. Out of the deadness of her womb, Sarah did bear a child. He was named Isaac and he was circumcised the eighth day. For years, whenever they called the child, they would be reminded of the circumstances of his birth, as God brought life out of the deadness of Sarah's womb to fulfill the promise.

f. The Test of Faith

Some time later God tested Abraham saying, "Take your son, your only son Isaac, whom you love, and go to the region of Moriah. Sacrifice him there as a burnt offering on one of the mountains I will tell you about." Abraham obeyed. He knew the meaning of sacrifice for sin. He knew Isaac was not sinless, being circumcised, and that he himself needed a sacrifice for sin, and could not be the sacrifice for Abraham's sin. Further, he loved Isaac, and would sooner give up his life for Isaac than give up Isaac's life for his own. He knew also the power of God in the birth of Isaac and that the promise was through Isaac and no other. He believed that one day God would raise him (Abraham) from the dead to fulfill his promise. He therefore believed that God would raise Isaac from the dead, after the sacrifice, to fulfill the promise made through Isaac. He expected to return to his servants with Isaac and he was led to answer Isaac's question "Where is the lamb?" by saying, "God himself will provide the lamb for the burnt offering."

g. The Revelation

Abraham was a prophet. Prophets are given revelation by God of what God will do. Sometimes they are called to enact in their lives, without understanding at the time, what God will do. When he, the father, took the knife to slay his son, his only son, whom he loved, to offer him as a burnt offering for sin, he saw what God would one day do. Jesus said of Abraham, "Your father Abraham rejoiced at the thought of seeing my day; he saw it and was glad."[18]

h. The Explanation

The writer to the Hebrews, in exhorting others to faith and in explaining what faith is, said what was in the mind of Abraham: "Abraham reasoned that God could raise the dead, and figuratively speaking, he did receive Isaac back from death."[19] Faith therefore is not something above reason, or apart from reason, or against reason. Rather the highest expression of faith is the highest expression of reason. Abraham's faith grew as his understanding grew. His faith was tested as his understanding was tested. The details of his life showed how, by his worldview, he responded to and received new revelation, which in turn helped him to understand and respond to further revelation. Being raised from the dead was a necessary part of his worldview of creation, fall, and redemption, and an integral part of his experience of waiting for the promise. Offering Isaac as a sacrifice is not murder when viewed as a unique unfolding of redemptive revelation.

---

18. *John 8:56.*

19. *Hebrews 11:19.*

Chapter 7

———

DUALISM AND
LOGICALLY POSSIBLE WORLDS

DUALISM

DUALISM, ALONG WITH MATERIAL MONISM and spiritual monism, holds that all is eternal. In contrast to both forms of monism, it holds that both matter and spirit exist. In contrast to theism, it affirms that both matter and spirit are eternal, that there is no Creator God. Dualism has been widespread in Greek, Persian, and Indian thought. All who believe in the reality of the physical world and in personal immortality, and do not believe matter and souls are created, are dualists. Plato and Aristotle were dualists of different sorts, and their thinking exerted considerable influence on Christian thinkers like Augustine and Aquinas. Persian Zoroastrianism affirmed an eternal conflict between the two realities of spirit and matter and continued its influence in Manicheism. Indian thought affirmed dualism based on the Upanishads (*Madhva* Vedanta), and on Samkhya philosophy based on the yoga sutras of Patanjali. Mormonism is a form of dualism, not material monism, to the extent that matter and spirit are essentially distinguished; there is no creation *ex nihilo* in this belief system.

The Appeal of Dualism

Dualism has a natural appeal. Dualism is the next natural step beyond the problems of material monism and spiritual monism. It avoids some of the problems encountered by each form of monism. Dualism has an explanation for the problem of evil by locating the problem in the soul becoming involved in bodily existence. Dualism also allows for some kind of immortality as well as pre-existence to this life. But dualism has problems of its own, which it has not been able to overcome, both ethically and metaphysically. Ethically, it locates evil in bodily existence in contrast to the soul or spirit.

Objections to the Appeal of Dualism

There are several problems and/or objections to ethical dualism. 1) If the soul is inherently good, how did it become ensnared in bodily existence? Must there have been a lack (of knowledge) in the soul? 2) If the soul is eternal, how could there be a lack of knowledge in the soul? If the soul grows in knowledge in time and had infinite time, being eternal, how could it have lacked infinite knowledge? This raises associated problems of whether infinite time can exist (see the *kalam* argument), whether there can be unique events (e.g., growth in knowledge) in infinite time, and whether there is any escape from return to bodily existence by a unique once-and-for-all event of enlightenment or going to heaven. 3) If both matter and spirit are eternal, what is the basis for saying one is good and the other evil, as against saying they are merely different? If both matter and spirit are eternal, what is the basis for hoping one can win over the other (as against having an eternal conflict)? 4) Why should the body be considered the source of evil and spirit be considered good? One can conceive of having all bodily needs met and yet have an evil act (as in the Garden of Eden). And one can conceive of a spirit without a body as evil (Lucifer). In these cases, one might think the source of evil is the spirit, and not the body. 5) Why should the good be considered the condition of the soul separated from the body, that is, disembodied existence, apart from this world, a state in which the soul exists in a pure contemplative vision of the eternal forms (or in a beatific vision of God)?

Persistence of Dualistic Attitudes

Dualistic attitudes have persisted in the history of Christianity. The world is seen to exist in varying degrees of evil or lack of the good. It is seen to be positively a source of evil, to be avoided by monastic withdrawal and celibacy. Or, it is seen as a possible source of temptation and sin, particularly the sin of the body as against the sin of unbelief. (Socrates thought that because of all our bodily needs, we don't have time for philosophy. One could just as well say that because we didn't take time to philosophize, we now have all these bodily "needs.") Or, the world is seen as neutral ground, neither good nor evil in its institutions and practices (democracy and capitalism); what matters is one's attitude. Or, the world may be seen as a positive good, having been created by God, but it is not as good as the world to come after this life. An alternative to this other-worldliness of Christianity, as influenced by Greek dualism, is to regard creation and history as revealing God's glory, that the earth is full of the glory of God, and that the goal of mankind, through the work of dominion, is to fill the earth with the knowledge of the glory of God as the waters cover the sea. Consistent theism is not dualistic other-worldliness, but dualistic attitudes still permeate much of popular Christian theism.

Two Forms of Dualism

Greek dualism exists in two philosophical traditions: the dualism of Plato, in which matter and spirit are eternal and independent of each other, and the dualism of Aristotle, in which matter is eternal but dependent on spirit. In Plato's dualism, there are four eternal realities: the eternal forms, the divine maker, the souls, and matter. The divine maker (demiurge) is not the Creator of matter, but one who shapes matter according to the forms. Not being Creator, the demiurge lacks absolute power over matter and can only imperfectly reproduce the forms in matter. Knowledge for Plato is of the unchanging forms, which the eternal souls recollect dimly from previous existence. This knowledge, described in Plato's allegory of the cave, is attained only arduously in this life by breaking free from bondage to the senses, in order to contemplate the pure forms.

Plato's Dualism

The basic things about God and man and good and evil are not clear for Plato, or for Socrates, through whom Plato speaks. In the early dialogues, Socrates claimed not to know. In the later dialogues, Plato uncritically assumed that matter and the souls were eternal, as well as the forms and the demiurge. He used reason constructively to develop a worldview based on these four eternal realities. He used reason critically to show inadequacies in the views of those who claimed to know and to teach others. And Socrates was willing to die rather than give up the public role of gadfly to those who would live unexamined lives. Yet some of Plato's claims about basic things were unexamined. Plato's dualism, in contrast to Aristotle's dualism, may be called ordinary dualism. In this view, matter and the souls are both eternal and independent of each other. Plato offered no reason for believing the soul is eternal. And he did not consider any reasons against it. In this, he is not unlike many who hold basic beliefs without proof. We have seen reasons in the first argument against materialism for saying the material world in general, in its parts, and as a whole is not self-maintaining and therefore is not eternal. This is a sufficient defeater for ordinary dualism.

We have also seen reasons for saying that while the soul is everlasting—a position for which Plato argued[1]—the soul is not eternal, without beginning. The soul is in time in that we have one thought after another. If it were eternal, it would be eternal in time. The soul as finite in knowledge would be subject to growth in infinite time. But there can be no unique event in an eternal process in time, for it could not be explained why that event had not happened before, given an infinite amount of time. Therefore, the soul is either not eternal, or not finite in knowledge, or goes through an endless cycle of no unique growth in knowledge. Since it is clear we are not infinite in knowledge and we are unwilling to say we go through an endless, and therefore meaningless, cycle, we conclude the soul is not eternal. Hence the soul is temporal, that is, with beginning, and therefore the soul is created.

Aristotle's Dualism

Aristotle was the student of Plato. He did not accept basic parts of Plato's metaphysics or his epistemology. He affirmed a qualified form of dualism: matter is eternal, yet dependent on the First Cause of its

---

1. One can argue for the natural immortality of the soul by arguing from its incorporeality, to its indivisibility, to its indestructibility. In the *Phaedo*, Socrates seems to rely on such inferences. Plato, *Complete Works*.

actuality. Aristotle's position raises a question as to whether what is eternal is necessarily independent and self-existing. Aristotle arrived at his position starting from an analysis of change in ordinary experience. He analyzed change as a movement from potentiality to actuality, from a condition of lacking form to taking on form. An acorn becomes an oak tree. Brass becomes a human statue. The acorn is potentially an oak, and in the process of change, the matter of the acorn takes on the form (or essence) of the oak and becomes actually an oak tree. To change from potentiality to actuality the acorn (or brass) must be acted upon by outside forces. Water, sunlight, and soil act upon the acorn for it to become an oak. All change requires a cause. The chain of causation cannot go back in an infinite regress. There must be a First Cause or an uncaused cause, an unmoved mover or a Prime Mover, in order for anything to become actual. This Prime Mover is Pure Actuality without any potentiality. Since matter is subject to change, Pure Actuality excludes all matter. Pure Actuality is therefore spirit. To say spirit acts on matter is no different from the ordinary dualism of Plato, where the demiurge acted on an eternal and independent material world. In Aristotle's view, only the Prime Mover has pure actuality. Everything else received its actuality from the Prime Mover. What does this mean? The acorn at a certain time is actually an acorn. It was not always an acorn; it became an acorn, let's say, from a combination of certain atoms. The atoms themselves were not eternally atoms or we would be in ordinary dualism, subject to its objections. Before being atoms, we might say today that there was energy. But we cannot stop with an eternal, self-existing, and self-maintaining energy. If we go back further, we must go to pure potentiality, without any actuality. But how is pure potentiality, or having no actuality whatsoever, different from not being anything or from non-being?

Aristotle's analysis faces a dilemma: Either matter has some actuality without spirit, in which case this is ordinary dualism, not dependent dualism; or, matter has no actuality without spirit, in which case this is creation, not dualism. In either case, there is no material reality which is both eternal and dependent. What is eternal is independent, self-existing, self-maintaining, and self-explaining.

Aristotle's analysis of all change as a motion from potentiality to actuality does not sufficiently explain the change of decay and the change of coming into being. Aquinas accepted Aristotle's argument for the Prime Mover as a proof of the existence of God. He then had to reconcile the eternal dependence of Aristotle with creation having a beginning, as expressed in the book of Genesis. Aristotle, in his view, went as far as natural reason could go. Nature is completed by supernatural grace. For Aquinas, it took faith to believe the paradox that there never was a time that the world did not exist, yet the world came into being. Aquinas could have said that time began when the world began. This, however, would mean creation, a doctrine which Aristotle failed to grasp because of a failure to use reason critically at the basic level.

LOGICALLY POSSIBLE WORLDS

We have critically examined the assumptions of three worldviews which affirm all is eternal. Before going on to examine the alternative that only some is eternal, we should consider whether there are other views that remain to be examined. Are there other worldviews that have come to expression in history, or could come to expression, or are at least logically possible, even if it is unlikely they will ever come to expression in any significant way? Since the argument has been proceeding by eliminating what is not logically possible, for the sake of soundness we must consider all the types of logically possible worlds. Historical worldviews have been examined in terms of their view of what is real/eternal. Alternatives to historical worldviews can be classified in various forms.

Forms of Logically Possible Worlds

1. Several forms, aspects, dimensions, and variations on the theme of skepticism have been considered, including various forms of anti-realism. These generally reflect uncritically held assumptions along with claims about the limits of reason, usually based on the failure to critically use reason sufficiently. If skepticism is not an explicit worldview in itself, it can be recognized as a characteristic posture. It no doubt will recur. The question is whether it will recur in any essentially new form. If or when it does, it must be critically examined for its assump-

tion, beginning with its view about what is reason, man's need for meaning, and about knowing by reason and argument.

2. A second set of alternative views revolves around the concept of being and non-being. Historical worldviews have affirmed the concept of being, in saying some (being) is eternal. The denial of being in philosophies of becoming (e.g., *Madhyamika*) and in phenomenalistic conceptions of being (Berkeley, Kant, Derrida) have been considered. They generally fall back into skepticism and silence, or an appeal to an unknown, or to a dogmatic assertion of one of the historical views.

3. Some alternative views affirm being, but without specification. Parmenides' *One* cannot be named. This is true also of the *One* of Plotinus. Lao Tzu's *Tao* cannot be named, nor Anaximander's *Apeiron*, nor Spinoza's *God*, nor Shankara's *Nirguna Brahman*, nor Hawking's *Singularity*. In common, they affirm "all is one" and "all is eternal" and thereby deny God the Creator. The way to the One appears to be required by reason, but the arguments are based either on begging the question, or on incoherent definitions, or on distinctions without a difference. This set of alternatives can either be classified under one or another historical form of non-theism, or set in a distinct class as appeal to an Unknown One. As such, this appeal places itself beyond rational thought. Insofar as reasons are given for the move to this unknown, these reasons can be criticized. Attempts to draw inferences from the unknown become purely arbitrary.

4. If a worldview must answer the basic questions about being, what might an alternative to the historical views look like? Being is either temporal (with beginning) or eternal (without beginning). Is there a third possibility? Can existence be neither temporal nor eternal, neither *a* nor *non-a*? By the law of excluded middle, there is no third possibility. Can existence be both *a* and *non-a*, at the same time and in the same respect? By the law of non-contradiction, it cannot be. By not identifying it as either *a* or *non-a* is to not form a concept of it by the law of identity. It is an unknown, and a matter of silence.

Is there something which is not matter (that which is extended and non-conscious), or not spirit (that which is non-extended and conscious), or is both matter and spirit (at the same time and in the same respect), or is neither matter nor spirit? As with the predicates temporal and eternal, the laws of thought apply here in the same way. The four historical worldviews—material monism, spiritual monism, dualism, and theism—exhaust the logical possibilities. This is to be expected if history is an outworking of the internal and external challenges of reason in the human quest for meaning.

5. Philosophers talk much about logically possible worlds. By this they do not mean logically possible worlds in a basic sense, but variations within a given world. It is often asked, "Is this the best of all possible worlds?" Could there be a world with less evil in it? Could there be a world with fewer persons, one in which, for example, I did not exist? This often gets into the question of God's goodness, God's freedom, and the application of some form of the Principle of Sufficient Reason. Our interest lies in showing basic things are clear in the actual world. If basic things are clear, then there is only one logically possible world in a basic sense. Variations within a world are of interest if they raise questions about basic issues. And since what is less basic depends on what is more basic, if there is agreement on what is more basic, there will be agreement on what is less basic, on questions about variations within this world.

6. Sometimes a world is spoken of in a subjective sense. In this sense, each person's world is said to be different, even to the point of not being comparable (incommensurability) with any other world. We have spoken of the variations of views earlier in saying there are many different degrees of consciousness and consistency with which a basic belief is held. While we interpret our experiences in light of our basic belief, the degree of consciousness and consistency of our basic belief is affected by our personality and life goal (artistic, philosophical, or practical), our culture (economic, educational, friendships), and in any given circumstance our mood (focus on self or the good). Differences admit of degrees and our values are reflected in a predictable pattern of association. Being more or less conscious and consistent does not place us in another worldview or in a worldview of our own. Variations in degrees assume an underlying commonality in content. Variations in kind assume an underlying formal commonality.

7. Perhaps the most engaging sense of logically possible worlds is presented in literature in the form of myth, whether in the past (*Lord of the Rings*) or in the future (*Star Wars*). The nature of ultimate reality is not always transparent. Is the Force personal or impersonal? Is the Force good or evil or neither? Does it make sense to say "May the Force be with you" if the Force is impersonal? If the Force is personal, can it have a dark side as well? Does its appeal lie in its mystery? Is the world of *Star Wars* one of a mystical materialism? Is the world of the *Rings* dualist or theist or a genuine alternative to all historical worldviews? Does the world of fantasy and magic rely on uncaused events, or on hidden or occult forces, or is the appeal mediated by symbolism and allegory? Whatever approach is taken, literature does not take us beyond the historical worldviews. We are warranted therefore in proceeding to examine the last remaining worldview, based on the belief that "only some is eternal."

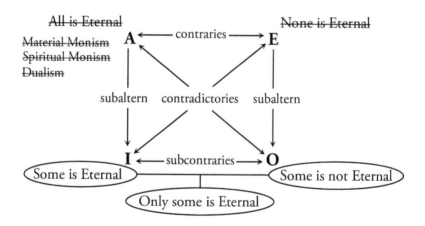

Chapter 8

———

THEISM

INTRODUCTION

WE HAVE LOOKED AT THE HISTORICAL forms and the logically possible forms of the view that "all is eternal" in some form or another. All showed logical incoherence at the basic level. It would appear that "only some is eternal" must be true. What is eternal brought into existence, or created, what is not eternal. Belief in a Creator is theistic belief in God. However, theism is thought by many to be logically incoherent and to fail to preserve meaning as other worldviews have failed. Belief without seeing what is clear, and without being able to show how theism preserves meaning, is to believe without proof and without understanding. Fideism empties belief of meaning. It is not an alternative to skepticism, since man's deepest need is for meaning. Theism therefore must respond to the challenge of being charged with incoherence or lose its public, as well as personal, relevance.

In speaking about theism, one cannot speak as a fideist. To appeal to belief in God on the basis of scripture without proof from general revelation encounters several problems. *First*, it begs the question. How does one know that scripture is God's word if it is not known that God exists? Why is there any need for the existence of scripture and, how does one know that this book rather than some other book is divine revelation? These are longstanding challenges that have not been met. Appeal to scripture as immediately, and without inference, self-attesting and the source of belief in God, does not explain how unbelief is inexcusable for those who have not had exposure to scripture.

Second, if the existence and nature of God are not clear from general revelation, then unbelief is excusable. To say that deep down everyone knows that God exists and that this knowledge is being suppressed, does not show how the unbelief used to suppress the truth is inexcusable. One consequence of the loss of inexcusability is that good and evil become emptied of meaning, and therefore also the idea of divine justice and mercy.

Third, fideism fails to represent the teaching of scripture which affirms the inexcusability of unbelief on the basis of clear general revelation, the responsibility to give a reason for one's hope to those who ask, the call to take thoughts captive which are raised up against the knowledge of God, and the goal of glorifying God in all that by which he makes himself known.[1] For these reasons, when speaking about theism, we must begin by speaking about what is clear from general revelation.

The term "God" has different meanings in atheism, pantheism, dualism, and polytheism. In theism, it is generally understood that God is a Spirit, infinite, eternal, and unchangeable, in his being, wisdom, power, holiness, justice, goodness, and truth.[2] God is personal, having knowledge and will. God is omnipresent as an infinite spirit, spiritually present everywhere. God is omnipotent, having absolute power over what he brings into being. God is omniscient, knowing all things exhaustively, knowing the end from the beginning. God has moral attributes of goodness and justice in an infinite and eternal and unchangeable way.[3] The attributes of infinite, eternal, and un-

---

1. See *Romans 1:20* on the clarity of general revelation; see *1 Peter 3:15* on reason for one's hope; see *2 Corinthians 10:4* on taking thoughts captive; for historic Christian creed, see *Westminster Confession of Faith 4.1, 5.1,* and *Shorter Catechism Question 1, 101.*

2. Derivation and defense of these attributes are appropriate for philosophy of religion, which is not being undertaken here explicitly. Assuming, from earlier proofs, that matter is not eternal, and that only some is eternal, it would follow that what is eternal is spirit, which by nature is personal, and has knowledge and will. The knowledge and will of an eternal Creator would be infinite and unchanging. More can be added, but here the focus is to be on the problem of evil for traditional theism, where this definition is common ground in the dispute (see *Shorter Catechism* above, Question 4: "What is God?").

3. Must God be infinitely good? If God is Creator *ex nihilo*, then God is infinite—having absolute power over, and knowledge of, what he brings into being from nothing. If evil is to act contrary to one's nature, then the question becomes: "Can God be infinitely evil?" If God were infinitely opposed to himself in every act, he could not act to do anything at all, and hence could not act to create. Could God be neither good nor evil? If God created man's moral sense with infinite, deliberate wisdom, God could not be morally indifferent. He would be concerned about what is moral, and hence he would be moral and not indifferent. If God cannot be evil or indifferent, then God must be infinitely good.

changeable apply to all other attributes of God. They are possessed by God alone and cannot be communicated to any creature. Human beings are the image of God, having the same attributes which God has (being, wisdom, power, holiness, justice, goodness, and truth) in a finite, temporal, and changeable way. All these attributes of God are manifest in the general revelation of creation and history. The first and fundamental attribute is the eternality of God, and with this, his aseity (completeness in self-existence).

These attributes, understood in certain ways, have caused puzzles. Some are merely intellectual puzzles, like the paradox of omnipotence—can God create a stone so large that he cannot lift it? Some raise questions about the personhood of God: If he is in timeless eternity, is he without passion (Open Theists)? Some raise questions about God's omniscience: If he knows the future, is there human freedom? Some raise questions about the simplicity (unity) of the troubling divine attributes, particularly of justice and mercy. But the question that is perplexing to all who think about God is: "How can God be all good and all powerful and there be evil in the world?" This is the classic problem of evil.

PRELIMINARY PROBLEMS

Before addressing the problem of evil, there are a few preliminary problems which should be addressed.

Creation *Ex Nihilo*

Creation *ex nihilo* is literally creation from nothing.[4] Creation *ex nihilo* is not forming an already existing material reality, as in dualism. Creation is not a transformation of God's being in which each being is part of God (pantheism). Creation is not an eternal dependence (Aristotle). Creation is not an emanation of the one into a hierarchy

---

4. The arguments in Chapters 4–7, if sound, show that only some is eternal, that is, that some is eternal and some is not eternal. What is not eternal came into being, but would not have come into being from non-being (see Chapter 4). It could then only have been brought into being by what is eternal. To bring into being is to create *ex nihilo* (to bring into being from no pre-existing being or substance). What is eternal therefore created *ex nihilo* what is not eternal.

of being (Plotinus). If it is none of these, then it appears to some to be a magical act of being from non-being, which was rejected as impossible. Creation *ex nihilo* differs from the view that being came from non-being in two ways. In the latter, nothing is eternal and all came into being from non-being. In the former, God is eternal. God did not come into being from non-being. In the latter, there is an uncaused event. In the former, being came into existence by the act (will) of God. Coming into existence by an act of creation is not uncaused.

Analogies of Creation *Ex Nihilo*

Creation *ex nihilo* has often perplexed those who think about it. How can God who is spirit create matter which is so unlike spirit? And how can God create spirit other than himself rather than from a part of himself? There are analogies to creation in human experience. In analogies there is an element of likeness as well as unlikeness, and these are bound together. In univocal cases they are altogether like; in equivocal cases they are altogether unlike. Man, as the image of God, is said to be like and unlike God. Man is like God in having wisdom; rocks and plants do not have wisdom. Man's wisdom is unlike God's wisdom in that man's wisdom is finite and God's wisdom is infinite. In the being of man, which is analogous to God's being, analogies to creation can be seen. In man, matter affects the mind in the transition from a neural impulse to a mental image (see *The Third Argument Against Materialism*, Chapter 5). How this occurs at some point cannot be specified. For in every chain of causal explanation, a complex cause is explained in terms of simple causal links, none of which, by virtue of being simple, can be explained in terms of a series of simpler causal links. As matter affects mind, so mind affects matter. A mental event (the intention to move my arm) can cause a physical event (the movement of my arm). In the act of intending, power radiates from the mind, and becomes physicalized in neural impulses, which move my arm and put energy into the physical world around me. The self is not decreased in the act of intending by which neural impulses are formed. Similarly, with the question of spirit, in procreation life flows from the parents, and becomes other than the parents, without the parents being decreased. The new life, which is the same as the soul, is other than the parents. Like creation, a new life comes into being.

Unlike creation, man participates in a process that is already highly structured, over which he has no control.

Creation as a Unique Event

It has previously been argued that there are no unique events in an eternal being in time. Creation appears to be a unique event in time, prompting questions like, "What was God doing before he created?" and "Why didn't God create before he did, given that God had infinite time?" These questions assume that God is eternal and in time, and that time is not itself created. Time is not a being, but an aspect of beings.[5] It is a relation among beings or within a being. Outer time is a relation among being in motion. If there is no motion whatsoever in any physical being, then there is no passage of time, no before or after, no getting older, no being late or early. And all the more, if there is no physical being, there can be no motion and therefore there would be no outer time. Inner time is a relation between ideas in finite minds, which occur one after the other. If there were no finite or created minds, there would be no inner time. Since both the physical world and finite minds came into being, there was no time (inner or outer) before creation.

Creation is the beginning of time. Time began with creation. There is a logical or atemporal order in timeless eternality, not a temporal order. If time must begin with creation, it makes no sense to ask what God was doing before creation, that is, before time began. It can also be said that there never was a time that the world did not exist, without denying that the world, and time, had a beginning. As for unique acts of God in time, such as the parting of the Red Sea, there is a natural explanation why that act must come in a particular relation to another event (the exodus of the people from Egypt), and not one year before or after it did happen.

---

5. The argument here (as is often the case elsewhere) is by good and necessary consequences from things which are commonly agreed upon. Concerning time, it is commonly accepted that time is not a being, but an aspect of beings. The analysis proceeds from there to its conclusion. What may not occur in many cases is the step-by-step analysis by way of which a particular conclusion is reached. The reader is being asked to examine each step in the analysis.

Why Did God Create?

It is commonly thought that when a person acts, that person acts to fulfill some need. God also, being a person, acts to fulfill a need, so it is thought. The need, however it is conceived, implies some lack in God, which is incompatible with divine infinitude and aseity. The question assumes that one can be without expressing one's being, that we can "be" without "being." It also assumes that like human persons, God is in time and acts in time. God is wise and is acting wisely. He is being wise. There is no separation of God's essence, act, and being. One can say then that God creates because he is Creator, or simply because He is. In creating, God is being God. It may be asked, "Why then did God create this world rather than some other world, a world, say, with less or more evil?" This is seeking for a reason sufficient to explain what we observe in the world.

The question of sufficient reason and theodicy will soon be addressed specifically. Here, more generally, it can be said that the act of God expresses the nature, essence, or attributes of God. Some avoid talk about attributes, but it is the attributes of God (mentioned earlier) that are revealed, and it is the attributes therefore that are to be known; and, it is the attributes that have not been sufficiently known and that have been the subject of disputes and divisions for centuries. Whether the knowledge of God is more mystical than cognitive, and whether there is knowledge of God without knowledge of his attributes, and vice versa, is discussed under arguments used in support of fideism.

The wisdom, power, justice, and goodness of God are revealed in creation, necessarily. Creation is revelation. This world reveals the divine glory, in fullness, but not exhaustively. Creation, being finite, can never exhaustively reveal God. The finite cannot exhaust the infinite. Yet there is fullness to this revelation. The whole earth is full of the glory of God. The particulars and circumstances of creation are therefore to be understood on the principle of plenitude of revelation.

THE PROBLEM OF EVIL:
DAVID HUME'S PRESENTATION

We turn now from preliminary problems of theism to look at the principal objection to theism based on the problem of evil. David Hume, in his *Dialogues Concerning Natural Religion*,[6] has given an extended presentation of the problem and offered solutions based on the perspective of the three participants in the dialogue. We will look at Hume's treatment at some length because it attempts to treat the problem comprehensively and with some insight, even where we may disagree with him. Following this, we will look at the Free Will solution to the problem of evil and objections to it. Last, we will propose a solution, which, in light of the nature of the problem and the nature of evil, is called the "Ironic Solution."

The problem of evil is one part of a larger dialogue concerning the existence and nature of God. The three speakers represent the three ways of speaking about God. Demea, the orthodox believer, speaks analogously about God: God is like and unlike man. Cleanthes, the rational empiricist, speaks univocally about God: God is essentially like man. Philo, the skeptic-mystic, speaks equivocally about God: God is said to be totally unlike man. Demea and Philo begin by agreeing that religion arises from a sense of misery and that the world is full of misery and wickedness. Philo then drops the problem of evil on Demea, and then all three look at solutions proposed by each, raising objections consistent with their particular perspective. In the end, no proposed solution is acceptable. Let us see why.

Religion Arises from a Sense of Misery

Demea and Philo agree that religion arises from feeling and not thought. This is not an uncommon view. It is a cliché that there are no atheists in foxholes. When the going gets tough, even the tough get religious. Religion is the opiate of the masses, in Marx's view. It is a matter of comfort and solace, a drug to relieve the pain of alienated existence. Religion is a crutch for the weak, an infantile dependence, in Freud's view. We project, from our fears and desires, a heavenly father

---

6. David Hume, *Dialogues and Natural History of Religion*, ed. J.C.A. Gaskin (Oxford: Oxford University Press, 1993), 95-115.

who will care for us in a hostile world. We call upon God in our trouble and turn away when we are at ease. Nietzsche thought the Christian religion was a religion for the weak, a slave morality. Churches attract the more emotional and vulnerable members of society. The best and, indeed, the only way to bring anyone to a due sense of religion is by the just representation of the misery and wickedness of life. And for that, what was needed for religious teaching, Philo thought, was not a talent for reasoning, but a talent of eloquence, in order to make people feel more keenly the misery they are already aware of.

Demea goes along with Philo in his assumptions, but need not, and should not. Do all or only some religions arise from the sense of misery? Are there some non-miserable persons who are religious? That would be hard to deny unless misery arises, not from circumstances, but from lack of meaning. Perhaps some religion arises from a sense of misery, for example, the religion of mammon or material success. But that would not compare favorably with the religion of Job, who from the depth of his misery cried out, "Though he slay me yet will I trust in him." Job does not serve God for God's outward gifts, or leave God when he loses all God's natural blessings. Job's religion does not arise from a sense of misery.

But there are further problems in Philo's view, in his concept of religion itself. What is religion? Are only some religious, and can religion arise? If religion is the belief or set of beliefs one uses to give meaning to one's experience, then, since all give meaning to experience, all are religious.[7] Theistic belief as well as non-theistic belief (an-

---

7. The definitions of religion proposed in the past two centuries by Schleiermacher, Weber, Marx, Durkheim, Frazer, Otto, Freud, etc., are much discussed in the academic study of religion. Recently, under the influence of Postmodernism, the notion of definition itself has been questioned. Here, we have to get back to the deeper, skeptical assumptions of the existence of essences (Is there any permanence?), and the existence of objective knowledge (Is reality a construct of ever-changing states of consciousness?). These assumptions of skepticism have been critically examined throughout this book (see Chapter 4 on eternality, and Chapter 6 on anti-realism). The definition of religion as an attempt to state the meaning of a term is bound up with one's larger framework of meaning, i.e., one's worldview. That is to say, one's definition of religion reflects one's religion (meaning framework) held more or less consciously and consistently. Insofar as one is not consistently skeptical and given to nihilism, common ground remains. There are commonly accepted examples of religion (Hinduism, Buddhism, Confucianism, Judaism, Christianity, Islam) from which common features of religion may be identified. Belief in a higher power is not a common feature of all of these, but giving meaning to one's experience in light of one's basic belief (true for both theism and atheism/secular humanism/naturalism) is common to all of these religions. This

titheism, pantheism, and dualism) function formally in the same way and are equally religious. Further, what one regards as misery depends on one's basic belief, so religion cannot arise from "the experience of misery." Since we never find ourselves existentially to be in a world without meaning of some sort or other, we must say religion does not and cannot arise, although religion may change.

The World Is Full of Misery and Wickedness

That the world is full of misery and wickedness is agreed to by Demea and Philo, but resisted by Cleanthes, who represents popular common sense. "Full" seems too strong and most would deny that the world is full of natural evil (misery) and moral evil (wickedness). Philo intends "full" in a strong sense, beyond ankle deep or waist deep. I will add to Philo's list of arguments by speaking on behalf of Demea, the orthodox believer, in the following seventeen points. The first thirteen are Philo's in essence, and the last four are added for the sake of showing the fullness of evil for the theist.

1. *Nature vs. nature.* Nature is red in tooth and claw. Larger animals devour smaller animals. The lion devours the lamb. The sparrow-hawk devours the sparrow. Insects sting larger animals and flies would lay eggs in the horse's eye. We are inclined to regard this as natural, not natural evil. Yet in a world created by God we naturally ask, must this be so? Insensitivity to animal suffering is a way to avoid seeing the extent of evil in the world.

2. *Nature vs. man.* If man has mostly overcome being devoured by larger animals, there yet remains much toil and woe. Drought and famine have ravaged and continue to ravage mankind. Earthquakes and extremes of weather, storms, and floods, destroy or leave man helpless. Diseases and plagues continue to devastate man in spite of technological advances.

---

applies to variations within any tradition (both classical and popular levels—there are many Christianities, many Islams, many Buddhisms), as well as to mixtures between traditions (syncretism), which is to say, worldviews are held more or less consciously and consistently.

3. *Man vs. man.* Man is the greatest enemy to man. Rich oppress poor. Arrogance of the proud is insufferable in every form it takes. The law is twisted by bribes. Wars consume man through history: the last century, being the most enlightened, was the worst. Acts out of cruelty, malice, and spite, and for personal glory, bring as much disaster as wars for ideology and utopian ideals.

4. *Man vs. woman.* In the most intimate of relationships, what often begins as true love ends in true hate. Marriages fail at an increasing rate. The pain of divorce is often worse than the pain of death. Those marriages that survive do so barely, or become a comfortable convenience. Naiveté is soon replaced by cynicism. The institution of marriage is put into question by serial polygamy, same-sex relations, and prolonged bouts of promiscuity, neither sex being the happier for it.

5. *Man vs. self.* The greatest enemy to man is himself. Where there are no real enemies, man invents his own. Men have lived in fear of gods and demons, and have sacrificed their children to placate the wrath of the gods. The more depressive and psychotic create hellish torments for themselves. Whole cultures and civilizations have been held captive for centuries by the contents of their own imaginations.

6. *Bad attitude.* Some might say that the world is not as bad as it is being made out to be. Things are actually quite good, but bad attitudes keep us from seeing this. This only shifts the focus of the problem and actually makes it quite worse. If there is nothing to complain about, then the complaining becomes a gratuitous source of evil.

7. *Ignorance is bliss.* It is said that some few persons (artists, poets, etc.) are sensitive to evil and spread their discontent among the masses. But if by being more sensitive to life one suffers all the more, then only the ignorant can be blissful, which is not a high estimate of life.

8. *Island of bliss in a sea of misery.* Some may say that they see misery in the world round about them, but they themselves are happy. They are in effect an island of bliss in a sea of misery. One wonders how this is possible if a person has even a slight degree of compassion. That

person surrounded by a sea of misery is to be congratulated on being so happy a singularity.

9. *Suicide.* That the world is full of misery and wickedness has been strenuously objected to by appeal to the mass of mankind, who, rather than choose escape by suicide, seem to find the world attractive enough to pursue their lives in this world and cling to it, rather than flee it. Hamlet contemplated suicide. He did not pursue it though, not from attraction to this world, but from fear of the afterlife. "What dreams shall come . . . must give us pause." We are terrified, not bribed, into continuing our existence.

10. *Hope.* Men everywhere seem to hope that the future will be better than the past. They hope not to repeat the mistakes they have made in the past. But we seldom learn from history, whether from our collective history or from our personal history. And there are always new errors to be made, even when we avoid old errors. Retirement, so longed for by many, is often regretted soon thereafter. We vainly hope to drain from the dregs of life what the first sprightly running could not give. "Hope springs eternal in the human breast. Man never is but is always to be blessed." Sisyphus has absurd hope that he could roll the rock of melancholy up the hill to stay.

11. *Family.* Some suggest looking on the bright side of life. Family is a source of human happiness. Many find purpose in family life and sacrifice much for it. They affirm family values and find haven in home and hearth. But families are subject to death by disease, accident, and misfortune (Job, Chekov's *Rothchild's Fiddle*), and can leave us in despair. Strife occurs with self-will. Children often become rebellious in growing up. Family members become co-dependent, reciprocally enabling each other in their fantasy life. Few attain old age in love of spouse, a lack which is often a source of distress and pain. Often enough, life settles into mere comfort and convenience—which is hardly friendship (the effect of mutual commitment to the good).

12. *Culture.* Some look to cultural achievements (literature, art, architecture) as a source of pleasure, the finest in human glory. The glory that was Greece and the grandeur that was Rome are mournful

monuments of human striving to rise above oblivion. Solomon, who tried all that man could desire, found nothing new under the sun, but vanity and vexation of spirit. Dilettantes find distraction in culture ("In the room, the women come and go . . . ."). Rock concerts, sought out as a place of excitement, are but a diversion from tedium.

13. *Nature.* If not man, then nature. Few besides religious hermits and social recluses find nature inviting enough to be wholly immersed in nature. Most find nature a recreational relief, as some find amusement parks. Thoreau did not remain at Walden Pond. Integration into nature as the Taoist sage or the eco-mystic is to give up on human society as irredeemable.

14. *Knowledge.* Many claim knowledge, even enlightenment, but seldom rise above mere belief without proof or understanding. Skepticism is the default position for those who want to distance themselves from fideism. What knowledge is found is mostly utilitarian (technology) and not of interest in itself. Teachers who transmit knowledge are often burnt out by mid-career and show little to no sign of intellectual growth. With much knowledge, in a natural sense, that is, for man "under the sun," in the words of Solomon, the wisest of men, comes much sorrow.

Beyond Hume: The Full Extent of Misery and Wickedness in Historic Theism

15. *Natural evil—Physical death.* All men die. Death is regarded by most men as natural. Ordinarily all men seek instinctively to avoid death as an evil. For theism, death is not merely natural. Physical death is a natural evil. It intensifies and magnifies the problem of moral evil. If there were no moral evil, there would be no natural evil. In simpler terms, if we were morally good, we would not get old, sick, and die. This is completely foreign to the common view of things. Yet, a little reflection shows that it is in accord with our instinctive sense of things. We naturally expect the absence of all evil in a world created by an all good, all powerful God. If God were all powerful, he could create a world without physical death. If God were all good, he would create such a world. Historically, theists have believed that God did

create the world without any evil, including physical death, especially so for rationally self-conscious beings. In this view, natural evil was subsequently imposed by God on man as a call back from moral evil. As such, it supports the view in Hume's dialogue that the world is full of misery (natural evil) and wickedness (moral evil).

16. *Deicide.* This is the radical nature of moral evil in Christian theism. Mankind is generally ready to recognize moral evil in a variety of forms, but not in its radical form. The origin of sin in the fall of man and its effect upon mankind is often affirmed in historic theism. The assumption of the clarity of general revelation, underlying the origin of sin and the inexcusability of unbelief, is less often affirmed. Moral evil, or sin, is an act contrary to human nature; it involves the rejection of reason to avoid what is clear about God. It is rejection of logos, the life of God in man as reason, a rejection present in all forms of unbelief. The clearest and fullest expression of evil is necessarily personal, and, according to Christian theism, occurred in the crucifixion of the Logos incarnate. The radical nature of evil, beginning in human autonomy and the rejection of the life of God in man, culminates in deicide. A greater moral evil cannot be conceived.

17. *Spiritual death.* The reality of moral evil is realized in the experience of its inherent consequence. What is inherent, and therefore always present, in the rejection of reason is meaninglessness, and with it, boredom and guilt. This is the condition of spiritual death, the destruction of the self or the soul of man, spoken of symbolically as hell. This spiritual condition is described in the imagery of darkness (of mind), burning (of desires), and torment (of conscience—the worm that does not die)—unendingly (the bottomless pit). The reality of natural and moral evil is therefore not mitigated, but maximized in historic theism. This is the context in which the problem of evil must be framed and responded to.

The Problem of Evil Stated

Having argued (1) that religion arises from a sense of misery and (2) that the world is full of misery and wickedness, Hume, through Philo, springs his trap on the unsuspecting Demea. Demea, the orthodox believer, expects from (1) and (2) that everyone should naturally turn to God in their misery and need. But given the reality of evil, to what kind of God shall they turn? To a God who is all good and all powerful? Philo presents the problem of evil in its classical form. If God is all powerful, he can prevent evil. If God is all good, he would prevent evil. So, if God is both all good and all powerful, why is there any evil at all? To assert all three—infinite power, infinite goodness, and evil—is either to assert a contradiction or a mystery, which leaves theism in no better position than other competing views. Hume does allow that, for all we know, there might be an easy solution. In his dialogue, Hume considers five solutions, none of which are acceptable. We will briefly look at each.

Hume's Five Solutions and Responses

The *first* solution, proposed by Philo, the skeptic/mystic, is an appeal to an unknown. God's goodness is perfect, but incomprehensible. To say God loves us as a heavenly father is not to say anything meaningful. An earthly father would do all in his power to help his sick child because he loves his child. If God loves us and does all in his power to help us, why do we yet die from our sickness? A common reply is to affirm God's love, but to assert that his ways are far above our ways (i.e., God's goodness is perfect, but incomprehensible). The bold assertion that God loves us is killed by a thousand qualifications. But if God's goodness is incomprehensible, then all religion ends. We would not know what to pray for or what to praise God for, since what is good in our eyes may not be good in God's eyes. And without prayer and praise, religion comes to an end. This solution is therefore inadequate.

The *second* solution is proposed by Demea, the orthodox believer. This life, he says, is short in comparison with the next. Here, we know in part; there we will see the whole. We will trace through all the "mazes and intricacies of providence the divine benevolence and rectitude of God."[8] Demea supposes what is presently unknowable about a future life in order to prove the existence of an all good, all powerful God. This is hope, not proof. Furthermore, it is questionable hope. Demea's solution presupposes that to know why there is evil

---

8. Hume, *Dialogues*, 101.

now, I must know everything. I must be able to trace "all the mazes and intricacies of providence." But, as a finite being, I cannot know everything, even in the future life. So, on Demea's reckoning, I will in principle never know why there is evil. Demea's solution is therefore also unsatisfactory.

Cleanthes, the rational empiricist, proposes a *third* solution based on the amount of evil in the world. He believes there is more good than evil. But the amounts in comparison are uncertain. We cannot measure the amount of animal pain there is, or our own pain compared with our pleasure. Who has passed out from pleasure? Furthermore, why should there be any pain at all, if God is all good and all powerful?

This leads Cleanthes to propose a *fourth* solution. God, he says, is not infinitely powerful, but only very powerful. Being finitely powerful, he adjusts means to ends within limits. One cannot expect all things from God. Still, one could expect more from one who is very powerful. And there is the problem of gratuitous evil, which it seems a finitely perfect being could easily enough prevent. But for theism, God cannot be Creator *ex nihilo* and be finitely powerful. So, this solution does not work in the final analysis.

Finally, Philo proposes a *fifth* and last solution. No natural evil is necessary. The original source of all things is as indifferent to good and evil as to heat and cold, and light and darkness. Philo gives four reasons. *First*, animal pain is not necessary. If an animal can be without pain for five minutes, then this time can be extended indefinitely. The pain of hunger is not necessary to move someone to eat. Pain is not necessary in death—one can die in one's sleep. Pain is not necessary for learning. One does not have to learn the hard way. One can learn by instruction and by mild discomfort to avoid sources of harm. There need not be accidents, since there need not be rocks in our path on which to stumble, or there can be angels to guard us from such accidents. And finally, pain is not necessary in order to appreciate pleasure. Pleasures are various, and the absence of one pleasure is not the presence of pain, but could be the presence of other pleasures.

Philo's *second* reason is that secret divine intervention can prevent a great deal of pain without overthrowing the natural order. Caesar could have been drowned in the Adriatic Sea with one wave higher than the other, and Republican government could have been pre-

served in the West. Hitler could have been accepted into art school.
A fly could have landed on the eyelash of Lee Harvey Oswald before
he fired the fatal shot which killed President Kennedy. Small miracles
would not destroy the present natural order of things.

Third, greater natural diligence in work could have been bestowed
upon man. We could have been like the ants, instead of going to the
ants to learn their ways. Many social problems would be eliminated
or relieved by an instinctual (rather than moral) motivation to indus-
triousness, although moral motivations are expected to be overriding.

And *fourth,* the excesses of nature are not necessary. First, it is too
dry, then too wet; then too hot and too cold. One can conceive of an
island in which there is much variety easily accessible, into which one
can choose to enter as one pleases, with the absence of excess.

The conclusion of these considerations for Philo is that the original
source (impersonal) is indifferent to moral concerns. But given the
earlier view of God as Creator and personal, it is not possible to be
Creator of man's moral sense with infinite, deliberate wisdom and at
the same time to be indifferent to the moral sense he wills to be in
existence. This last solution, also, therefore does not work. A solution,
if any, must be sought elsewhere than in Hume's proposals.

THE FREE WILL SOLUTION

The most commonly accepted solution to the problem of evil by theists has been the free will solution. It begins by accepting Hume's conclusion that no natural evil is necessary and the expectation that there
should be no evil in God's creation, at least originally. Natural evil, in
the free will solution, is not original in creation. Natural evil came in
only after moral evil, and was imposed because of moral evil. Natural
evil is due to moral evil. Moral evil in turn is due to free will. And free
will is necessary for human dignity. Automatons lack dignity. And
a world with dignity and evil is better than a world of automatons
without evil. This is one version of the best possible world theodicy.
Does it work?

Objections to the Free Will Solution

There are several objections to the free will solution. *First,* free will makes evil possible, not actual. One can be free without the possibility of evil for a period of time. Thus, free will may be necessary, but it is not sufficient for evil, like oxygen, with respect to fire. *Second,* if evil is actual, that does not make evil necessary. Actuality is not necessity and does not imply necessity without sufficient reason. *Third,* free will does not have to make moral evil possible (or actual, or necessary). God is said to be free without the possibility of evil. And man, in his final state of blessedness, is said to be free without the possibility of evil. (This is not the counter-causal freedom of libertarianism, where freedom is the ability to do otherwise. Freedom here is the liberty to do as one pleases.)[9] *Fourth,* one can pass from a state of innocence to virtue, without moral evil. One can be tempted without sin, as was the case with Christ's temptation in the wilderness (or Adam's temptation in the Garden of Eden). A theodicy of soul-making, in which a lower order (natural) evil justifies a higher order moral good, such as patience and love, is therefore unwarranted.

So far, we have looked at many of the standard responses and objections to the problem of evil. It would appear that theism faces the same incoherence as other worldviews, if there is no further response. We are left somewhere in the continuum of skepticism / fideism / relativism / pragmatism, descending into nihilism, depending on how

---

9. Libertarian freedom of the will is the ability to do otherwise; "ought" here implies "can." Libertarian freedom requires absence of cause; it is incompatible with cause and is called contra-causal freedom since, if the cause is present, the effect necessarily follows—it could not have been otherwise. Contra-causal freedom, or the absence of cause, if held consistently, eliminates causes generally (see causality, Chapter 4). There could be no causal connection in perception, or thought, or agency. An uncaused event is not *my* act, hence not my *free* act, and therefore not anything for which I am responsible. Libertarian incompatibilism purchases freedom at the price of intellectual chaos (William James, *The Dilemma of Determinism* (Whitefish, MT: Kessinger, 2005). James said that indeterminism—lack of cause—"offends only the native absolutism of my intellect," whereas determinism "violates my sense of moral reality through and through." The dilemma, however, is not a choice between determinism and indeterminism, but between compatibilism and incompatibilism. Compatibilist freedom grounds freedom of the will in desires: *can* assumes *want*—I did what I wanted to, without external constraint. I can use my reason critically if I want to, in order to find lasting meaning. I always get what I want, all things considered. And if I get what I wanted, then I am free and responsible, and without grounds for complaint of any injustice.

conscious and consistent we happen to be. A response to this is to appeal to mystery. The answer is beyond humankind, utterly. There is not a contradiction here, it is said, only a paradox, wrapped in mystery. For all we know, there is a good reason why God allows evil, and just so much evil (13 turps in Plantinga's reckoning),[10] but he has not chosen to make it known to us. Another solution, more promising than an appeal to the unknown, is along the lines of Hume's suggestions that, for all we know, there may be an easy solution. This is worth exploring, particularly if we proceed presuppositionally.

AN IRONIC SOLUTION

There are some assumptions we can bring in any approach to the problem of evil. *First*, the problem of evil presents itself as an intellectual problem, not a practical one. The concern is to make sense of things, to know why there is evil, not how to avoid or remove evil. It is a problem for man as a rational being, not for man as an animal. *Second*, the problem of evil is not an abstract problem; it is an existential problem for man as a rational being. Evil is not just objectively there in the world; it is subjectively here in the one asking the question. It affects the questioner as a rational being. *Third*, evil has the effect of going against the nature of things and it affects our thinking by reversing our conception of things. We are thereby inclined to call evil good and good evil. Any solution therefore will be existentially difficult, while being objectively easy. Given the nature of evil to reverse things, any solution would be ironic. It would be what we should expect, but in fact did not expect. And any solution must be intellectual, requiring a clearer, more consistent understanding of good and evil at the most basic level.

How then shall we understand "good" and "evil," key terms in the problem of evil? In general, as an *a priori*, good for a being is according to the nature of that being, and evil is what is contrary to the nature of that being. Good for a horse is according to the nature of a horse; good for a rabbit is according to the nature of a rabbit; and good for a man is according to the nature of a man. Man, by the very

---

10. Alvin Plantinga, *God, Freedom and Evil* (Grand Rapids, MI: Wm B. Eerdmans, 1994), 55-63.

intellectual nature of the problem of evil, is a rational being. What then is good for man, as a rational being? Good for man, as a rational being, would be the use of his reason to the fullest. Since reason is used to grasp the nature of things, good for man, as a rational being, would be to understand the nature of things. Since thinking by nature is presuppositional, that is, we think of what is less basic in light of what is more basic, the good would be to grasp, first of all, the nature of basic things in light of which all else is understood. Since the nature of things created reveals the nature of the Creator, good for man is the knowledge of God. Evil is the failure to use reason to the fullest, the failure to understand basic things which are clear. It is the failure to know God. This definition assumes the clarity of general revelation, that only some is eternal. It is consistent both with the notion of the objective clarity of general revelation and the inexcusability of unbelief, as well as the subjective difficulty, for anyone who fails to see what is clear, to acknowledge one's failure.

This definition of good and evil for the problem of evil can be illustrated by applying it to the well-known parable of the prodigal son,[11] paraphrased as follows:

There was a man who had two sons. When they grew up, the younger son said to his father, "Father, give me my share of the estate." Sadly, the father gave him his share and the young man took his money and left home. He went on a long journey to a distant land and there he fell in with other young men, and they gave themselves up to riotous living.

Eventually his money was spent. His friends forsook him. There came a famine in the land and he began to be in want. He hired himself out and was sent to the fields to feed pigs. He longed to fill his stomach with the pods the pigs were eating, but no one gave him anything. He came to his senses and thought, "How many of my father's hired men have food to spare and here I am starving to death. I will set out and go back to my father and say to him, 'Father I have sinned against heaven and against you. I am no longer worthy to be called your

---

11. *Luke 15:11-32.*

son; treat me like one of your hired men.'" So, he got up and went to his father.

But while he was still a long way off, his father saw him and was filled with compassion for him; he ran to his son, threw his arms around him, and kissed him. The son said to him, "Father, I have sinned against heaven and against you; I am no longer worthy to be called your son." But the father said to his servants, "Quick! Bring the best robe and put it on him; put a ring on his finger and sandals on his feet. Bring the fattened calf and kill it. Let's have a feast and celebrate. For this son of mine was dead and is alive again; he was lost and is found." So, they began to celebrate (the response of the older son to follow).

How does this illustrate the problem of evil? Why is there evil? The younger son was in a state of unbelief with regard to his father's teaching. Day and night, for all his life, his father, by word and deed, lived out the way of life before his sons. Yet the younger son did not see or hear or understand what was clearly laid out before him. He had his own fantasy vision of things. His eyes were on the ends of the world. He turned his back on his father's teachings and way of life, and left home. His unbelief was inexcusable and therefore evil. Evil, as unbelief, serves to obscure the clear revelation to the person in unbelief.

The condition of unbelief is allowed to work itself out in the prodigal's life. As a result, the revelation of justice (his way came to naught in the pigsty) and of love (his father forgives and receives him back) are deepened. If he had second thoughts about possible dangers and hardships of his way the first night away from home, he could have reconsidered and returned with his fortune intact. He could have returned all to his father, simply acknowledging gratefulness to know that he had the freedom to leave if he wanted. In that case, there would be no deepened revelation of justice and mercy. Evil, as unbelief, serves therefore to deepen the revelation of justice and mercy.

The older son refused to celebrate his younger brother's return. He also failed to see what was clear, and was reproved by his father. He failed to see his own failure and need of grace. He thought he had earned his standing before his father and had his own righteousness on which to stand. His attitude was that of a slave, working for wages, and not that of a son who is heir by grace. He chose the way of "justice" over mercy, and lived out his life without knowledge of his father's way. His life of unbelief also deepened the divine revelation of justice and mercy.

Applied to evil in world history, evil, as unbelief, obscures the clear revelation of God's nature and will. It serves also to deepen the revelation of divine justice, seen in the relation of sin and death, and the divine mercy, seen in the call back, return, and restoration. If evil is removed abruptly, the revelation will not be deepened; and if evil is not removed, the revelation will not be seen. The solution is to remove evil gradually. Evil, in every form of unbelief, and in every degree in combination with belief, is allowed to come to expression in world history, in the various civilizations and cultures, and in the various stages of their development and interaction with other cultures. In an age-long and agonizing spiritual war between good and evil, between belief and unbelief, good gradually and eventually overcomes evil. This applies to mankind as a whole, not to each individual or culture.

This solution to the problem of evil has certain assumptions. It assumes *first*, in the definition of good and evil, that there is a clear general revelation that only some is eternal, that God the Creator exists. It assumes clarity and inexcusability.[12] The arguments against material monism, spiritual monism, dualism, and logically possible worlds, if they are sound, show this clarity. It assumes, *second*, that there is no other way to deepen the revelation of the divine justice and mercy. Some things cannot be known except by experience—such as hunger or pain, both physical and spiritual. A book version of human history, or a movie version, cannot supply this experience, and is incomprehensible without it. Virtual reality works insofar as it is indistinguishable from reality. Some experience is necessary for imagination to work, so there is no way to deepen the revelation apart from providence in the fall and redemption of mankind.

Thirdly, it assumes that the deepened revelation and knowledge of this revelation is worth the suffering. This third assumption is not so

---

12. The clarity of general revelation is necessary to establish the inexcusability of unbelief. St. Paul's prolegomenon to redemptive revelation appeals to this principle (*Romans 1:20*), as also the historic *Westminster Confession of Faith 1.1*. The need for clarity to establish inexcusability is assumed in J.L. Schellenberg, *Divine Hiddenness and Human Reason* (New York: Cornell University Press, 2006). Graham Oppy, *Arguing about Gods* (New York: Cambridge University Press, 2006). Both deny clarity and affirm inculpable or reasonable non-belief.

clear because it can be asked before or after the revelation is seen, and it can be asked of those who do see it and of those who never come to see it. Here, testimony is relevant. Job struggled before seeing, and after seeing, was silenced in awe and repentance. Paul the Apostle said the sufferings of this life cannot be compared with the glory that is to be revealed. Many throughout the ages have confessed the same. The figure of the pearly gates symbolizes that through suffering we come into the knowledge of the glory of God. The answer to the question "Is it worth it?" is a presumed, unqualified, yes.

Asked of those who do not see it, the relevant question can only be: Is the divine justice an excellence to be revealed, inseparable from all the other excellences? And, is justice revealed in the reality of sin and death? Understanding sin as rooted in not seeking and consequently not understanding what is clear about God, understanding death as meaninglessness, boredom, and guilt inherent in sin, and understanding human freedom and responsibility in using or avoiding the use of reason, are necessary to begin thinking clearly about the divine justice. This requirement means that the question must be dealt with existentially and not abstractly, and there we must leave it.

Some other questions remain however. We have attempted to answer "Why is there moral evil?" But why is there natural evil? Natural evil consists of the sources of human misery which come from outward circumstances, from the environment. Individually, it consists of toil in regard to nature, strife in regard to other human beings, and of old age, sickness, and death. Collectively, it occurs in famine, war, and plague. Natural evil was not originally placed on the creation. This would be inconsistent with the infinite power and goodness of God the Creator. And natural evil (physical death, to be short) is not inherent in moral evil. Spiritual death, not physical death, is inherent in moral evil. Physical death therefore was imposed by God upon mankind after moral evil, and because of moral evil. And it was imposed not as punishment, which is inherent, but as a call back from moral evil. Besides the inner call of conscience resisted by self-deception, and the outward call by others resisted by self-justification, the suffering of natural evil is the final and continuing call back upon all of mankind, to stop and think deeply about basic things.

Natural evil therefore is divine mercy calling man back from moral evil. Physical death calls man back from spiritual death. Natural evil serves multiple purposes in regard to moral evil. It serves to re-strain, to recall from, and to remove moral evil, and accomplishes these purposes variously in different persons, in different states and stages of their lives. The visible analogously reveals the invisible. There are many implications to be drawn from natural evil about the inner human condition and about the expectation of divine mercy, but the fundamental purpose in natural evil is to call man back from moral evil. This purpose of a call back ceases at death. After death, there is no more natural evil and no more call back.

The Ironic Solution Stated

The ironic nature of this solution to the problem of evil can now be approached. If we consider the original statement of the problem of evil, with the understanding of good and evil as explained above, the problem becomes transformed. The problem is not resolved; rather, it is, ironically, dissolved:

1. Because of all the evil in the world, I cannot see how it can be said that God is all good and all powerful.
2. Because of all the unbelief in the world, I cannot see how it can be said that God is all good and all powerful.
3. Because of all the unbelief in me, I cannot see how it can be said that God is all good and all powerful.
4. Because I have neglected and avoided the use of reason, I cannot see how it can be said that God is all good and all powerful.
5. Because I have shut my eyes, I cannot see what is clear about God.

———

PART III

ETHICS

———

Chapter 9

———

THE GOOD AND
THE MORAL LAW

WE COME NOW TO THE THIRD AND LAST of the basic questions of philosophy: What ought I to do? The answer to this question builds upon the answers to the questions of epistemology and metaphysics. Given the many different conflicting answers to this question, we are led to ask if knowledge in the area of ethics is possible, and if so, how are these knowledge claims to be justified. If there is justification, it seems that it would require knowledge of the nature of being (metaphysics).

DEFINITION OF ETHICS

We begin by proposing a definition of ethics with an explanation for this proposal. Ethics is an area of philosophy concerned with giving rational justification for an answer to the question "What is the good?" Why do we speak of "the good" and of rational justification? Ethics assumes choice. If there were no choice, there would be no ethics. Choice assumes values. We choose what we believe to be of greater value, all things considered. Hierarchy of values assumes what is of the highest value, the greatest good (the *summum bonum*) or, simply, the good. When we choose something, we choose it either as a means to something else or for its own sake, as an end in itself. What is chosen for its own sake, and not as a means to something else, is the good. The good is what we want above all else. It is the good that is ultimately sought through choice. Ethics therefore is and must be concerned with "the good."

But there are many views about the good and there are many justifications given for our views, and rationalizations made for our choices and actions. If knowledge of the good is possible, and if the possibility of knowledge of the good is necessary for ethical accountability, then the many conflicting views about the good cannot be equally justified. The justifications are not equally rational. And if the good is of the greatest value, and most to be desired, we would not want to come short of what truly is the good and have in its place something which merely appeared to be good. We would desire to have the real thing and to have assurance that it is the real thing. We would desire and need rational justification, not mere rationalization, or *prima facie* justification. And in the face of conflicting views and consequent challenges to justify our actions and the moral claim made on others in the name of the good, we must be able to justify any knowledge claim concerning the good. For all these reasons, ethics must be concerned with giving rational justification for an answer to the question "What is the good?" For rational justification assures that we have knowledge.

ON THE NECESSARY CONDITIONS FOR RATIONAL JUSTIFICATION IN ETHICS

If rational justification is necessary for ethics, then there are certain conditions which are necessary for the possibility of rational justification in ethics. There are certain metaphysical, personal, and epistemological conditions which are necessary in order to make rational justification for ethics possible.

First, there must be a metaphysical basis for rationally distinguishing between good and evil. There must be a metaphysical absolute in contrast to what is not absolute. This absolute must be eternal, and only the absolute is eternal. In material monism, all is one and all is eternal. While persons who are materialists make distinctions between good and evil, the question is whether these distinctions are rationally justified. In material monism, all is part of nature. All that comes about, being part of nature, is natural. Birth and death, consuming and being consumed, wars, famines, and plagues, are all part of nature and are natural. In the realm of the natural, the distinction between good and evil cannot be rationally justified. Likewise, in spiritual monism, where all is one, the distinction between good and evil cannot be rationally justified. The more consistent materialists and spiritual monists become, the less they speak of good and evil. In the case of dualism, where both matter and spirit are eternal, a dualist may claim spirit is good and matter evil. But how this goes beyond a metaphysical distinction is hard to imagine, and how matter, a principle incapable of choice, can be called evil is even more unfathomable. A necessary condition therefore for rationally distinguishing good and evil is the metaphysical condition that only some is eternal. "Only some is eternal" implies God the Creator, for what is eternal would have brought into existence, or created, what is not eternal.

Second, there must be personal immortality. If there were not personal immortality, if death were the end of personal existence, and if I and everyone else could cease to exist at any moment, then I could not rationally justify to myself one course of actions over another. If one were to pursue personal pleasure (let's eat, drink, and be merry, for tomorrow we die), I could not come up with a rational objection, even if I chose not to go that way. Continuity of my being, to experience future consequence of my choice, is necessary to justify one choice over another. Or else, I must argue that choices are without consequences, internal or external. But such choices are inconsequential and meaningless, and not subject to any rational consideration. Furthermore, immortality must be personal, not impersonal, such as in reincarnation/karma. These theories affirm consequences (karma), but allow the agent to disappear through the loss of personal consciousness in reincarnation.

Third, there must be freedom in choice if our actions are to be considered moral. But there are different views of what freedom means and what is necessary to be free. In the libertarian view, freedom means the ability to do otherwise: if I *ought* to have done otherwise, then I *could* have done otherwise. Libertarians hold that freedom (as ability to do otherwise) and causality are incompatible. To be free, there must be nothing causing, and therefore necessitating, my act, so that I could not have done otherwise. Libertarian freedom requires the absence of cause; it is contra-causal freedom, and must argue for the absence of cause (Kant's noumenal world) or absence of a chain of external causation (William James's block universe). But the absence of cause implies uncaused events and makes for an unintelligible universe, as well as the elimination of the self as causal agent. The alternative is a compatibilist view of freedom, where causality is compatible with freedom in that my act was caused by me, in that I did what I wanted to, all things considered. And what I considered reflects my willingness to use reason to consider basic things which are clear. At any given time, I can use my reason if I want to. At this level of freedom, *want* implies *can*. Freedom here is doing what I want. The ability to do otherwise (can) is secondary and contingent upon want.

Fourth, it must be objectively clear what the good is. If it is not objectively clear, then we are left with skepticism, and a justification for moral relativism. Clarity is necessary (and sufficient) for inexcusability, that is, for moral accountability. If what we ought to do is not clear to (that is, required by) reason, then as rational beings we cannot be held accountable for doing it. As rational beings, we ought to be rational. The connection between clarity and inexcusability is intuitive, and commonly accepted in ordinary moral and legal affairs. This assumes we are rational beings (i.e., thinking beings) capable of using reason to see what is clear if we want to, and that we ought to give rational justification for our choices. What is objectively clear can be known by anyone who does not neglect or avoid the use of reason. What is objectively clear need not be subjectively clear, that is, actually seen and understood. One does not have to actually know in order to be responsible; it is sufficient that one could know if one wanted to.

Fifth, there must be rationality, since rationality is necessary for thought, for knowledge, and specifically for knowing what is clear. Knowledge is not achieved by testimony apart from a justifying context. Nor is knowledge achieved by sense experience by itself (which gives appearance and not reality), or by intuition by itself (which assumes a sign is accompanied by its reality in a morally ideal world). By reason we can think constructively (i.e., systematically) by good and necessary consequences, and by reason we can think critically (i.e., presuppositionally) and examine basic beliefs for meaning. What violates a law of thought cannot be meaningful and therefore cannot be true. Reason is natural, ontological, transcendental, and fundamental (see earlier discussion on *Reason in Us*, Chapter 1). And one has to neglect, avoid, resist, and deny reason to avoid what is clear. One has to deny one's nature as a rational being to avoid knowing and doing what is good.

THE MORAL LAW

In light of previous reflection on the questions of epistemology and metaphysics (in Parts I and II), and in light of the prerequisite for rational justification for answering the question "What is the good?" assumed in the reality of choice, it can be affirmed that there is a moral law which is clear, comprehensive, and critical. It is *clear* because the good and the moral law, by which the good is to be achieved, are grounded in human nature, which is easily knowable. In theistic terms, the law is said to be written on the hearts of all men. "Written on the heart" means that the moral law is structured into human nature. It is *comprehensive* in that it applies to all choices, since choices as such are grounded in rational deliberation concerning values, aimed at achieving the good (Aristotle). And it is *critical*, since the consequences of achieving or not achieving the good required by human nature are a matter of (spiritual) life or death.

In showing this moral law which is clear, comprehensive, and critical, we begin in each law with certain universal concepts and show the origin of these concepts in basic features of human nature. From this, we proceed to an analysis of these concepts. We will speak of the nature of the good, of work, of authority, etc., in order to have a fuller and clearer view of what is meant in each case. From this analysis, we achieve a clearer understanding of basic concepts on the basis of which we derive a moral judgment, which is a statement of the moral law regarding those concepts. Application of this law is made in several ways (we limit ourselves to seven applications) in order to more fully show the significance and comprehensiveness of the law. Lastly, we draw out the consequences which are inherent in observing or not observing the law, to show how consequences are a matter of (spiritual) life or death, individually and corporately.

Chapter 10

———

MORAL LAW 1:
THE GOOD AND GOD

ORIGIN IN HUMAN NATURE

THE FIRST MORAL LAW IS ABOUT the most basic concept in ethics and about the ground (rational justification) of this concept. It is about the moral absolute and its ground in the metaphysical absolute. It is about the good and the real, or the eternal. It is about the good and God. Ethics (and the moral law which prescribes what we ought to do) assumes the reality of choice. Moral consciousness in human nature is grounded in the reality of choice—by nature we make choices. This is common ground in any moral discussion and is not disputed. What may be disputed is whether or not the choice is free, and this depends on one's view of freedom (see Chapter 9 on prerequisites of rational justification in ethics). Choice in turn assumes values and values assume the good (the highest value). When we choose something, we choose it either for its own sake or for the sake of something else. We choose it either as an end in itself or as a means to an end. What is an end in itself, chosen for its own sake, is the good. (Here we speak of the good in singular terms. Whether the good is one or many will be examined soon.) So, beginning with the reality of choice in human nature, we must affirm the concept of the good—that which is chosen for its own sake and not for the sake of something else.

ON THE NATURE OF THE GOOD AND GOD

1. The Good Is Not Virtue

The good must be distinguished from what is other than the good. The end in itself is not a means to the end. The means to the good is virtue. The good is not virtue and must be distinguished from virtue; the end is not the means. The idea of the end in itself, or the good, is not a strange idea. It is present in philosophy in Plato's *Republic* and in the opening words of Aristotle's *Nicomachean Ethics*, and in theology in the opening words of the *Westminster Shorter Catechism*: man's chief end. The chief end here is higher than all other intermediate ends; it is the end in itself, chosen for its own sake and not for the sake of anything else. We can begin to set aside many casually held views about the good. If something is not and cannot be chosen for its own sake, then it is not and cannot be the good. Since money is not and cannot be chosen for its own sake, but only for the sake of what it can buy, money cannot be the good. Money is sought as a means to other things (what money can buy—house, car, food, services, etc.). It is *a* good, but not *the* good. It is a means to the good. As a means to the good, it can be called a virtue, understanding that there are different kinds of virtues. Money (and what money can buy) would be an *instrumental virtue* and valued as a means to the good.

Another person cannot be the good, although in romantic love a person is often viewed as the good. The good is achieved by choice. While a relationship may be achieved by choice, another person is not achieved by choice. Furthermore, the good is for persons, therefore persons and the good are to be distinguished. A person may be good, but a person is not the good. Furthermore, love is not the good, but is to be understood in relation to (or relative to) the good. If we love someone, we seek the good for that person (according to their nature). Love therefore is not the good, but a means to the good; it is a virtue. Love is a *moral virtue* and its achievement is considered morally praiseworthy. Love is perhaps the greatest of the virtues given its connection between the good and persons, and brings all the other virtues to bear in seeking the good for the other.

Other virtues, as means to the good, are not to be mistaken for the good. Wisdom, courage, and justice (in its many forms) are moral virtues, which make the achievement of the good possible. Existence itself, understood as survival, is not sought for its own sake. We do not survive in order to survive. We do not seek to prolong mere vegetative or animal existence. We live for a purpose, to achieve and to enjoy the good. Therefore, survival is not the good. Health, talent, and beauty are *natural virtues* in that we are born with these as capacities, which we may or may not develop or enhance. And each, in different ways, contributes to the good.

All of this is to point out the difference between the good, as the end in itself, and virtues, as the means to the end. The good is not virtue. Deontological theories of ethics identify the good with virtues and are for that reason deficient. Virtues (of liberty, equality, and fraternity) or duties (of truth telling and promise keeping) may conflict if they are not held together in unity by the good. What is right must be understood in relation to the good, and ultimately to the real, in order to be rationally justified. Moral intuition against murder may be agreed upon, but may be applied differently, with differing conceptions of the good and human nature. Virtues may become vices if they are not directed toward the good. The vices likewise (seen for example in the seven deadly sins) must be understood in relation to the good if they are to be understood as vices. Mere declarations and expressions of feelings do not constitute rational justification for one's choice. And the pursuit of virtues (family values) as a means to happiness, apart from the good, become legalistic and eventually prove inadequate for happiness.

Before leaving this distinction between means and ends, it may be asked, "Must there be an end in itself?" Can something be both means and end, or neither means nor end? Means and ends are being applied here to the category of choice. Outside of choice, the distinction is not being considered here. A person may be thought of both as means to achieve the good and as an end for whom the good is to be achieved. But a person is outside the category of choice itself, and odd characterizations occur when this category is misapplied to persons. Health may be considered to be both a means and an end in itself. But one may be willing to suffer affliction in the loss of health (Job, John Donne), if that furthers the good in one's life. So, health is not in the same category as the good. And finally, if we were to give up the idea of an end in itself, we would have to give up the idea of means also. And the idea of choice, with no end in mind whatsoever to be achieved, makes rational deliberation in choice, and therefore choice itself, unintelligible.

2. The Good Is Not Happiness

It is often thought that pleasure or happiness is the good. This common view is embodied in hedonic theories of ethics, both individual (ethical egoism) and collective (utilitarianism). It is considered a consequential theory of ethics in contrast to deontological, which calls for duty to be done for its own sake. If happiness could be sought directly, independent of beliefs about the good, then happiness could be the good. But happiness (or pleasure) is not and cannot be sought directly. Happiness is a consequence, or an effect, of believing we possess the good. The good is what is of highest value, and believing we possess this highest value, given our capacity for belief and desires, brings happiness.

If belief about the good changes so that we no longer believe we possess the good, then happiness ceases. Happiness is relative to the good and conditional upon the good. It is not independent of the good. It lasts as long as belief concerning the good and possession of the good last. If happiness itself were the good, it would not be altered by belief. If happiness were the good, it would be sought directly. There are attempts to directly produce pleasurable states, through drugs for example. But this is considered artificial and requires the obliteration of ordinary conscious awareness, and becomes self-defeating upon return to ordinary consciousness. This is true of all forms of artificially-induced euphoria, from fantasy to hypnotic states, where we believe, temporarily, that we possess the good.

Relief (from pain or sorrow) and rest (from work) are necessary for health, and some form of recreation may allow a season of enjoyment, either by way of pursuit of thoughtless euphoria or by thoughtful experience of the good. Hedonism, the pursuit of pleasure as the good, is held up as the alternative to deontology, but this is merely an antinomy. The synthesis of duty leading to pleasure, apart from the good, fails because the connection between virtue and happiness is not inherent (Plato's Thrasymachus, Kant's postulate of God). So, pleasure apart from the good is not lasting.

3. There Is One Good for Each Person

The good is the source of unity in each person and, as such, must be one. The tension between two alternatives in choice is resolved by the good. If there were two goods (not merely two aspects of the good) so that they were equal and independent, and to gain one were to forfeit the other, there would be no rational way to choose. If we were rational, we would be frozen in inaction. It is sometimes said in certain current natural law theories that there are several goods (John Finnis, Robert George et al.), such as friendship and health. But these, as we have seen in the case of health, and shall see in the case of friendship, are to be understood not as instances of many goods, but in relationship to the good.

4. The Good Is One and the Same for All Persons

There is not just one good for each person, but one good for all persons. It is the source of unity in each person, as well as between two persons, and between groups of persons. It is expected that as rational beings we should be able to settle disputes—and ethically, we should do so—by reason. The good therefore must be one and the same for all persons. The intuition that the good is one and the source of unity arises out of our human nature, and can be made explicitly. The good for a being is based on the nature of that being. The good differs for each kind of being (horse, rabbit, human, etc.). The good for a human being is based therefore in human nature. Since human nature is the same in all humans, there is one good for all human beings. Difference in gender, talent, age, and ethnicity, do not override what is common, and therefore more basic, in all human beings. As the diversity within each person is not a source of conflict, so diversity of the kinds mentioned here among human beings is not a source of conflict. Human nature is one; therefore, there is one good for all human beings.

5. The Good Is Clear

If the good were not objectively clear, there would be no rational basis for morality. Skepticism, which denies clarity, leads to relativism and eventually to nihilism. Fideism, as an alternative to skepticism, cannot avoid relativism. Belief without proof is not subject to public examination and therefore must be kept private. Multiculturalism, the contemporary expression of classic skepticism and cultural relativism, affirms the moral equality of all cultural practices, and tolerance and inclusivism as cardinal virtues. The covert absolutism within each culture is brought into closer proximity in the process of globalization as culture wars and clashes of civilizations are occurring. This is not what one should expect if the good is the source of unity, based on a common human nature, and is objectively clear. All sides seem to agree in principle on the connection between clarity and morality. If a moral standard is not objectively clear, one cannot (as a rational being) be held accountable for living by it. If there is a rationally justifiable good, it must be clear, that is, easily enough knowable by all who seek to know.

6. The Good Is Based on What Is Real

While the good must be objectively clear, it need not be, and most often is not, subjectively clear. The good is not actually known by all men, given the many views of the good that there are, and the general lack of concern to think critically about basic things on the part of most persons. One's view of the good is based on one's view of human nature. And this in turn is based on one's view of what is real. What the good is in actuality is based on what human nature is in actuality, and this is based on what is real or eternal in actuality. The moral absolute is based on the metaphysical absolute. One cannot engage in ethics (as far as giving rational justification is concerned) without engaging in metaphysics. Speaking of the good requires us to speak of the ground of the good in what is real.

7. It Is Clear That Only Some Is Eternal

In Part II, under *Metaphysics*, arguments were given to show what is eternal. There must be something eternal. The contradictory "nothing is eternal" is not possible. It has been argued that matter exists (vs. idealism) and that matter is not eternal. It has been argued that the soul exists (the mind is not the brain) and that the soul is not eternal. By critical analysis for meaning, the premises in the arguments were shown to be true by *reductio*, by showing that the opposite was not possible. It is clear to reason then that only some is eternal. What is eternal brought into existence or created what is not eternal. Therefore, the Creator (i.e., God) exists. Preliminary objections against the existence of God were responded to and considerable attention was given to the problem of evil. Finally, an ironic solution was proposed based on the assumption that it is objectively clear that God exists.

MORAL LAW 1

Given the existence and the nature of the good as grounded in human nature, and given human nature as grounded in God by creation, the first moral law can be stated as follows: God, as Creator of human nature, is the determiner of good and evil for man. Good and evil cannot be spoken of apart from human nature, and human nature cannot be spoken of apart from God, who determines human nature by creation. Therefore, God the Creator determines good and evil for man. It must be underscored that this determination is not apart from, but in and through, human nature, which is created by God.

APPLICATIONS OF MORAL LAW 1

Several applications follow from Moral Law 1 and the manner of its derivation. These applications are best seen in understanding what is opposed by this moral law.

1. Theism vs. Non-theism

Belief in God the Creator (theism) is opposed to all forms of non-theism. Theism is opposed to atheism, pantheism, polytheism, and animism. Philosophically, it is opposed to all forms of material monism, spiritual monism, and dualism. Theism vs. non-theism is the major dividing point for mankind. Ethics must address this division. The good, as the source of unity, when rationally justified by its ground in God, overcomes this first major division.

2. Objective Clarity vs. Skepticism and Fideism

We have maintained that clarity is necessary for morality, that this clarity is by reason, and that it is clear to reason that only some (God) is eternal. This clarity is objective, available to all who seek diligently to know the basic things about God and man and good and evil. Clarity therefore is opposed to skepticism, which denies that basic things are clear to reason. It is also opposed to all forms of fideism (theistic and non-theistic), which hold basic beliefs without proof or understanding what is clear. One has to neglect, avoid, resist, or deny reason to avoid basic things which are clear.

3. Subjective Clarity vs. Emotivism and Voluntarism

While it might be admitted that clarity is necessary for morality, it is often enough questioned, and sometimes denied, that knowledge is sufficient for morality. It is sometimes maintained that we knowingly do evil. Our feelings are independent of our knowledge (emotivism) or can override our knowledge (R.C. Sproul—priority of the heart). Or, our will can be separated from our knowledge (voluntarism), by weakness ("For what I would, that I do not."[1]) or by rebellion (knowing the truth and suppressing it). What more is needed remains an unknown outside the realm of knowledge and raises questions about human accountability.

The objections of emotivism and voluntarism are based on impressions from our ordinary experience. This experience of division between knowledge and feeling and will needs to be interpreted in light of our being more or less conscious and consistent in our beliefs. Beliefs can be contradictory at the level of implied meaning. Understanding is often mixed with misunderstanding of which we are not aware. This division in thought, within the intellect itself (as t1 and t2), is reflected in our feelings (as f1 and f2) and in our will (as w1 and w2). We may be aware of opposition between t1 and f2, without noticing the connection between t2 and f2, or the division between t1 and t2. (Peter had divided thoughts and feelings: he affirmed that

---

1. *Romans 7:15*. St. Paul expresses here what is sometimes taken as a classic statement of the weakness of the will. This should not be taken so as to negate other passages which speak on the subject.

Jesus was the Christ, but denied Christ must suffer; David's adultery arose in the context of not pursuing the good in his call as king to engage in war: "At the time when kings go to war . . . .") There are lines of thought in Greek philosophy (Socrates: no one knowingly does evil), and in Christian theism (Jesus: "You shall know the truth and the truth shall make you free."[2]), which maintain the sufficiency of knowledge for morality.

4. Theonomy vs. Autonomy

Theonomy affirms that God as Creator is the source of the moral law. It is opposed to all forms of autonomy, in which man, understanding himself apart from God, determines good and evil for himself. In intellectual history, particularly in the West, several forms of autonomy are recurrent. These forms reflect personality traits, and the degree of consciousness and consistency with which presuppositions are held.

a. *Ethical Egoism* views happiness/pleasure as the good and seeks to maximize pleasure for the self. Thrasymachus in Plato's *Republic*, Thomas Hobbes, and Ayn Rand affirm the position of ethical egoism.

b. *Utilitarianism* views pleasure as the good and seeks the greatest amount of pleasure for the greatest number of people. This view is exemplified in Jeremy Bentham, John Stuart Mill, and in the socialist theory of Karl Marx.

c. *Deontology* holds that the will is to be guided by reason apart from desire. Duty, or what is right, or virtue is to be pursued for its own sake, independent of consideration of consequences in contrast to ethical egoism and utilitarianism. This view is exemplified in Kant and W.D. Ross.

d. *Existentialism* maintains that the determination of good and evil is by an act of will (choice) independent of reason. The essence of things is not determined by God and/or grasped by reason, but determined in or by choice. According to Kierkegaard, the will of God is beyond

---

2. *John 8:32.*

reason; according to Sartre, there is no God and man must fill the role of God to determine good and evil by authentic choice.

e. *Naturalism* affirms individual instinct as a sufficient guide for action. In his natural state, man is good. Artificialities of human society are the source of corruption. This is exemplified in the writings of Lao Tzu and Rousseau.

f. *Tradition* affirms the collective instinct of a group as a whole, worked out over a long time, and embodied in traditions which are handed down as the guide for life. This is exemplified in Confucius (in contrast to Lao Tzu) and in most cultures.

g. *Humanism* affirms the fulfillment of human nature as a whole in contrast to one or another aspect (desire, will, intellect as above). Human nature here is understood in naturalistic terms (Abraham Maslow) or in Greek dualistic terms (Aristotle).

h. *Stoicism* seeks to limit the satisfaction of desires to those over which we have control (Epictetus), or seeks the ascetic limitation of desires to avoid self-indulgence (Gandhi).

i. *Mystical Contemplation* seeks direct knowledge of ultimate reality beyond sense experience and discursive reason, constituting enlightenment, beatitude, or release from bondage. Plato's direct vision of the highest forms, the beatific vision of God in this life or the next, and enlightenment in Hindu and Buddhist traditions, exemplify mystical contemplation.

5. Theonomy vs. Heteronomy

The moral law given in human nature is opposed to heteronomy. Kant was opposed to heteronomy in which the law is seen as given externally and is viewed as a burden. The law in theonomy is written on the heart and is a delight (a yoke which is easy, and a burden which is light). The law is not something foreign to man as a rational being, imposed upon man by another, contrary to our nature. But the law is in our nature and is known in the exercise of reason. Where there is misconception of the good and of human nature, the law is felt as a burden, as something foreign, being imposed upon us. Being rational, we feel naturally we should be guided by the light of reason. To set aside reason is to go contrary to our nature. Laws which are understood and presented in ways that minimize our reason are heteronomous and are naturally resisted and resented. Laws which only appear to go against reason and laws which do go against reason can be sorted out by the process of dialogue.

6. Theonomy vs. Divine Command Theory and Positivism

The moral law given in human nature, and knowable by reason, is opposed to the divine command theory (DCT) and positive law. Positive law is not grounded in human nature and is arbitrary or conventional, and can be known only by proclamation. In opposing DCT, it is not the case that God wills it because it is right, as if there were some standard apart from or above God, as the Platonic Forms. Nor is it the case that whatever God wills is right, as if having created human nature, God could will stealing or lying to be right. Creation is according to what God is pleased to reveal of himself and the law is according to the nature of the thing created. Some recent theonomists, who argue for the divine law as given in the scriptures and knowable only from the scriptures, and who neglect or avoid the objective clarity of the law from general revelation, are inclined to make the will of God independent of God's nature and the law of God independent of man's nature.

7. Teleology vs. Deontology and Consequentialism

Teleology is goal oriented. It is thinking, desiring, and acting to achieve an end—the chief end or end in itself. Teleology in ethics is ethics focused upon the good, the moral absolute. Virtues and happiness are understood in relation to the moral absolute and not the other way around. Virtues and happiness are not and do not become the central concept in teleological ethics. Much discussion in ethics has been categorized in terms of virtues or happiness as the good, from Epicureans and Stoics to Kant and Utilitarianism. Much of contemporary ethical discourse is carried on in either deontological or consequential terms. These faulty distinctions fall into the category of antinomies: in religion, legalism is opposed to antinomianism; in popular talk, the duty of virtue ethics is opposed to freedom in pleasure-seeking. A formal distinction between means, ends, and effects requires a formal corrective at a basic level, which will affect thinking in ethics fundamentally. Progress in overcoming the antinomy of duty and happiness cannot be attained until the formal question "What is the good—the end in itself—the highest value?" is settled. If formal distinctions between good, virtue, and happiness, between end, means, and effect cannot be made, or can be obfuscated when made, then ethical discourse loses rational justification and slides into skepticism, relativism, and nihilism.

CONSEQUENCES OF MORAL LAW 1

There are inherent consequences to observing or not observing this moral law. There are inherent consequences to acting according to one's nature or acting contrary to one's nature. Since good for a being is according to the nature of that being, evil is what is contrary to its nature. Evil for man as a rational being is to neglect, avoid, resist, or deny reason in the face of what is clear about basic things. In theistic context, evil begins in *neglect* in which one does not regard or seek God. One therefore does not understand what is clear about God, and consequently does not do what is right. Evil increases to *avoidance* of seeking by self-deception. It grows still further to *resist* the charge of being irrational by self-justification. It culminates in the *denial* of one's reason through shutting one's eyes and closing one's ears to avoid what is clear. Evil is an act of self-destruction in the denial of one's nature as a rational being.

Since reason is the laws of thought, to not use reason is to not think. It is to perceive, but not understand the meaning of things. It is to be unaware of contradiction and absurdities in one's thinking. It is to have a mind which is darkened, devoid of the life of reason. The darkened condition, devoid of the life of reason, is spiritual death. It is the condition of meaninglessness inherent in the failure to use reason to seek, and in the failure to understand. Since reason is fundamental to other respects of human personality, meaninglessness in thought results in boredom in desires. What is devoid of meaning cannot satisfy the human need for meaning, as rational beings. And excess in pursuit of what is empty deepens boredom.

As rational beings, the misery of meaninglessness and boredom must be accounted for. Attempt is perpetually made to avoid responsibility for one's self-inflicted condition. The torment of guilt is inescapable. Every attempt to avoid one's condition, without taking responsibility for it, only deepens that condition. Meaninglessness, boredom, and guilt become a bottomless pit, the inherent consequence of moral evil. Inherent consequences are present and continuing; they are not to be understood as something essentially future and imposed. To misunderstand inherent consequences is to misunderstand justice in the world. Inherent consequences are just consequences. More than that can only appear arbitrary.

The consequence of living according to one's nature as a rational being is to gain understanding of basic things which are clear. It is to live a life which is full of meaning, a life full of joy in enjoying meaningful participation in every aspect of life, and a life full of peace, the opposite of the consequences of evil. Because humans are finite, temporal and, in themselves, changeable, consequences are experienced in a finite, temporal, changeable manner, consistent with human nature. One can increase in good or in evil, and in the consequences of life or death, both in this life and after this life, unendingly.

At the end of this basic explication of the first moral law, it can be seen more clearly what is meant by saying that there is a moral law which is clear, comprehensive, and critical. It is derivable from human nature in the reality of choice. Human nature can be known because it is grounded in what is real, which is clear to reason. The law is applied to overcome basic divisions within metaphysics and ethics. And finally, its consequences are a matter of life and death.

Chapter 11

_____

MORAL LAW 2:
THINKING AND PRESUPPOSITION

HAVING ADDRESSED THE MAJOR DIVISION between theists and non-theists, the second moral law addresses the divisions within theism. It addresses the question of how we are to think about God. We shall continue the format used before by first deriving the origin of the basic concepts of this law from human nature, by analyzing the nature of things referred to in these concepts, and then by deriving the law from this analysis. We will again look at seven applications of this law and the consequences of observing or not observing this law. This will be the format for each law that will follow.

ORIGIN IN HUMAN NATURE

By nature we think, and by nature we think about the infinite and the eternal, those attributes which are applied properly only to God. It cannot be doubted existentially that we think. Doubting that one is thinking is self-referentially absurd. And even if we do not always think, we do naturally think, unless what is natural is hindered by accident or by the supernatural. And it cannot be doubted that in thinking we have and apply the concepts of both finite and not finite (or infinite), and temporal and not temporal (or eternal), to beings we think about. A being is either finite or infinite, temporal or eternal. And some being must be eternal. The concepts which apply to God are inescapably in our thinking. In this sense, at least there is a sense of deity (_sensus divinitatis_) in all who think. So, by nature, we think about God, either by thinking God exists or God does not exist. Following Moral Law 1 then, we will consider here the views of the nature of God held by those who think God (the Creator) exists.

ON THE NATURE OF THINKING AND THE NATURE OF GOD

1. Thinking Is Presuppositional

Thinking by nature is presuppositional. We think of the less basic in light of the more basic. We think of truth in light of meaning. We interpret experience in light of basic belief. In argument, we base conclusions on premises. At the level of concepts, we think of the finite in light of the infinite, and the temporal in light of the eternal. In regard to disputes in general, if there is agreement on what is more basic, there will be agreement on what is less basic. Lack of agreement on what is less basic is due to lack of agreement on what is more basic.

2. Presupposition and Longstanding Disputes About the Knowledge of God

In regard to disputes about God in general, there are longstanding divisions on secondary matters which have hardened over centuries because more basic issues (about good and evil, for example) have remained unexamined. In regard to disputes about God based on scriptures, there are longstanding divisions which have not been overcome because the layers of contexts presupposed in hermeneutics have not been noticed, agreed upon, and critically examined. The context of general revelation in approaching special revelation has not been examined and agreed upon. The context of foundational revelation (in Genesis 1–3) in approaching subsequent revelation has not been examined and agreed upon. The context of a statement within a book is often overlooked or is disregarded.

3. Presupposition and the Possibility of the Knowledge of God

There are pre-theistic claims against the possibility of the knowledge of God (we cannot think rationally about God) because the infinitude of God cannot be grasped by the finite mind. God is infinite it is said, and the infinite is all inclusive. It includes even opposites. No limit is to be placed on God. These are based on misunderstandings. God is not merely infinite, but infinite in his perfections. He is not merely infinite (including both wise and unwise), but infinite in wisdom. The perfection of God excludes, it does not include, imperfection.

The exclusion principle is sometimes taken to mean that the infinite excludes the finite, as if to be finite were to be imperfect. But perfection as infinitude is an attribute of an attribute, which must be specified. Finite in wisdom is not the same as unwise; a lack in knowledge is not the same as holding to error. And a lack in knowledge (ignorance in some respect) does not imply ignorance in all respects. Infinite knowledge, to be infinite, must include finite knowledge. The exclusion interpretation of infinite therefore is unwarranted. It has been applied to the being of Christ to deny Christ can be both finite and infinite. Furthermore, the incomprehensibility of God does not mean the finite cannot grasp the infinite at all, but that the finite cannot grasp the infinite exhaustively, i.e., infinitely. We can know in part, otherwise we know nothing at all.

4. Presupposition and Direct Knowledge of God

There are sub-theistic claims that infinite and eternal (in a timeless sense) cannot be applied to persons—that if God is a person, God cannot be infinite or eternal. Open Theists claim that God is in time and that his knowledge, like ours, grows in time. To be a person is to be like a human person, that is, the infinite must be understood in light of the finite. A timeless person, it is said, is incomprehensible, even in part. While it is true that a finite and temporal mind cannot include the infinite (the relation is asymmetrical), or know anything in a timeless way, that would be just to say man cannot know God except by God's self-revelation. To deny God's self-revelation in the work of creation is to deny either that creation is revelation, necessarily and intentionally, and therefore truly, or to deny creation altogether. The *via negativa* of medieval mystical theology disregards the validity of creation (and history) as true revelation, and seeks direct immediate knowledge of God in a cognitively contentless beatific vision (Aquinas and Al Farabi). Logical order, which is timeless, need not be reduced to sequential order in time for there to be order at all in eternality.

MORAL LAW 2

We are to think about God presuppositionally. We are not to think about the infinite in light of the finite, but the finite in light of the infinite. We are not to liken the infinite Creator to the finite creature, but to understand the finite creature in light of the infinite Creator. God is not to be made in the image of man, but man is to be understood as the image of God. Nor is the finite (man) to be understood in light of finite nature—man is not the image of the animal. History abounds with this reversal. God has been made in the image of man (in the Greek view—Zeus, and in the Mormon view), and descends further to be made in the image of the animal—birds, beasts, and creeping things. God, who is Creator, is a Spirit, infinite, eternal, and unchangeable in his being, wisdom, power, holiness, justice, goodness, and truth.

God, in relation to man, is to be thought of analogically, not univocally or equivocally. God is infinite, eternal, and unchangeable in his attributes; man cannot be infinite, eternal, and unchangeable—these are incommunicable attributes, possessed by God alone, by virtue of being Creator. Man is finite, temporal, and changeable in these same attributes of being, wisdom, power, holiness, justice, goodness, and truth. These are the communicable attributes of God given to man, not to the rest of nature, by virtue of which man is the image of God. God is not totally unlike man (as equivocal and unknowable). And God is not totally or essentially like man (as univocal and known, differing only in degree). God is both like and unlike man in being infinitely wise. Infinitely wise is one attribute with distinguishable, but inseparable parts. Analogical predication has been the occasion of heated debate among theologians (Gordon Clark and Cornelius Van Til, for example) when more basic issues have not been settled. The difference of infinite and finite is qualitative and not merely quantitative, yet the nature of wisdom is identifiably the same (wise in contrast to unwise, and wise in contrast to non-wise, as in saying the attribute of power is in the category of the non-wise). Likewise, God is analogically not only infinitely good, but infinitely just and holy as well. The attributes, in God, are not in any sense in tension with each other, but exist in perfect unity or simplicity, and are to be thought of in this way if we think presuppositionally about God.

Divisions within theism are rooted in multifaceted disputes concerning the attributes of God. What does it mean to say God has attributes, what are these attributes, and what are the implications of any infinite attributes? The major division within belief in God the Creator is first between deism and theism. Within theism, the divisions are between Judaism, Christianity, and Islam. Within historic Christianity, the main division is between Catholic and Protestant. Within Protestant, the main division is between Reformed and non-Reformed. If we think presuppositionally about God, believing the good to be the source of unity between two persons or between groups of persons, we should be able to overcome divisions among theists concerning the nature of God. Presuppositionalism is not merely recognizing differences in presuppositional starting points and the ensuing difference in worldviews due to different presuppositions. This is a fideistic, not a rational, form of presuppositionalism. Abraham Kuyper recognized differences in systems due to palingenesis (regeneration). B.B. Warfield went further in apologetics to argue against alternative views. Recognizing meaning as more basic than truth, and reason used critically as the test for meaning of a basic belief, *rational presuppositionalism* seeks to settle the objective side of disputes, as a good and necessary consequence of belief in the clarity of general revelation and the inexcusability of unbelief.

APPLICATIONS OF MORAL LAW 2

1. Presuppositionalism vs. Non-Presuppositionalism

Presuppositional thinking, in general, is opposed to the non-presuppositional epistemologies of rationalism and empiricism. Correspondence theorists cannot compare experience with the real world known apart from experience. Empiricism fails to recognize the basic beliefs assumed in interpreting experience. This includes common sense, science, and religious experience. Rationalism often uses reason constructively first and not critically first, as a test for meaning of basic belief. Coherence theorists operating with a set, rather than a system of beliefs, are unable to identify more basic beliefs in that which is merely a set.

2. Deism and Divine Justice

Deism is opposed to theism. Deism affirms that God has created the world and rules by a general providence, but denies any special act of God in divine providence. Deism opposes the theist view (1) that God acts in history and (2) that God has revealed himself redemptively in history in scripture. Specifically, deism denies the divine justice, goodness, and power in its understanding of natural evil. Natural evil exists in the reality of the death of human beings. But natural evil was not originally present in the creation of the world. If God is all powerful, he could make a world without natural evil. If God is all good, he would make a world without natural evil. If God could and would, then he must have made a world without natural evil. And if he must have, then he did make the world without natural evil. Natural evil is therefore not original at creation.

Natural evil is not inherent in moral evil. The inherent consequence of moral evil is spiritual death, not physical death. Since physical death is neither original in creation nor inherent in moral evil, it must be imposed by an act of God. And if it was imposed upon man by an act of God, then God acts in history, contrary to the claim of deism. By assuming physical death is natural in creation, deism fails to understand the infinite power and goodness of God. It thinks of the infinite in light of the finite, rather than the finite in light of the infinite. Deism fails to think presuppositionally about God.

Natural evil is not imposed by God as a purposeless act. It is imposed for a reason. It is imposed on man because of a moral change in man. Natural evil is imposed because of moral evil. Since all have died, it was imposed from the beginning upon the first man. Because the act of one affected all, the origin of natural evil implies representation of all by the first man. Since natural evil is not imposed as punishment for moral evil, it must be imposed as a call back from moral evil. Moral evil in theism is rooted in the failure to seek and understand what is clear about God. Suffering from toil and strife, and old age, sickness, and death is a call to stop and think. As a call back from moral evil, natural evil is imposed as an act of mercy. In ordinary human consciousness, natural evil, in any degree, is thought to be anything but an act of mercy. As a continuing and final call back, the imposition of natural evil assumes man's resistance to any prior call back of conscience or by others in human society. Natural evil is a silent, constant, inescapable, universal, and final call to stop and think.

Man is not being left in the state of spiritual death. Since divine justice is infinite and eternal, it cannot be set aside by mercy. A call back implies divine forgiveness in mercy. But how God can be both just and merciful to man at the same time is a mystery to man. If man is to respond to God as both just and merciful, this will require a special revelation from God. Natural evil, as mercy, requires redemptive revelation which shows how God is both just and merciful to man. The scripture of biblical revelation, accepted by theists, presents itself to mankind as this redemptive revelation. Theism therefore affirms the necessity for and the existence of scripture by an act of God, over and against deism. Besides the necessity of scripture, we can know what in general terms must be the content of scripture, and what must be the origin of scripture. And given the necessity, content, and origin of scripture, it can then be determined whether or not biblical revelation constitutes scripture from God.

3. Islam and Divine Justice

The major divisions within theism are among Judaism and Christianity and Islam. Islam professes to build on Judaism in the Old Testament and Christianity in the New Testament, yet it differs from both in fundamental ways—from what is central to both and to the idea of scripture itself as redemptive revelation. A religion expresses itself in its holy days, and the most holy day in Judaism is Yom Kippur, the Day of Atonement. In biblical Judaism, the high priest takes the blood of the slain animal and sprinkles it over the mercy seat within the most holy place in the temple, in order to atone for the sins of the people. In Christianity, in its most identifying symbol, the cross, the death of Christ as the Lamb of God who takes away the sin of the world is remembered.

For both Judaism and Christianity, atonement for sin through the death of another is central. Redemption from sin and death through vicarious atonement, by a representative other, answers the question which makes scripture necessary: "How can God be both just and merciful at the same time?" Islam, while professing to build on the Old and New Testament, denies the necessity for and the actuality of atonement. Presuppositionally speaking, this central teaching regarding the atonement is the dividing point between Judaism and Christianity on the one hand, and Islam on the other. And presuppositionally speaking, this dividing point entails significant difference in understanding the nature of God's justice and mercy.

Islam affirms both the justice and mercy of God. God is just in condemning unbelievers to the everlasting punishment of hell, conceived of as future and imposed. God is seen as merciful in forgiving the sin of those who go to heaven. The penalty due to sin is not paid; it is simply forgiven by Allah as compassionate. The central question of how God can be both just and merciful is answered, not by mercy satisfying justice through vicarious atonement, but by mercy setting aside the requirements of justice. In this understanding, God is not infinitely, eternally, and unchangeably just by nature. God is not bound by nature to be just. God has no nature by which he is bound. God has many names, such as just and merciful, but is not infinite, eternal, and unchangeable in justice and mercy. If he were, justice would need to be satisfied; it could not be set aside by mercy.

God's will is not bound by his nature because God has no nature. God then would be a natureless being. A being without essential properties, by which that being is identified, cannot be conceived. A being which cannot be conceived cannot be conceived to exist. The alternative, if anything is to be said of God, would be to say God is not infinite, eternal, and unchangeable, but finite, temporal, and changeable in justice. But this is no longer theism. Or, one could attempt to sketch a view of divine justice that did not require everlasting punishment. To alter this fundamental doctrine would involve a change throughout the entire Islamic worldview, so as no longer to be recognizable as such. Varying conceptions of divine justice have been tried in other theistic worldviews, but it cannot be said that these attempts achieve basic coherence. Or, Islam's disavowal of atonement, by which it distinguishes itself from its predecessors, and justifies its separate existence, must be revised. (There are other distinguishing traits and claims of Islam—its view of the Koran, the Trinity, the Incarnation, Sharia, jihad, the clarity of general revelation, natural evil, etc., which can be questioned. Here, the focus is restricted to the most basic issues in thinking presuppositionally about God.)

4. Judaism and Divine Justice

Christianity professes to be a continuation and fulfillment of the promise made in the Jewish scriptures. Judaism rejects this claim. It rejects that Jesus is the promised messiah. More basically, it rejects a conception of messiah as the Lamb of God who takes away the sin of the world. It affirms the promised messiah. Identifying the common core of Judaism today is notoriously difficult; yet identifying beliefs held historically in Judaism is not so difficult. Although classical rabbinic Judaism is not creedal, Moses Maimonides' statement of Jewish belief comes as close as anything to a summary of historically held beliefs in Judaism. And, while Temple and priesthood stood, biblical Judaism affirmed atonement as observed on the Day of Atonement. Post-biblical Judaism (after the second Diaspora of 70 C.E.) affirms atonement by one's own suffering, good deeds, prayer, and physical death, rather than by vicarious atonement through the animal sacrifice (Neusner).

Two questions are raised about divine justice by these two approaches in understanding atonement. What is common is that there must be payment for sin. *First*, concerning the post-biblical view: Is the suffering of natural evil (physical death) to be considered punishment for sin in divine justice, or is it a call back in mercy? Regarding physical death as punishment raises questions about what is moral evil and its inherent consequence. It raises questions about the existence of mercy if all pay by death. It raises questions about proportionality of the suffering of natural evil in relation to moral evil. And it raises questions about the resurrection of the body if physical death is punishment and punishment is everlasting. Atonement by prayer and good deeds raises questions whether good deeds can be considered payment for bad deeds; whether, for example, kindness to one person pays for murder of another.

Second, in biblical Judaism: Is the animal sacrifice on the Day of Atonement to be considered actual payment for sin, or is animal sacrifice symbolic? If vicarious atonement in animal sacrifice is considered actual payment, this raises questions about the nature of evil, and about clarity and inexcusability and its inherent consequence—spiritual death. It raises questions about representation—can an animal substitute for a human being? Can one animal substitute for all? Is one sacrifice sufficient for all sin, or for past sin only?

Given the assumption of human representation implied in the origin of natural evil in connection with moral evil, must animal sacrifice be considered symbolic of another representative to come? The promise of a coming messiah is basic in historic Judaism, and needs to be connected with salvation and atonement. Is messianic salvation external, to be understood in social-political terms (in the restoration of the Davidic kingdom), or does it extend to the removal of the penalty and power of the inward reality of moral evil? To say the sacrifice is symbolic, in the sense that it is to teach moral truth, does not do justice to the idea of atonement as payment to satisfy divine justice. It also assumes these moral truths are not sufficiently objectively clear from general revelation, in which case the existence of inexcusability and of morality itself is called into question. If messianic salvation extends to sin, then messiah, as man's representative, must suffer the penalty of sin.

5. Christianity: Purgatory and Divine Justice

Christianity affirms Jesus as the Christ, the Savior of the world. In biblical revelation, he was promised from the beginning, after the fall of Adam, as the seed of the woman in the place of Adam, who would undo what Adam did and do what Adam failed to do. Man is forgiven on the basis of the death of Christ and accepted as righteous on the basis of Christ's righteousness (seen in the covering of man's nakedness by the skin of animals). Man is sanctified by knowing the truth through suffering (seen in the expulsion from the Garden). Man lives under the curse and the promise. There will be a spiritual war between belief and unbelief, which will be age-long and agonizing, in which good eventually overcomes evil (the seed of the woman will crush the head of the serpent).

Christianity expanded from Judea in Palestine to become worldwide. It has faced many challenges, both internal and external, through the centuries. In the 16th century, a major split occurred within Western Christianity. (This is not to discount an earlier division between Orthodox and Latin Christianity.) In 1517, Martin Luther protested the Church's teaching regarding the sale of indulgences, for relief from the penalty of sin in purgatory, by posting his *95 Theses*. This raised the question of divine justice and mercy. How is sin paid for? Is the work of Christ (grace) sufficient for payment of sin? Luther denied both the teaching of purgatory and the efficacy of indulgences to forgive sin. This challenge in turn raised questions about authority in teaching and the sufficiency of faith, apart from works, for justification. Protestants, following Luther, affirmed the principles of *Sola Scriptura*, *sola gratia*, and *sola fides*, in contrast to the teaching of the Roman Catholic Church.

Purgatory was said to be a place in the afterlife where the soul suffers for its own non-mortal sins committed in this life, which were not removed by sacramental grace. Suffering for one's sins is a matter of justice in payment of a penalty, not a matter of cleansing from sin. If suffering were for cleansing, then cleansing could not and should not be interrupted by the purchase of indulgences. The sufferings of purgatory are not inherent, but imposed, and that for a time only. Repentance and faith are not sufficient to receive the grace of forgiveness. One must do penance in this life or the next. This raises the question of the nature of sin and death, and the purpose of imposing natural evil. Natural evil, being imposed, is not a part of divine justice, but of mercy, as a call back. The call back, through imposed suffering, naturally ends with death and does not continue into the next life. That natural evil is not payment for sin, and that natural evil ends with death, is inconsistent with the idea of purgatory as payment through temporarily imposed suffering in the afterlife. If the sufferings of purgatory were not imposed but were inherent, then they would be permanent and not temporary. And if they are permanent, then indulgences as an external transaction cannot remove them. The grace of redemption accomplished objectively, and applied subjectively inwardly, is necessary to remove the penalty and the presence of sin and death. Purgatory and indulgences are inconsistent with the nature of sin and death and infinite justice.

6. Popular Theism: The Doctrine of Hell and Divine Justice

Popular views of divine justice in theistic religions conceive of punishment as future, in a physical place called hell, often pictured as a lake of fire. Taken literally, without much thought given to context, as is often the case in popular thinking, divine justice is seen as future and imposed. Hell, thus conceived, is the utmost degree of imposed natural evil and is thought to be therefore consistent with infinite justice. This view, promoted by those who read the text literally, has been rejected by non-theists and by some theists as inconsistent with either the divine goodness or with the divine justice, or in some cases, with both. Objections arise from a sense of moral repugnance against the literalist view, from the practical incoherence of this view, from contextual reading of the text, and from alternative passages which address the divine justice.

Moral repugnance would be justified from a consideration of general revelation, and all the more so if the literalist view were a misinterpretation. There are the alternatives of universalism (all are saved, eventually), and annihilationism (the cessation of suffering through the cessation of one's being) used by some to avoid the repugnance. It is sometimes pointed out that a soul cannot be affected by a physical fire, and that a resurrected body is either imperishable or unaffected by flames, or, if affected, is immediately annihilated. In response to the problem of immediate annihilation, a continuous re-creation in the face of continuous destruction is offered as the divine solution. How opposing conditions can simultaneously recur is hard to imagine and is held (if it is held at all, since few go this far in order to hold a literal view) by faith *sans* understanding.

Textual counter-indications to a literalist view are prominent, to indicate which textual passages must be cited. The devil, as a spirit, is said to be cast into the lake of fire (*Revelation 20:10*), in which case, the fire becomes a spiritual fire. At this point, a spiritual fire is no longer a literal fire or a literal lake, in any ordinary sense of the term. And when Death and Hades, which are neither physical nor spiritual beings, are cast into this lake of fire (*Revelation 20:14*), the mind can no longer hold to a physical or to a spiritual fire. But the mind is not left merely perplexed. The lake of fire is described as the second death in the book of *Revelation* (*20:14*).

The second death assumes there are two kinds of death, physical and spiritual (*John 11:25-26*), and that the second death is spiritual death, continuing on after physical death is removed by the resurrection of the body. It is spiritual death that is affirmed as the wages of sin (*Romans 6:23*), inherently connected with sin ("in the day you eat you will surely die") and present in this life ("you that were dead in your trespasses . . . ."), as a condition out of which a person is brought by the supernatural act of regeneration, referred to as the first resurrection. Spiritual death is the death of the soul, inherently connected to acts contrary to our nature as rational beings, and the subsequent effect on other aspects of the soul. It is meaninglessness, boredom, and guilt, the inherent consequences of not seeking and not understanding. The soul destroys itself in acting contrary to its nature. Fire is the apt symbol of destruction. The destruction is not annihilation of being, or cessation of activity, but futility and waste, in the self-contradictoriness of sin. To be given up to the futility of one's choice reveals the divine justice: a man reaps what he sows.

7. Presuppositional Thinking About God Is Opposed to All Forms of Idolatry

While focus has been on misconceptions of the divine justice which divides theists, there are misconceptions about God in many other aspects. While some misconceptions develop into what is called gross idolatry in the form of visual images, some misconceptions remain in the realm of mental idolatry. Since moral evil remains in man until death, left to oneself, misconceptions of God persist, even in the human activity of praise and worship of God. This problem becomes acute in corporate worship, where one's deficient conception of good and evil, and the worldview based on this, becomes embedded in songs of praise used in worship, the essence of which is to acknowledge God as he is. Worship is no longer thought to be regulated by any principle of worship, but is regulated by a presumption of one's sincerity. Conception of heaven as the good has done much to promote an other-worldly view of life, which in turn has been dismissively rejected for the antinomy of a merely this-worldly vision of secularism.

CONSEQUENCES OF MORAL LAW 2

A deficiency in our concept of God occurs when we come short of the infinitude of God. A deficiency left uncorrected leads to distortions in one's concept of God, which have far-reaching consequences over time. In time, distortions, by going to the left or to the right, bring division. Divisions left uncorrected allow distortions to develop into caricatures of God. When people fail to see beyond the caricatures, these straw men become occasions for justifying apostasy, a way of life without God. Human beings in a state of apostasy descend into the pit of meaninglessness, boredom, and guilt. Without God, and without meaning, cultural decay sets in. A culture in decay does not inspire effort to defend it. When challenged from the outside, the culture collapses. Many cultures have gone through cycles of distortions, divisions, apostasy, decay, and collapse, until they disappear from history into oblivion. Moral evil, when it has fully developed, brings about the death of a culture.

Where there is acknowledgment of the continuing presence of moral evil in oneself and in the world, and watchfulness against unbelief, it is possible to overcome unbelief and to grow in understanding. The outcome of this way is increasing understanding, accumulating through succeeding generations. Instead of increasing divisions and death, there is increasing unity and life. If theists were to overcome the causes of division among themselves, those in apostasy would be drawn to consider and would come to understand what is clear about God.

Chapter 12

MORAL LAW 3:
INTEGRITY AND KNOWLEDGE

THE GOOD IS THE SOURCE OF UNITY in a person, between two persons, and between groups of persons. In Moral Law 3, we come to unity in a person.

ORIGIN IN HUMAN NATURE

There is a natural unity in our being. Each person is by nature one person. In and through all the diversity of our being, there is a fundamental unity. This unity of being is so natural and so basic that it is taken for granted and not argued for. To act according to one's nature is to act consistent with our natural unity of being.

ON THE NATURE OF INTEGRITY AND
ITS RELATION TO KNOWLEDGE

1. Integrity is a concern for consistency in what we say and do.

If we have integrity, we will act according to what we profess. We will not say one thing and do another. Integrity, as a concern for consistency, preserves and expresses the natural unity of our being.

2. What we say is both explicit and implicit.

Some things we say explicitly in spoken words. Some things are so deeply held that they go without saying. Our most explicit statements are expressed in vows at the height of a solemn, that is, thoughtful, ceremony (for example, in marriage vows, in taking an oath of office, and in swearing an oath in a court of law). We take oaths and vows to assure others that we will do as we say we will do. God is called upon as a witness to the truth of what we promise and to hold us accountable if we break our vow. Some other things are held implicitly. We believe some things to be true of ourselves, or we want to believe they are true, and we want and expect others to believe these things to be true of ourselves. We want to believe we are rational beings who have a serious interest in knowing the truth, and we want and expect others to believe that of us. We don't say to others, "I really don't care about being rational; I don't really care to know the truth." And we don't want others to believe that about us. We like to believe we have integrity and we want others to believe we have integrity.

3. Integrity is a concern for consistency, not only in outward act, that is, in our outward behavior, but in our inward or mental acts.

It is a concern for consistency within our thoughts. It is a concern to avoid holding mutually contradictory beliefs. The self is not to be divided against itself in its beliefs. We are not to be double-minded. What violates a law of thought is meaningless and cannot be thought. The critical use of reason as a test for meaning in one's own basic beliefs, that is, the examined life, is the beginning of integrity.

4. Basic things about God and man and good and evil are clear to reason.

Since reason is ontological and applies to being as well as thought, what violates a law of reason cannot be, and it is clear to reason that it cannot be.

5. Integrity, as a concern for consistency, is necessary and sufficient for knowledge.

If one is not particularly concerned for consistency, one can hold a view which is self-contradictory and not become aware of it by critical self-examination. Therefore, integrity is necessary for knowledge. And since basic things are clear to reason, integrity is sufficient for knowledge.

6. Integrity is not merely sincerity.

Sincere persons will act consistently with their feelings and may therefore have strong convictions, which are mistaken for integrity. But it is possible to have strong feelings and convictions without knowledge. Objectively, a person's belief, strongly held, may not withstand critical scrutiny. It is possible to have zeal without knowledge. Zealots may kill or be killed in the name of their ideal, but their ideal may turn out to be a form of idolatry. Job was said to be the most righteous man in his time. He felt he had integrity, and in his affliction, he questioned God's justice. When questioned by God, he found that he came short in his seeking and understanding God's revelation of himself in his works. He then felt self-abhorrent, and humbled himself, and repented in dust and ashes. Subjective sincerity is not objective integrity.

7. Integrity is necessary for dialogue.

Concern for consistency requires a commitment to reason, and commitment to reason is necessary for dialogue. Dialogue involves reasoning together in search of understanding and truth. Willingness to dialogue is an ordinary aspect of self-examination. It is possible to think one is committed to reason in search of truth, whereas one may be more committed to defending oneself as already being rational. We seek to maintain the appearance of integrity by shifting the burden of proof (rather than sharing it), by linguistic quibbles and appeals to unknowns, by irrelevant counter-examples (red herrings), and by straining at gnats while swallowing camels (uncritically held assumptions). These are common ways to avoid and resist rather than engage in the use of reason in dialogue.

MORAL LAW 3

We should have integrity. We should not lightly and thoughtlessly disregard that by which we can come to knowledge of the truth (or else we should make the truth of our intentions, that is, our disregard of reason, known). We should diligently seek to know and to understand.

APPLICATIONS OF MORAL LAW 3

1. Integrity and Self-Examination

Integrity is opposed to professing to want to know without engaging in self-examination. Our most implicit profession is that we want to know. The following argument is one of self-examination:

> If I had integrity, then I would know basic things which are clear to reason.
>
> I do not know basic things which are clear to reason.
>
> Therefore, I do not have integrity.

Lack of integrity applies to all instances of failure to seek and to understand basic things which are clear. It applies to all forms of skepticism (basic things are not clear) and fideism (belief without proof or understanding). Integrity is opposed to the thoughtlessness and complacency of tradition without self-examination. Integrity would agree with the dictum, "The unexamined life is not worth living."

2. Integrity and Commitment to Reason in Dialogue

Integrity is opposed to dialogue without commitment to the use of reason. To neglect, avoid, resist, and deny reason in dialogue, in the face of what is clear, is to forfeit the right to speak or to be taken seriously. One has the obligation to remain silent if one is without commitment to reason, and therefore to withdraw from dialogue. One has a moral right to insist on commitment to reason as a precondition for dialogue and to terminate and withdraw from dialogue where this commitment is not present.

3. Integrity and Accepting Implications

Integrity is opposed to professing a position without accepting the good and necessary consequences of that position. To deny any of the necessary conditions for morality without accepting moral nihilism is a lack of integrity. To object to behavior without also objecting to the thought leading to that behavior is to deny the integrity of that person. It is to divide between thought and consistent implication, between belief and practice. Integrity recognizes that all of one's life is an integrated whole and not an aggregate of fragments. It recognizes the connection within foundational beliefs, between foundation and worldview, between worldview and one's cultural identity and values, and between culture and practice in public institutions.

4. Integrity and Discipline

Integrity is opposed to professing a position without the discipline to put it into practice. In discipline, a long-term goal is achieved by a gradual process of accomplishing a series of short-term goals. A long journey is accomplished one step at a time. Life is lived one day at a time. Extraordinary ends are accomplished through the daily use of ordinary means. A seemingly impossible task is achieved through easily possible small steps. Integrity in professing high ideals is seen in continued willingness to take small steps toward these ideals. Romantic and utopian idealism must be replaced by a rugged gradual idealism, which recognizes the full extent and degree of evil in the world, and with patience and perseverance works to overcome it and to achieve the ideal. Lack of discipline in taking the small steps necessary to overcome moral failure, or to achieve moral ideals, reveals lack of integrity.

5. Integrity and Vows

Integrity is opposed to making vows and not keeping them. For deep and long-term commitments, we make our promises most explicit by vows made before God and witnesses. Yet vows are taken often enough, as in marriage vows, and are not kept. The argument here is this:

> If I have integrity, then I will keep my vow.
> I did not keep my vow.
> Therefore, I do not have integrity.

Vows are to be made with great thoughtfulness, understanding the implications and costs. One must possess at the time, at least in principle, a willingness and determination to keep one's vow, "for better or for worse." A light and thoughtless taking of vows does not permit nullifying one's vow. The content of vows must be consistent with what is morally required or permissible. A person is morally required to have integrity with respect to one's vow, and is held accountable by the one called upon in the vow.

6. Integrity and Hypocrisy

Integrity is opposed to the self-deception and self-justification of hypocrisy. Every failure to do as one professes is not hypocrisy. It is the avoidance of acknowledging one's moral failure that leads to hypocrisy. The avoidance of the shame felt in one's conscience as a call back from moral failure requires self-deception. The avoidance of guilt in being held accountable by another for moral failure requires self-justification. Moral failure accompanied by self-deception and self-justification constitutes hypocrisy. Self-examination and discipline in accepting consequences and correction are necessary to avoid hypocrisy. To the extent that hypocrisy remains in us, the sufferings of natural evil work to produce self-examination and discipline.

7. Integrity and Primacy of the Truth of the Good

Integrity is opposed to placing practical and personal concerns above concern for the truth of the good. Love of money and love of persons cannot be placed above love of the good. Inconsistencies and double-mindedness remain in us. When these inconsistencies in us become manifest in a choice between holding to the truth and compromising the truth for other apparent goods, one is to affirm the primacy of the truth. Holding to the truth enables a person to grow in the truth. And it is knowing the truth in a deeper sense that sets a person free from present inconsistencies. A person is transformed by knowing the truth. Money and what money can buy—some measure of relief from natural evil—is not the good. Another person, or love of another person, is not the good. But true love, which is unconditional, is to seek the good for the other person, unconditionally.

CONSEQUENCES OF MORAL LAW 3

There is a moral law which is clear, comprehensive, and critical. Its consequences are a matter of life and death. As integrity decreases, stupor increases. And, as self-deception and self-justification increase in hypocrisy, integrity and the ability to see what is clear decrease. The mind becomes darkened. The obvious is not seen. Nothing is clear. All is opaque. The search for truth is abandoned as futile. Without meaning, the desires go awry in becoming excessive, perverse, and eventually exhausted in boredom. No finite being can satisfy the appetite for the infinite. To account for the misery of the human condition, grand theories (metanarratives), not built upon the foundation of what is clear, are constructed and as easily deconstructed, in which we excuse or accuse the other. Nihilism and despair, without end, are inherent consequences of abandoning integrity.

As integrity increases, clarity increases. As finite, temporal, and changeable beings, we know in part, we grow in knowledge, and errors of misunderstanding can be corrected. As we walk with integrity in the measure of light that we do have, inconsistencies become apparent and corrected. Change by way of correction allows for more growth, which in turn brings more change. As errors of misunderstanding are corrected through a concern for consistency, basic things become progressively clearer. A person's life becomes more full of meaning, more joyful, and more peaceful as integrity increases. Divisions within the self dissipate and the unity and integrity of the person is restored.

Chapter 13

MORAL LAW 4:
WORK AND HOPE

ORIGIN IN HUMAN NATURE

T O BRING INTO BEING AND TO SUSTAIN in being requires effort, that is, work. Human beings are brought into existence by pro-creation, which involves work. And for beings brought into existence, work is required to sustain that person in being. Work, then, is a universal for all human beings, in all cultures, grounded in the nature of our being.

ON THE NATURE OF WORK AND HOPE

1. On the Nature of Work

Work is not an end in itself. It is a means to the end in itself. Persons are not the good, but the good is achieved by persons and is sought for persons. By work we are brought into being and sustained in be-ing, and by the work of persons, the good is achieved for persons. But perhaps work is only an instrumental virtue to provide wealth in order to have the necessities for a leisured existence. We may be unleisurely in order to be leisurely (Josef Piper), the life of leisure being the source of contemplative culture, which is the good life. In that case, an aris-tocratic class may be supported by a class of workers or slaves, as has been the case through much of history. But if the good is grounded in human nature, which is universal (the same for all persons, everywhere, at all times), then the good is for all, equally. And if the good is grounded in choice, then the good is to be achieved by the choices of all. So, the good is by all and for all. But whether this good is achieved individually and separately, or individually and corporately, will depend on what the good is.

2. On the Nature of the Good

Up to this point with the moral law, the good has been considered only from the point of view of its broadest formal features. There are other formal characteristics of the good which must be considered in order to understand the relation between work and the good. Ten formal characteristics, at least, are required of the good, and may together be sufficient to characterize the good.

a. *The good must be continuing.* The good must be something we can take with us beyond this life. Without personal immortality, there can be no rational justification for morality. But more is needed. The acts of the agent must have consequences beyond this life. If there are no consequences beyond this life, or consequences for only one or a few choices, then choices without consequences, for the good that lasts, become meaningless. There is only one thing from this life that we can and must take with us, and that is knowledge. If the good must be continuing, then knowledge must be the good.

b. *The good must be inexhaustible.* The good must not only continue beyond this life, but must continue forever. And it must increase according to our finite and temporal nature, which grows forever. That which can grow forever must be inexhaustible, that which cannot be exhausted or completed. Knowledge which continues beyond this life is inexhaustible. A finite being cannot have exhaustive knowledge of anything, not merely of everything, or of the infinite. The understanding of all aspects of one human life, in relation to all aspects of all other human lives, cannot be exhausted. Hence the common saying: the more you know, the more there is to know. This is not said of anything else. If the good must be inexhaustible, then knowledge must be the good.

c. *The good must be comprehensive.* The good must be complete and lacking nothing. As the object of all choices of all persons, it must be inclusive of all aspects of life concerning which choices are made. But no one human being can encompass in one's life all the variety of life. No one is poet, philosopher, athlete, and engineer, nor can one achieve mastery in all areas equally. If we cannot participate in all areas, shall the good exclude some areas of life and be restricted to a few areas, namely areas of our own interests? Which sport, or which art, shall be excluded? We cannot go that way and achieve the fullness of the good, and we do not need to. There is one thing which is as broad as (or broader than) life, and that is knowledge of life. Through knowledge we can participate in and receive from all areas, even when we do not participate to achieve in all areas. Knowledge is comprehensive, and only knowledge is comprehensive, therefore knowledge must be the good.

d. *The good must be inalienable.* The good must be something which cannot be taken from us, by intent or by accident. We must not fear losing the good now or in the future by anything which lies beyond our control as moral agents. What we possess outwardly can be taken from us. But what is possessed inwardly cannot be taken from us. Knowledge which is possessed inwardly cannot be taken from us. Although brain states altered by diseases, injury, or drugs, can hinder the pursuit of knowledge here, they do not hinder the mind, freed from its connection to this mortal body, in the afterlife. Since knowledge is inalienable, knowledge must be the good.

e. *The good must be corporate.* If the good is comprehensive, it requires others to achieve it. It cannot be achieved by oneself without others. The good therefore is corporate, not individualistic; it is achieved by individuals working in cooperation. This cooperation is not only within one's own culture, but by individuals in other cultures as well. For the diversity of our humanity, in response to the world, is not exhausted by one culture. Since all persons in a culture contribute in various ways to the culture, the good as corporate includes all persons. What is achieved cooperatively are not essentially material artifacts, but cultural accomplishments contributed to and preserved in the knowledge achieved by culture.

f. *The good must be cumulative.* The good is not achieved by one generation, but is increased by transmission from generation to generation. What is possessed today, by way of cultural achievement, has accumulated from the earliest days of human history. Fire, the wheel, metallurgy, music, language, writing, printing, medicine, mathematics, and much more, have been invented or discovered, transmitted and accumulated, and have become, in the form of knowledge, the common inheritance of mankind. Therefore, knowledge, as cumulative, must be the good.

g. *The good must be communal.* It must be something which can be shared with others and yet not be decreased through sharing. Since the good is comprehensive, and achieved only in part by individuals, it must be communal. Since each must receive from others and build upon others in the process of further achieving the good, and in turn transmit one's own achievement to others, the good must be communal. And since in love one seeks the good for the other, the good must be communal. Knowledge is communal and is actually increased by sharing it. Other things cannot be received, increased, and transmitted, as knowledge can be. Therefore, knowledge must be the good.

h. *The good must be fulfilling.* It must be satisfying. It would be most satisfying. And it would be the only thing which satisfies. It is what satisfies in all instances of finding satisfaction. Childhood is often said to be the happiest time of life. Childhood is the time of the greatest growth in knowledge. It is a time of constant new discoveries, which fill the mind with wonder. Childhood is wonderful because it is full of wonder. In wonder, knowledge is in its purest sense, enjoyed as an end in itself. The pleasures of travel are a continuation of wonder as we seek out places of special attraction. The pleasures of cinema are the pleasures of seeing the drama of the conflict of good and evil told over and over again. The pleasures of spectator sports are in watching excellence displayed. The pleasures of sex are in the intimate knowledge of the other. The alluring pleasures of drugs, fleeting and illusory as they are, are in the revelation of new states of consciousness, but are not lasting because they have only an appearance of knowledge. The pleasures of the sensuous/aesthetic order in new experiences of taste, color, sound, scent, and beauty—natural and artistic—are in new states of awareness of reality. In short, what satisfies in the many senses of pleasure is knowledge. Knowledge, therefore, must be the good.

i. *The good must be ultimate.* It must be connected to what is ultimate, that is, to what is infinite and eternal. If it is not connected to the infinite, the finite soon loses its significance and ceases to satisfy. The connection that man, as a rational being, has with the infinite is by way of knowledge. The connection that the finite has with the infinite, relevant to man as a rational being, is that the finite reveals the infinite. Since the infinite and eternal is God, the good must be the knowledge of God.

j. *The good must be transformative.* The good must have power. It must have the greatest power. Power to rule over nature and power to rule over others are great, but not as great as the power to rule over the one who rules, that is, over oneself. Power to control and to change oneself is the greatest power. It is knowledge of the truth that sets us free from various forms of bondage. Nothing else has this power. And it is particularly the knowledge of God which transforms a person to become like God. By steadily contemplating the glory of God's justice and goodness, one becomes just and good. The good as transformative, therefore, must be knowledge—specifically, the knowledge of God.

3. The Good Is Achieved Through Work

Creation is revelation. Being expresses itself and thereby reveals itself in act. The acts of God reveal the nature of God, necessarily. Since God acts in creation and providence with infinite, deliberate wisdom, creation and history are revelation, intentionally. The finite cannot know the infinite apart from the self-revelation of the infinite. And revelation, given with infinite wisdom, is not unnecessary, so that it may be neglected. There is no other revelation which allows one to bypass this revelation. Creation is revelation, exclusively. Man is called to know this revelation which is given necessarily, intentionally, and exclusively.

Since creation is revelation, knowledge of creation is by the work of dominion. In exercising dominion, man is to rule over the creation in such a way as to develop the powers latent in the creation and in himself. In developing the powers latent in himself and in the creation, man comes to know the creation, and thereby comes to know God who reveals himself in the creation. The powers, which are latent, cannot be known apart from developing them and bringing them to expression. The power of sight cannot be known apart from the exercise of that power. The power of understanding cannot be known except from the exercising of the understanding. Therefore, the knowledge of God, who is revealed in the creation, is by the work of dominion over the creation.

4. Dominion and Knowledge

While all lives reveal something of human nature, which in turn reveals the nature of God, not all lives achieve an equal measure of dominion. Some lives are cut off in infancy. Some lives fail to develop dominion to any great extent due to neglect of opportunities. Some lives develop dominion in achieving a natural understanding of some things, apart from understanding the relation of those things to God. And some lives exercise dominion in both the natural and the moral order, so as to come to know and to make known the self-revelation of God. There exists in the world, by divine providence, a great deal of moral and natural evil. Evil does not negate revelation, but deepens revelation. And evil does not negate the need for dominion, but calls for a greater dominion. The understanding must be exercised in a greater way in the presence of unbelief, to take captive every thought which is raised up against the knowledge of God.

5. Work and Hope

Work for the good requires hope. Work is not an end in itself, but is undertaken with an end in mind, in the hope of achieving that end. The end in mind here is the knowledge of God, to be achieved through an age-long work of dominion by all mankind. To work for this long-term goal requires hope. And given the age-long and agonizing war between good and evil, there is all the more need for hope that the end will be achieved, and that work will come to an end. This hope, which is necessary to endure in the face of what seem like overwhelming odds, is not a bare conjectural hope based on mere wish and longing, but a certainty based on understanding the nature of things. From the nature of things, it is certain that the good will be achieved.

6. Hope and Certainty

It is certain that the good will be achieved. This hope is based on faith, which understands the nature of things.

a. The nature of man requires the good. As a rational being making choices, the good as the end in itself is required. As a rational being, made in the image of God, the knowledge of God as the good is required.

b. The nature of the good requires dominion. Knowledge of God is only through the work of dominion. This was true originally, apart from evil, and all the more true in the presence of evil as unbelief.

c. The nature of God as infinitely good requires that good overcome evil. Infinite goodness is infinitely active in regard to evil. Evil is permitted to an extent and degree to deepen the revelation of divine justice and mercy. It serves the divine purpose and will be removed according to the divine purpose. Infinite goodness itself is the guarantee that the good will be achieved through the work of dominion. Everything that is opposed to the knowledge of God will be subdued.

d. From considering the past, there has been progress. Belief in God the Creator, and in the truth of redemptive revelation, has grown over the past four millennia, from the time of the patriarch Abraham to the present. This is true even when outward belief without true understanding is discounted. It is also true when progress has been uneven.

e. From considering the present, significant challenges remain. Over the past three hundred years, there have been challenges to theism which have been unmet. The principal challenges concern the clarity of general revelation (faith vs. reason/science) and secularism (this-worldliness vs. other-worldliness). As a result of challenges not being met, unbelief has become established where belief was once established. This is not cause for despair, but for deepening one's understanding and engaging the challenges. Challenge and response has been the common pattern by which understanding grows.

7. Work and Rest

When the work is completed there will be rest, naturally. The rest consists in the enjoyment of the work accomplished. As God worked and completed the work of creation, so man, made in the image of God, will complete the work of dominion. As the work of creation is revelation, so the work of dominion brings the knowledge of this revelation. The outcome of this work is variously described in biblical revelation. It is described in terms of fullness: "The earth shall be full of the knowledge of God as the waters cover the sea."[1] It is described as a city, the city of God, the completion of human culture under God. The city is of unimaginable size and splendor, which is a figurative expression of the good fully realized.[2]

MORAL LAW 4

We should work for the good with true hope. As this work is corporate, cumulative, and communal, preparation for work, renewal of commitment to work for the good, and reaffirmation of hope for achieving the good, should likewise be corporate, cumulative, and communal.

APPLICATIONS OF MORAL LAW 4

1. True hope is opposed to false hope.

False hope believes that the good can be attained without the work of dominion. The popular belief is that heaven is the good, and that one attains the fullness of blessing upon death, when one enters heaven. Heaven is equated with eternal life and with the absence of any suf-

---

1. *Isaiah 11:9.*

2. *Revelation 21.*

fering. Heaven is equated with being with God, perhaps even seeing God, and being with those we love.

Since God is a spirit, God cannot be seen. And since eternal life is to know God,[3] and God makes himself known through his works of creation and providence, the popular view cannot give a positive account of the good of heaven. Heaven, as a place after death, is not the final state, but an intermediate state in which the disembodied soul is awaiting the resurrection and the restoration of bodily existence. Eternal life, as the knowledge of God, begins in this life, not in the afterlife. Eternal life increases in this life as one increases in the knowledge of God. Eternal life is the same in essence as it continues in the afterlife, and grows in the afterlife, as it did in this life, through the work of dominion. Here, one grows by active participation in the work of dominion. There, one grows as witness to the providence of God in the work that has been and is being done on earth. Attempt to possess the good apart from the work of dominion is false hope.

2. True hope is opposed to no hope.

Work without the good is no hope. For most who work, there is no conscious connection between work and the good. Work is seen mostly as a necessity for providing for material needs, something to be endured or escaped if possible. Some work is done to alleviate suffering or to make the world "a better place." But this is done by way of instinct, not by rational justification. If death ends it all, or if heaven is the good, "Why polish brass on a sinking ship?" it is asked. It would be better to get as many passengers as possible into lifeboats.[4] Regarding work without the hope of the good, the popular attitude toward work is that of hopeless resignation: "I'd rather be fishing, or skiing, or anything but work." Work without the good is a grin and bear it

---

3. *John 17:3.*

4. Dwight. L Moody, a prominent American evangelist of the latter part of the Nineteenth Century said, "I look upon this world as a wrecked vessel . . . God has given me a lifeboat and said to me, 'Moody, save all you can.'" In light of heaven as the good, the work of dominion, being separated from the knowledge of God as the good, came to be seen as futile—as polishing brass on a sinking ship. "The Second Coming of Christ," *The Best of D. L. Moody*, Wilbur M. Smith, ed. (Chicago, Moody Press, 1971), 193-95.

type of existence, a grim endurance to the bitter end, a life of quiet desperation, or one of sound and fury, signifying nothing.

3. True hope is opposed to revolutionary utopianism.

In utopian views, man is seen as basically good. Evil is considered as coming from the environment. Attempts are made to create an ideal society by changing the environment, rapidly, through the use of force, if necessary. The revolutionary fervor of the modern period has been built on this false conception of evil. Rousseau, in his sentimentalism, promoted this view of man. Man is not fallen. Evil is not unbelief in the face of what is clear. Divine grace is not necessary to bring man out of a state of sin and spiritual death. Hence totalitarian dictators liquidate all who oppose "the cause." Scores of millions have perished at the hand of dictators, aided and abetted by those who have been seduced by utopian ideology. Man's work, without God's work, to bring about an ideal society is worse than futile. It is suicidal.

4. True hope is opposed to supernatural millennialism.

Many theists long for an ideal society, not simply in the afterlife, but in this life, in history on earth. Popular Christian theism longs for the coming of the kingdom of God, seen as a future millennium during which God rules directly over the nations. In this view, man's work does not avail in bringing about the kingdom. It is by the supernatural work of God apart from man's work. In this view, divine grace does not work in and through man's work of dominion, as the ordinary means to achieve this end. In popular Christian theism, in contrast to historic Christian theism, it is not understood that the kingdom is now present, now growing, and will gradually grow to its fullness, displacing the kingdom of darkness. As the Church fails to be salt and light, as it fails to meet challenges, as it fails to exercise dominion and take thoughts captive, it loses ground and becomes the tail of the culture. Loss of ground in popular theism is taken as a sign that the end is near. In desperation, false hope in supernatural millennialism increases. This false hope is buttressed by a non-contextual, literalist reading of certain passages of scripture on the coming of Christ and his millennial rule.[5] Without a view of the good as the knowledge of God through the work of dominion, supernatural millennialism becomes the antinomy of revolutionary utopianism, and vice versa.

5. True hope is opposed to the hope of salvation by works.

Many have believed that if one is morally good enough in this life, one can merit admission to heaven in the next life. This view, widespread in mankind throughout history, is based upon a superficial understanding of good and evil and life and death. Morality here is seen as transaction between virtues and rewards and vices and punishment. Virtue is rewarded by happiness, apart from the good. The diligent who hold this view spend their whole lives in works, which they believe will merit the divine favor.[6] When salvation is seen as a gift—not of works, but of grace—the discipline of work is directed to fulfill one's calling, by which God is glorified.[7] Works-righteousness (whether full Pelagianism or synergistic semi-Pelagianism[8]), in contrast to an imputed righteousness received by faith, is false hope, since human acts of righteousness, given the continuing presence of sin in man, cannot withstand the divine scrutiny. Much less can acts of supererogation merit divine favor for another.

---

5. Passages on the first resurrection before the millennium (*Revelation 20*), and the war of Armageddon (*Revelation 19*) are taken as literal rather than spiritual occurrences.

6. Saul of Tarsus, upon conversion, became Paul, an apostle of Christ. Before his conversion, he sought to be accepted by God based upon the righteousness of his obedience to the law, as taught by the Pharisees in his day. Martin Luther, before his conversion, sought to be accepted by God based on obedience to the teachings of the Church in his day.

7. Max Weber, and Stephen Kalberg, eds., *The Protestant Ethic and the Spirit of Capitalism* (Oxford: Oxford University Press, Incorporated, 2007). When work is freed from the goal of achieving salvation by the Protestant doctrine of salvation by grace alone, received by faith alone, it was directed to the end of glorifying God. Work received a greater dignity and worth than before. Glorifying God, however, has not been commonly understood in relation to knowing God in all that by which he makes himself known, that is, in all his works of creation and providence.

8. Pelagianism is the doctrine that salvation is based solely on human effort. It was taught by Pelagius, a British monk of the Fifth Century, who opposed the teaching of Augustine that salvation is by grace alone. Semi-Pelagianism taught that salvation, in some part at least, is based on human effort, if only in not resisting the grace of God.

6. True hope is opposed to all forms of fatalism.

Fatalism denies the efficacy of human effort by virtue of a determinism, in which ends are effected apart from any (ordinary) means of human effort. Determinism may be impersonal and cosmic (astrological), or impersonal and natural (biology or geography is destiny). Or determinism may be by God, whether in Islam (*kismet*) or in Christianity (predestination),[9] or by the gods, as in Greek tragedy. Cyclical fatalism sees a sequence in human society from a golden age in the past, to the present end age, to inevitable cataclysm, followed by renewal in a golden age, in a beginningless and endless cycle (Hindu cycles or eternal recurrence). Sometimes human effort is nullified by local spirits or nature and must be appeased by man through sacrifice, or by use of occult forces appropriated through magic. Much human effort has been prevented or wasted through fatalistic superstitions.

7. True hope is opposed to all forms of mystical ecstasy.

Mysticism seeks an immediate union with or vision of ultimate reality as the source of full blessedness. There are mystical approaches to the divine in all religions. The knowledge of God is not viewed as coming through the work of dominion. Rather it is viewed as coming through the monastic contemplative life, through negative theology, through the Dark Night of the Soul, through whirling dances, through bacchanalian ecstasies, through mantras and incantational prayer, and through magic-mysticism of convergence in "sacred places." Poetically, the beatific vision is depicted in Dante's *Paradiso*, in the *Divine Comedy*. Non-theistic mysticism has been pursued through yoga and meditation to realize the unity of the self with ultimate reality through an intuitive awareness, which realizes the suchness and emptiness of all being, and through immersion in the way of nature, which realizes the primordial oneness behind all duality. All distinctions are transcended in a total immanence. The subject/object duality in thought is extinguished in mystical consciousness. There is no sense of self, of thought, of choice, of values, or of the good. Mysticism moves

---

9. While both Islamic and Christian theologies teach predestination, they differ in their view of whether both ends and means are predestinated. In the former, one may be lost, apart from one's desire to be saved; in the latter, one is not saved apart from one's belief and desire.

beyond thought to silence. It isn't is; it isn't isn't; it isn't both; it isn't neither. Silence!

CONSEQUENCES OF MORAL LAW 4

There is a moral law which is clear, comprehensive, and critical. The consequences of this law are both individual and cultural, both present in one lifetime and cumulative in history, both in history and beyond history. The work of dominion in pursuit of the good is the work of all mankind throughout history. A person's life ends when one's work is completed. History ends when the work in its entirety is completed. Work apart from the good is empty. Effort becomes minimal. There is not individual or cultural development. Life stagnates in the mind-numbing repetition of tradition or the mind-numbing pursuit of directionless progress. There is no rest from work, or enjoyment of the fruit of one's labor, which is not mind-numbing.

Work for the good is fulfilling. Fullness is achieved in developing one's own capabilities and in giving to and receiving from all others. Work done in accordance with the good, and to achieve the good, is never in vain. It is cumulative, until fullness is reached and rest in completion is achieved. There remains, after work, an unending enjoyment of God in the inexhaustible knowledge of God.

___

Chapter 14

MORAL LAW 5:
AUTHORITY AND INSIGHT

ORIGIN IN HUMAN NATURE

ALL HUMAN BEINGS ARE BORN IGNORANT. Authority is grounded in the fact that we are born ignorant. Being ignorant, we need to be taught the good and the means to the good. Authority is expressed fundamentally in teaching.

ON THE NATURE OF AUTHORITY

1. Authority is rational, not personal.

Since what is to be taught is the good and the means to the good, teaching ought not to be subjective. It ought not to depend arbitrarily on the mere wish of one person, or a few persons, or many persons. Ignorance is removed, not by happening to receive right opinion, but by knowledge, grounded in understanding. What is known must be rationally justified. Rational beings are ruled by reason through the understanding, not merely by the wish of others.

2. Authority is based on insight, not might.

It is based on insight into the good and the means to it, in any sphere of life. Might does not give one the right to rule, since the good cannot be achieved by blind force. One may overpower another and subject the other to one's own will through fear. Power and victory in battle may establish a *de facto* rule but not a *de jure* rule. It does not establish the mandate of heaven.

3. Authority is not established through agreement by contract or by consent of the governed.

Consent is subject to confirmation through rational discourse. The voice of the people is not the voice of God. All of these can be present with little or no connection to the good.

4. Authority is not established by duly agreed upon laws.

A constitution may be adopted without understanding the good and without understanding laws in relation to the good. A law not aimed at the good is not a good law. No one is king above the law, but the law itself is not king. All human laws are subject to the moral law, grounded in human nature, and therefore knowable to all.

5. Authority is not established by following established procedure.

Laws may be upheld by courts, and persons may enter office by following procedure, but none of this guarantees connection with the good, or competence to rule.

6. Authority is not conferred by heredity, whether in kingship or priesthood.

Insight is not transmitted by birth, but by teaching. Those who rule should think deeply about basic things which are clear.

7. Insight, as the basis of authority, is historically cumulative, not individual.

The one who exercises authority in teaching should be aware of and build upon the achievements of those who have gone before, in one's field of authority. One is not to reinvent the wheel by trial and error; one should have proven competence before exercising authority.

MORAL LAW 5

Authority based on insight must be honored. Authority without insight must be changed where possible. Authority must be questioned to see if it has insight into the good and the means to the good. The one in authority should be able to offer rational justification for one's view of the good, in contrast to alternative views, and to explain how this good is to be achieved. Where there is insight, one must submit to its oversight and teaching. Where there is not insight, there is no obligation to submit. Where someone is already in a position of authority without insight, seeking change in authority, for the good, must be done according to the good. It must be done within the bounds of the moral law. One can never be morally obligated by the authority, or in seeking to change the authority, to do what is contrary to the moral law. There is an order for change, from more basic to less basic, in keeping with the moral law, which must always be observed.

APPLICATIONS OF MORAL LAW 5

1. Authority based on insight is opposed to authoritarianism.

It is opposed to persons without insight in positions of authority. In authoritarianism, authority is personal, not rational. It is opposed to authority without insight in family, state, school, and Church. Parents are naturally our first teachers. They have the greatest freedom and responsibility to teach the good. If the chain of teaching were unbroken, parents would pass on the wisdom of the ages. While the freedom is there, rationally justified teaching is seldom there. Yet parents expect their teaching that lacks rational justification to be heeded. Even the best teaching is resisted in the quest for autonomy. How much more then will merely personal authority (i.e., authoritarianism) be resisted?

In the state, those who make laws and enforce laws should be able to give an account of justice, and of the purpose of the state, and the boundaries of its jurisdiction. Where there are disputes, they should be able to identify what is basic to the dispute and what is clear. Justice is not reached by compromising worldviews, but by clarifying what is basic. Those who rule should be able to philosophize deeply.

Educators, especially, who stand *in loco parentis*, should be able to give an account of the good. And students should seek an account of how the discipline being studied is connected to the good. The academic tradition began with Plato and its spirit is embodied in his *Dialogues*. In *The Republic*, an account is given of justice, which in turn required an account of the good. Educators who are not easily familiar with *The Republic*, and with discourse about the good, lack historically cumulative insight. The life of understanding in the universities can be destroyed by fragmentation and specialization, and by the temptation to reductionism in a faulty quest to recover integration. The temptation to quantify all things is present in recent science. Mathematics, which underlies science, needs the focus of the good to avoid Pythagorean reductionism, that all of reality is in essence numbers.

Those who teach in the Church, which presents itself as the institution of redemption and restoration, should be able to give an account of the good and to rationally justify it. Members should ask of its teachers proof for the existence and nature of God. Without objective clarity regarding the existence and nature of God, there can be no inexcusability, and therefore no account of good and evil. Teaching becomes fideistic, personal, authoritarian, and divisive, without understanding. One is not obligated to submit to authoritarian dogmatism and one is obligated to change it where possible.

2. Authority based on insight is opposed to principles of authority as ultimate which are not self-attesting.

It is opposed to testimony (by scripture or tradition) and to experience (by common sense, science, or intuition) as self-attesting. Reason, as the test for meaning, is self-attesting. As the laws of thought, reason cannot be questioned, but makes questioning possible. It is immediately self-attesting. Tradition is taken as authoritative in many cultures. Yet traditions differ, and traditions change. Tradition therefore cannot be an ultimate principle of authority. There are likewise many competing and mutually exclusive claims of what is to be considered scripture. Many persons present themselves as prophets,

speaking in the name of God. They all cannot be scriptures or prophets and must be tested, and are therefore not self-attesting. A test of
new revelation is that it must be self-consistent, consistent with what
is clear from general revelation, and consistent with previously given
special revelation. It is by reason that meaning and consistency are
grasped and tested.

Experiences, both inner and outer, both ordinary and extraordinary, are given in immediate states of consciousness. The cause or
causes of these states of consciousness can and have been variously interpreted by way of realism or anti-realism (idealism). In realist views
of the physical world (as in science), the cause of what exists now in
observation is explained by the past (which is not observed), by way
of the assumption of uniformity, rather than non-uniformity. No experience is meaningful without interpretation. Every interpretation
(including that of uniformity vs. non-uniformity) can and must be
tested for coherence of meaning by reason. It is reason, as the laws of
thought, which is the test of meaning, and is therefore self-attesting.

3. Authority based on insight is opposed to reversing the order of authority in each person.

There is a natural order in the human personality between intellect,
emotion, and will. Thought, feeling, and action are not, in the economy of human personality, independent. (All living beings act. Some
beings which are sentient feel and act. Only man thinks and feels and
acts. And in man, these three are ordered.) What we think *about the
good* directs desires and feelings. (At least some feelings arise from
belief systems. There are feelings which arise from intuition and from
bodily states.) Thought and feeling direct and move the will. (It is the
belief that God rewards those who diligently seek him that leads to
seeking him.[1]) Moral evil brings a split in the understanding, as well
as in the desires, and the will. Not recognizing the inconsistencies in
one's thought, and how subsequently desires and the will are split,
these aspects are mistakenly thought of as independent of beliefs or as
controlling beliefs. Since thought directs the other aspects of feeling
and will, the order can be spoken of as an order of authority. So, as far

---

1. *Hebrews 11:6.*

as the economy of the human personality is concerned, it can be said that the intellect rules.

4. Authority based on insight is opposed to reversing the order of authority within an institution.

The order that is within each human personality becomes the basis for the order among human beings operating within an institution. In an institution, the philosophical must lead the psychological and the practical. Order does not, as is often thought, imply subordination. When it is seen that way, it justifiably provokes extreme resistance in the name of equality. Gifts based on dominant aspects of personality become manifest in function and ministry.[2] In any institution, the person of vision must lead in terms of the good. When the good is lost sight of, the goal becomes what is valued in the psychological or what is valued in the practical. In education, with the loss of vision of understanding worldviews through critical thinking, there has been an alternative emphasis on self-esteem and on skills. Since only a small percentage of a society is philosophical, and since the tendency to lose sight of the good is great, the tendency to inversion of order in an institution is very great. Once it is in place, the inversion is hard to reverse without a crisis.[3]

5. Authority based on insight is opposed to totalitarianism among institutions.

In totalitarianism, one institution rules over every aspect of life by becoming dominant over all other institutions. Each institution has a particular form and function which determines its competence, and its jurisdiction is restricted to its competence. No institution is over another, and each institution is equally under the moral law, according to its form and function. The state bears the sword to restrain evil outwardly. The Church teaches the Word of God to remove evil inwardly.

---

2. Prophet, priest, and king reflect these ministries and here too there is an order. There is an order of prophet, priest, and king in the Old Testament, and of knowledge, holiness, and righteousness in the New Testament. See *Moral Law 8*, on Talent.

3. William Strauss, and Neil Howe, *The Fourth Turning: An American Prophecy* (New York: Broadway Books, 1997), apply generational theory to cycles in history.

The family reproduces and nurtures human life. Business produces goods and services which provide the material needs of life—food, clothing, shelter. Each protects and promotes human life in different ways, according to its form and function.[4]

6. Authority based on insight is opposed to any form of government which would subordinate Church to the state.

Religion in totalitarian states becomes an instrument to further the power of the ruler, as in ancient Egypt, Babylon, China, and Rome. The ruler assumes divinity, with unlimited power to kill and to bless, as it serves his purpose. In communist and fascist states, all possible opposition to the state from Church or elsewhere is liquidated or made an instrument of state propaganda.

Authority based on insight is equally opposed to Church over state. Here, religion uses the state to establish and to extend its power to rule in the name of God. In Islam, divine laws (*Sharia*) are established through the state (the Caliphate). So too, papal authority was extended in medieval Catholicism. In post-Reformation Europe, after the peace of Westphalia, the religion of the ruler became the religion of the land. For a time, also, in colonial America there were theocratic states. The moral law, given in human nature, was not sought out or appealed to as the basis of law for all men, everywhere, at all times.

Authority based on insight is opposed to state over business and to business over the state. Command economies of socialist states lack the competence (insight) and the jurisdiction to engage in economic planning. Plutocrats and multinational corporations that would control the government are inclined to serve their own interests through the state. State, Church, and business are equally under the moral law.

7. Authority based on insight is opposed to the state over the family and to the family over the state.

It is opposed to tyranny of dictators, absolute monarchs, and aristocracies, which rule for their own benefit. The English, French, American, and Russian Revolutions have overthrown the power of one or a

---

4. Abraham Kuyper, *Lectures on Calvinism* (Grand Rapids, MI: William B. Eerdmans Publishing Company, 1943), 48-66.

few families, which have prevailed over the state for centuries. Author-ity based on insight is also opposed to the welfare state, which absorbs the function of the family and creates increasing dependencies rather than increasing responsibility. Without the culture and discipline of a work ethic, the rich who do not work, and the poor who do not work, use the power of the state to further their self-interest, to their own harm and the harm of others. The state should be kept free from abuse by either.

Authority based on insight is opposed to the state absorbing the function of the family in public education. The family has the prima-ry freedom and responsibility to educate its children. In establishing and regulating public education, the state goes beyond its competence and jurisdiction and undermines the primary means to achieving the good. Public education, by virtue of being public, must be religious-ly neutral. But public education, by virtue of being education, can-not be religiously neutral. Teaching facts which are uninterpreted is meaningless; but teaching facts which are interpreted naturalistically, in the name of science, is not religiously neutral. So, public education must be either neutral and meaningless or not neutral and religious, in which case it is not public. In either case, public education as reli-giously neutral education is not possible.

The dilemma of public education can be summed up: Is public edu-cation possible?

If it is public, it must be neutral.

If it is education, it cannot be neutral.

If it is public education, it must be and cannot be neutral.

When students in their most formative years should be learning to think critically about worldviews, they are either being indoctrinated in the worldview of naturalism, or their minds are being filled with meaningless facts, with resultant effects on the formation of their character and moral conduct. The way out of the dilemma of public education is to return education to the private realm where it belongs, according to the moral law on authority. The private sector has shown its competence historically, in that the best schools have been private, from grammar schools to graduate schools. Privatizing education (and reallocation of educational funding through vouchers, as a possible first step) increases choice and opportunities, especially for the least advantaged families. It permits freedom of thought, competition of ideas, and dialogue to occur as part of self-examination, necessary for integrity and knowledge.

CONSEQUENCES OF MORAL LAW 5

Authority without insight subverts and perverts the good. Effort to achieve the good is undermined by those in positions of authority who are without insight into the good. Something other than the good is put in place of the good. The substitute can never satisfy and lack of satisfaction leads only to excess and perversion. Attempts to challenge or change the powers that be are most often met with the fiercest defense of their prestige and privileges, unless they have already gradually become irrelevant by disregard. To give honor to whom honor is not due, by submitting to authority without insight, and to fail to challenge illegitimate authority by legitimate means, is to perpetuate the rule of darkness and oppression over human existence, through the generations, without end.

Authority based on insight protects and is productive of the good. When insight is manifest in removing thoughts that would oppose and obstruct pursuit of the good, and when it "prepares a highway in the wilderness," then rulers and people will come and rebuild the desolate places. When the people become concerned about insight in those who lead, and when they seek it out, then the way is open for the renewal of society, after ages of stagnation. Change begins with a solitary voice, then a small band, and when the time is at hand, it comes swiftly like a flood. The landscape changes. There are new rulers and authorities in place whose hearts have been inclined toward the good. And then there comes a renewal of all things.

Chapter 15

———

MORAL LAW 6:
HUMAN DIGNITY AND RATIONALITY

ORIGIN IN HUMAN NATURE

W E ARE BORN HUMAN. There is a set of qualities which distinguishes us from all animals. This set of qualities which sets humans apart is a difference of kind rather than of degree, and confers upon mankind a dignity of being and function above the creation. There is a hierarchy of being from rocks to plants to animals and to humans, in which the higher being includes the qualities of the lower, and more. This order is natural and not imposed, and commonly recognized, not conventional or contrived.

ON THE NATURE OF HUMAN DIGNITY

1. Human dignity consists in the capacity to understand.

We understand by reason. The capacity to understand, which is the ground of human dignity, is to be distinguished from the exercise of that capacity, which differs with time and circumstance.

2. Reason in itself is the laws of thought.

It is used to form concepts, judgments, and arguments, the forms of all thought. It is used as a test for meaning, to interpret experience in light of one's basic beliefs, and it is used to construct a coherent world and life view.

3. Reason in us is natural, not conventional.

It is universal, the same in all persons, everywhere, at all times—Eastern and Western, male and female, young and old, rich and poor, educated and uneducated, ancient and modern. As the laws of thought, reason is the same in all thinking beings.

4. The capacity to understand distinguishes humans from animals.

Humans, by the use of reason, form concepts and judgments; animals do not. Concepts, which are formed by acts of reason, are not images formed by the senses, which humans have in common with animals. Since concepts grasp the essence of a class of things, concepts are universal, the same in all persons and apply to all members of a class. Words, as conventional signs, express concepts, and differ from one society to another. The argument can be stated as follows:

> If animals could think, we would communicate with them as with other human beings. (The difference would be one of language—conventional signs only—not of concepts.)
>
> We cannot communicate with animals as with other human beings (at the rational level of concepts and judgments vs. at the sensory level of images and sensations).
>
> Therefore, animals do not think (however intelligent they may act at an instinctual level).

Humans think critically about meaning of basic beliefs; animals do not. Humans interpret experience in light of basic beliefs; animals do not. Humans construct and change worldviews; animals do not.

5. Human beings, as rational, act out of their system of beliefs.

We are immediately aware that we think and hold beliefs. And we are immediately aware of our beliefs as reasons which cause us to act, and that actions vary according to our beliefs. To change our actions, we must change our beliefs as reasons which cause us to act. Appeal to hidden and unknown causes which could be known by self-examination are different from unknown natural causes. Causes which are not reasons knowable to the agent may cause events, but these causes are not actions of rational agents.

6. Human beings, as rational beings, are free to use reason.

We are able to respond rationally to a whole range of situations, and we are therefore responsible for whether or not our response is rational. We can use our reason if we want to use reason. *Can* is not more basic than *want* at the basic level. We are instinctual and intuitional in some ways, but these do not apply to or override basic beliefs. As a free, conscious, rational being, man is capable of ruling over the creation, and is called in and by the constitution of his being to do so. In this capacity to rule, man reflects his divine origin and likeness, his dignity as *imago dei*.

7. Human society is a society of rational beings.

Participation in, or separation from, human society depends on the exercise of this capacity. Children, whose rational capacity is not sufficiently developed, are limited in their participation—they do not yet have the right to exercise certain freedoms. Humans who use force, instead of reason, are by force restrained from free participation in society. Companions who are unwilling to be reasonable about certain matters are not admitted to dialogue concerning these matters, or in sharing matters which are close to one's heart. We do not open ourselves to one whom we perceive is not open to reason.

MORAL LAW 6

We are to affirm human dignity in ourselves and in others. We are to treat others, and be willing to be treated, as having the capacity and responsibility for understanding.

APPLICATIONS OF MORAL LAW 6

1. Affirmation of human dignity is opposed to the use of force in murder and war.

Murder results from an accumulated lack of personal discipline in self-control. We kill in order to have what the other person will not grant us. We kill because we cannot persuade. Murder arises from a way of life in which what we want and how we get it have not been subject to the discipline of reason. Murder is evidence that external constraints against self-love were never internalized by discipline while growing up, to make one stop and think. Unchecked narcissistic beliefs were allowed to inflame desires to the point of lawlessness. Discipline in thought, leading to self-control in desire, prevents lawless conduct, including murder.

War results from accumulated collective failure to use reason on both sides. On the part of the aggressor, this is fairly easy to see, although who is the aggressor is often obfuscated by self-justifying propaganda of victim status. Wars are fought in the context of ideologies grounded in basic beliefs. War with Communism, Nazism, and Islam involved ideologies. Intellectual or spiritual war which destroys false ideologies prevents physical wars. Persuasion by force (terrorism) or by emotion (propaganda) bypasses the understanding and dehumanizes others. Many worldviews bypass the use of reason to persuade and resort to force to spread their system, insofar as their system of belief inherently deprecates the use of reason. Marx's dialectical materialism, Nazi's evolutionary superior race, and Islam's requirement of all to submit, have used force to spread their system. Their basic assumptions require intellectual engagement. Failure to take these thoughts captive over decades and centuries permitted war to occur and to recur.

2. Affirmation of human dignity is opposed to racism.

In racism, ethnicity is placed above our common humanity in reason. When what is common is lost sight of, only differences remain. Judgments based on differences, rather than sameness in rationality, result in judgments of inequality and in unequal treatment of others. Genocide and slavery have been based on denial of common humanity. Cultural differences are not understood in light of basic beliefs and use of reason, but in natural terms of genetics or geography, as if there were degrees of humanity. Racism has been profound and pervasive and destructive, not only between color lines, but within all color lines, between local tribal groups as well as between ethnic groups distantly separated.

Attempts to counter racism without addressing basic beliefs and the use of reason, continue to operate on racist assumptions. Affirming the equality of all persons and of all ethnic groups leads to, in light of ongoing postmodern academic skepticism, the equality of all views. Giving up on the possibility of knowing anything rationally, skepticism opts for a pragmatic theory of meaning and truth. All views are equally true, pragmatically speaking. They serve their purpose of satisfactory adjustment to one's environment equally well, given differences in environment. Affirming the equality of all views leads to affirming the equality of all cultures, with the expectation of the equality of outcomes, and resultant affirmative action programs to bring about equal outcomes. Lack of equality in outcome is taken as an *a priori* indication that one group has gained power by establishing its ideology, its grand theory, its meta-narrative as truth, and has used its power to its advantage by oppressing others. Correction of this presumed victim status must be made, if necessary, by the state through affirmative action programs.

Tolerance of all beliefs and cultures, as being of equal value, is the cardinal virtue of multiculturalism. True tolerance here is seen in the affirmation and celebration of all diversity. This is contrary to the affirmation of human dignity, in which human beings are to be treated as having the capacity and the responsibility to understand basic things which are clear. In the name of tolerance, a new oppression has emerged. Cultures are frozen in order to be identified, and persons of all ethnic backgrounds are expected to be identified by and with one's culture. One's ethnicity, not one's humanity, is one's destiny. Reductionistic views of what it is to be human identify persons in terms of one aspect of our being, disregarding or reducing other aspects to one aspect. Several aspects of human nature are to be recognized in order to avoid reductionism: our larger aspect (universal/formal—the capacity for holding basic beliefs), our narrower aspect (material content of basic belief), our triune personality (thought–feeling–will), our body/soul unity, our male/female diversity, our cultural/historical background, and our personal uniqueness *(haecceity)*. No secondary aspect should be allowed to override the most basic aspect, our capacity to understand.

3. Affirmation of human dignity is opposed to gender wars.

In gender wars, gender identity is placed above our common humanity in reason. In the feminist narrative, men have used "reason" to oppress women. Male thinking is said to be linear and hierarchical; women's thinking, to be holistic and collaborative. The patriarchy is said to be justified by the view of God as father. Earlier feminism sought inclusion on the basis of equality. Gender differences, understood as essentially physical differences, are considered insufficient to justify role differences. Later feminism rejects same-role model to affirm the uniquely feminine as superior to (because more life-affirming than) the masculine God. The goddess replaces God as father, or God as neither. Gender wars have called into question every aspect of male/female relation and have left things psychologically and practically unsettled.

Instead of questioning the beliefs held in the name of reason, and the extent to which reason is being used, reason itself is called into question. But if reason in itself is the laws of thought, then reason cannot be questioned. And one person or group cannot oppress another with respect to the use of reason, since we are always free and responsible to use our reason critically. Women have significant influence in shaping the lives of men as they grow up from childhood. Victim status for women is therefore not a given. In gender wars, we fail to hold each other responsible for the use of reason. We are first human, and then we are male and female.

In gender wars, we fail to understand the nature of male and female, both in their diversity and unity. Gender differences are fundamentally spiritual and not physical; the visible/physical reveals, manifests, and is a sign of the invisible/spiritual. Male and female are both in the image of God. God is both Creator and upholder of all things. All humans—both men and women—are in the role of the feminine in relation to God the Creator and upholder. The invisible relation between God and man is revealed in the visible relation between man and woman. The work of initiating and originating is complemented and completed by the work of upholding and nurturing. To have fruit, the work of planting and watering are both necessary, and ordered, without the latter being subordinated to the former. In pursuit of the good, male and female are both necessary and ordered, and exist in perfect unity. Without the good, there is no unity. Gender war, suppressed or open, is the result.

4. Affirmation of human dignity is opposed to abortion, euthanasia, suicide, and to life-support which disregards the loss of the capacity to understand.

The dispute over abortion is grounded in the dispute over what it is to be a person. There is a legal and a moral aspect to this dispute. The former concerns when human life begins. The latter concerns when human life ends. Current law prohibits infanticide. Societies in the past have permitted infanticide. In the current debate, there is common ground regarding the illegality of infanticide. The dispute turns on the question of the continuity or the discontinuity of human personhood, from birth going back to conception. In genetic terms, there is continuity from conception. In terms of capacity to understand, there would be continuity in the existence and development of that capacity, unless it can be argued that thinking is an activity of the brain, not the mind or soul, and that the soul is distinct from life, and is something added sometime after conception. (This has previously been discussed in Chapter 5, under theistic evolution: Is the soul the same as life?) Being a distinct human life in mind and body from conception, the fetus cannot be regarded as mere tissue any more than a newborn infant is mere tissue. Argument from inconvenience cannot override the legal right of a person to life.

There is another aspect of what it is to be a person, one that is assumed, but is not often articulated, that enters into the moral argument regarding abortion. It is the moral worth of human life in relation to whether or not human life, once begun, goes on forever. The dignity of human life is deemed less significant, or insignificant, if the death of the fetus marks the complete end of that person's existence. The dignity of the pre-born person is viewed differently if it is understood that that person's existence continues beyond physical death. As a person, the fetus grows and becomes aware of one's origin and destiny, and of the unique significance of human life on earth, which was taken away by abortion from the womb. No doubt then, there will be a future encounter with, and an account sought from, those who by choice deprived another person of the right to life on earth. The everlasting consequences of one's choice cannot be considered by the one who thinks human life is not everlasting. Without belief in personal immortality, there cannot be rational justification for morality, and the choice to abort cannot be considered a morally significant choice.

Euthanasia means a good death. A good death is thought to be a pain-free death. But if physical death itself is not natural merely, but natural evil, imposed by God on man as a rational being, as a call to stop and think, then a good death is a thoughtful death. Conscious awareness of the nearness of death should bring what is important in life into clear focus. It is a continuation and consummation of a life-long process of dying to self-centered existence. Far from avoiding or dulling one's awareness, thoughtfulness is to be protected. Pain is not to be avoided at all costs, but in relation to preserving the capacity to think. Euthanasia, as it is practiced, is the final act in seeking to avoid the call to stop and think.

Suicide is an act of despair based on a false conception of the good. The good, as falsely conceived, is seen as unattainable, and life without any hope of the good becomes unbearable. It could be circumstantial, as in Romeo's perceived loss of Juliet, or in a sculptor becoming a quadriplegic, or in the loss of honor in war or shame, or it could be an internal subjective feeling of hopelessness as in depression. Thoughts of hopelessness are a challenge to see the good more clearly, not an occasion to seek comfort through the false hope of suicide.

Some suicide may arise from intellectual despair—that life at its best is meaningless. It may be believed that intellectual honesty requires skepticism, and that skepticism, held with integrity, leads to nihilism. When the absurd arises, escape may be sought by a return to the unconscious, or by intellectual suicide of a leap of faith, or by ordinary suicide, or by becoming the hero of the absurd (Albert Camus, *Myth of Sisyphus*). If basic things are clear, then skepticism is a lack of integrity, not a requirement of intellectual honesty. Intellectual hopelessness, in light of the many conflicting worldviews held throughout history, assumes we are seeking to know. Skepticism can be tested by its response to the claim that some things are clear, that it is clear that something must be eternal.

Some intervention to save human life disregards the loss of the capacity to understand. Since human dignity consists in the capacity to understand, when the capacity is lost, the life that is being preserved by life-support systems is mere vegetative existence. Discerning the loss of this capacity can be difficult at times, but is clear when there are no brain waves for a 24-hour period. At one end of the spectrum, standards can be clear. There are degrees of the loss of the capacity to understand in relation to using life-support systems, which require further consideration. The question here is not whether ending life-support is justified, but whether continuing life-support can be justified. The burden of proof shifts with evidence of loss of capacity to understand.

The removal of life-support is not the same as the act of ending of life as in euthanasia. It is a case of letting nature take its course, or letting die, or leaving it in the hands of God. A person may elect, consistent with human dignity, not to use extraordinary means to prolong one's life. Organ transplants, cancer treatments, or invasive surgery go beyond the ordinary means of diet and exercise to maintain health. The natural instinct to avoid death cannot be made absolute, but is relative to the purpose of human existence on earth. Assuming that one has lived thoughtfully in light of one's specific purpose, it is more natural to desire to depart when one's work is completed, than to cling to life.[1]

5. Affirmation of human dignity is opposed to psychotherapeutic programs which disregard our interpretative assumptions and responsibility for our beliefs.

Psychotherapy has become increasingly widespread as skepticism, pragmatism, and the naturalistic worldview have increased.[2] Natural-

---

1. The dilemma of choosing to flee suffering by euthanasia or to cling to life through life-support is resolved by one's worldview in light of which the meaning of life on earth is determined. St. Paul resolved the conflict between desiring to depart or to stay in terms of meaningful work still to be done (*Philippians 1:23*).

2. Christina Hoff Sommers, and Sally Satel, *One Nation Under Therapy: How the Helping Culture is Eroding Self-Reliance* (New York: St. Martin's Press, 2006).

istic paradigms in explaining human behavior put feeling and sensation above thought (Freud, Skinner). The idea of human freedom and responsibility was lost with little protest. (Some voices of protest were raised: Thomas Szasz, *The Myth of Mental Illness* and Karl Menninger, *Whatever Became of Sin?*)

As the idea of right and wrong diminished and social pathologies increased, new non-moral categories of explanations were sought. Moral inhibitions were viewed as neuroses. The feeling of shame was rejected as an external imposition, damaging to the psyche, and was rejected as something toxic. Self-love in relation to the good was replaced by simple narcissism, self-fulfillment in being true to oneself and being in touch with one's feelings. Inhibitions were replaced by exhibitionism. Authenticity permitted transgression of social boundaries in the name of the "natural." Nurturing one's inner child and enhancing self-esteem replaced the discipline of virtue and honor. Asocial behavior was explained as a natural response of the oppressed, the disenfranchised, the victims of the blameworthy powerbrokers who control the social environment.[3] Underlying causes in a person's worldview are ignored or thought not to exist, or are considered symptoms which are to be treated or managed by a cocktail of drug therapies (by soma, in Huxley's *Brave New World*). By denying the place of reason and belief in human nature, there has come about an abolition of man.[4]

Background factors are occasions, not causes, of behavior. Two persons from the same background, including identical twins, can react differently to their life situations. They can hold different basic beliefs, with different values, and different life plans. The same person can undergo fundamental changes in basic belief and conduct his or her life very differently than before. While change can occur at a behavioral or psychological level in a way that relieves stress, deep change occurs at the level of basic belief, which brings about a more complete transformation in a person's life. Change in basic belief occurs when a person sees one's belief system is incoherent, that one's life lacks meaning, and that one is responsible for holding incoherent beliefs due to the failure to use reason in self-examination. When psychotherapy fails to engage persons in self-examination at the level of basic belief,

---

3. Frantz Fanon, *The Wretched of the Earth* (New York: Grove/Atlantic, 2005).

4. C.S. Lewis, *The Abolition of Man* (New York: HarperCollins, 2001).

it fails to treat persons with human dignity, as having the capacity and responsibility for understanding, and therefore fails to help persons to become whole.

6. Affirmation of human dignity is opposed to the view that capital punishment is dehumanizing.

In capital punishment, a person is separated from human society by death. The alternative that is offered in place of capital punishment is separation from human society by life sentence in prison. The specific difference between these two forms of separation is retribution as a principle of justice, which holds a person responsible for one's action. Objections to capital punishment would have to address, *first*, whether retributive justice in general denies human dignity, and *second*, whether the death penalty violates retributive justice. The concern here is not with judicial procedure and wrongful conviction, but with the principle and application of retributive justice.

Many responses to capital punishment do not address the principle of retribution. Any killing is seen as murder (including self-defense?). Vengeance is a barbaric motive (including deliberated judicial judgment?). The death penalty is cruel and unusual (in every form?). Utilitarian theory, by considering consequences only, can go in any of several directions, and is insufficient to account for justice. Rehabilitation theories are open-ended as to what constitutes rehabilitation, whether it is possible, and when the possibility ends.

Retribution is based on *lex talionis*, an eye for an eye. The principle is applied in cases short of the death penalty, where reparation is possible to the injured party in kind, or in equivalence, as in the cases of property damage or personal injury. The guilty party must forfeit as much as he has damaged. In the case of intentionally taking life, the guilty party must forfeit his life. Retributive justice is commonly practiced as holding a person accountable. Holding accountable affirms human dignity as being responsible for understanding the consequences of one's action. There can be no objection to the principle by those who accept it in practice. The question then, is whether life for life in the death penalty is a violation of the principle of retribution.

7. Affirmation of human dignity is opposed to the view that final separation from rational human society is a denial of human dignity.

Human society is a society of rational beings. Human dignity consists in the capacity to understand. In light of basic things that are clear, the use of reason brings us to the good and to unity. To neglect, avoid, resist, or deny reason brings denial of the good and disunity. Mutual opposition is inherent in opposing views. What one builds the other opposes and tears down. War will be constant unless one party changes or there is separation between the parties. The separation will continue unless one changes; and the separation is effectually final if there is no change.

Separation is inherent in differing views about the desirability for greater consciousness and consistency, that is, the need for understanding and meaning. Separation may be mutually accepted, perhaps mutually desired, where irreconcilable differences are mutually recognized.[5] It is not the case that one desires to use reason and wants to enjoy the company of another rational being and is being disallowed. There is no injustice in having what one desires. To affirm human dignity and to hold another accountable for the use of reason is to recognize the justice in being given up to, or not being restrained from, what one desires, even when the desire is to not use reason.[6]

CONSEQUENCES OF MORAL LAW 6

To deny human dignity in another, one must first deny it in oneself. Denying one's own human dignity is a form of spiritual suicide. It is an integration downward into the non-human, denying the distinction between humans and animals. It may also be done in the name of affirming the divinity of oneself, denying the distinction between the divine and the human. We lose our true self in either case. And

---

5. C.S. Lewis, *The Great Divorce* (New York: HarperCollins, 2001).

6. It is possible to desire not to use one's reason, or to regard the use of reason as a constraint on one's freedom. The failure here, to use reason critically at a basic level, goes unnoticed, or is disregarded, or is resisted. Milton's Satan thought it better to rule in hell than to serve in heaven. In this sense, it is possible to love darkness more than light, especially if one has to acknowledge one has come short in a basic way (*John 3:19*).

having lost oneself, we are incapable of communion with any other self. There is no more "thou." We are an "it" to them and they to us (Martin Buber). With personhood being denied, there can be no personal relationships. Human society comes to an end. To lose contact with humanity, our own and others, is to enter the heart of darkness. Kurtz (in Joseph Conrad's *Heart of Darkness*) entered that darkness, but also returned, when he judged it: "the horror, the horror." Things unspeakable arise from the heart of darkness, finding oneself at once a beast and a god over others.

To affirm human dignity in oneself is to affirm it in others. It cannot be recognized in oneself without being recognized and affirmed in others, since it is the same in all. Beyond ethnicity, gender, status, and education, there is a connection in our common humanity. We shift from power relations and explanation to natural relations and explanation. It is possible to communicate at the deepest level of concern for meaning and to realize the communion of friendship. It is possible to realize human society as a society of friends, who share the deepest concerns in a mutual commitment to the good.

Chapter 16

———

MORAL LAW 7:
LOVE AND FIDELITY

ORIGIN IN HUMAN NATURE

THE ORIGIN OF OUR BEING is from a sexual union of our parents. We are born of a sexual union of one man and one woman. Except for an original creation, all human beings come into existence by procreation. Through the nurture of our being, by our parents, the good is achieved. Upon being born, dependent and without knowledge, we need nurture and instruction to achieve the good, the end in itself. Those who gave us being from their own being are naturally the ones to nurture and to instruct us. This is so universally understood, accepted, and supported as to require no argument.

ON THE NATURE OF LOVE AND FIDELITY

1. Sex is a sign and seal of love.

There are many forms of love, depending on persons and circumstances, which are non-sexual, each in its own way connected to the good. In sexual love, two persons give themselves wholly to each other. Sex expresses the love of giving oneself and it confirms the love of giving oneself wholly to the other. There is giving and receiving simultaneously. It is not a taking without being given or a taking without giving. Sex is not love; it is the sign and seal of love. The sign is not the reality; it is possible to have the sign without the reality and the reality without the sign. Since the sign is the expression and confirmation of the reality, it derives its significance from the reality. To express and confirm what is not there is to empty the sign of significance and to mislead and deceive the other (and oneself). In matters so deep and near to the heart, the sign without the reality is worthless. Sex without love is regarded as contemptible. Where conscience has not been deadened, it is commonly regarded as degrading to separate sex and love. Human languages have many words to express this contempt and degradation.

2. A physical union is a natural sign of a spiritual union.

A human being is a union of body and soul, not merely a body, like an animal, and not merely a spirit that happens to be in a body for a while. The visible is a mirror representation of the invisible. Sight is spoken of in both physical and spiritual terms, as are terms like heart, life and death, and awake and asleep. There is a natural, not conventional, correlation between the visible and the invisible, between the body and the soul, between the mirror representation and the original. As the body and the soul are united and cannot be separated without harming the person, so the physical union and the spiritual union are united and cannot be separated without harming the person.

3. A physical and a spiritual union is together a full union.

One without the other is incomplete. There is not another dimension of one's being besides these two which exists, and which therefore can be exempt or reserved from union, so as to make it less than a full union. In this full union, the two become one. In the Edenic account of creation, the woman is taken out of man. What was one became two, and the two were to become one flesh. There is a full and constant sharing in the materiality and domesticity of human existence, not only in the occasions of sexual union. There is no private property here, although there are items of individual, exclusive, and personal use. Life plans and purposes are one, being a unity of diversity.

4. A full union is a union of persons.

Personhood and consent are essential to a union of persons. Personal identity is not submerged, but preserved and enhanced, as in a dance of man and woman together, which is a higher unity, made possible by the diversity of male and female. The details of one's particularity must be compatible, and one must be informed so as to be both able and willing in giving consent.

5. A full union of two persons is monogamous and lasting.

One is completed by the other and there is no place for a third or a fourth. A full union is therefore exclusive of all others, and any intrusion or inclusion of others into a full union becomes a displacement of a part, or the whole, of the life of one person in that union. Life is not divisible or separable into its parts. It is an all or nothing affair. Jealousy is natural where one is excluded from what is one's own, given by virtue of a full union. And life is not divisible into moments or periods of days and months and years. As one enters a full union with the whole of one's life, so the union is for the whole of life. A full union, like life, is naturally lasting.

6. A full union is the union of marriage.

Marriage is a full union of one man and one woman, which is monogamous and lasting. Marriage is constituted by a full union of two persons, where the sexual union is the sign and seal of love. A relationship may be in fact a marriage relationship, though it is not called marriage. And a relationship may be called a marriage, though it is not in fact marriage. A marriage relationship may not continue by reason of infidelity, but it does not mean there never was a marriage. Because there are moral rights and obligations mutually present to both persons, and to third parties, and especially to children born solely of this union, the public recognition of marriage is undertaken to protect, to promote, and to preserve that union of two persons, by which we are brought into being and nurtured in being. Marriage, as the source of our being, is both private and public, and must be protected and preserved both privately and publicly. Hence there is the public institution of marriage with benefits, rights, and responsibilities, sanctioned by civil law.

7. Love, in marriage, seeks the good for and with the other, and for those we bring into being.

Sex is naturally connected to love. Sex and love are naturally connected to marriage. Love and marriage are naturally connected to the good. Love, in general, seeks the good for another. In families, we seek the good for and with children and grandchildren, and succeeding generations, without end. Succeeding generations expand through marriage to ever-enlarging communities. Material and spiritual riches accumulated over time are transmitted as inheritance to succeeding generations. The continuation and completion of corporate, cumulative, and communal effort toward the good brings about the good, which is comprehensive and inexhaustible.

MORAL LAW 7

Marriage is to achieve the good. There is an order for marriage which protects it. Marriage itself is not the good. Since each person is to seek to achieve the good, two persons in full union are all the more to seek to achieve the good. The increase of mankind is to the end of increasing the good. To assure this end of marriage, care must be taken to protect marriage. By keeping the goal of marriage in focus, the order for protecting marriage is discernible. To seek to protect marriage without the goal of marriage in place is counter-productive. To protect marriage as an end in itself is merely to delay the inevitable buildup of forces which are destructive of marriage and any social structures lacking foundation. Recent focus on family values and on instilling virtue by training, as well as recent focus on redefinition of marriage and family, become antinomies, because neither get their focus on the good.

APPLICATIONS OF MORAL LAW 7

1. The good for marriage is opposed to regarding the other as the good.

In romantic love, the other is regarded as the good. The intensity of pleasure in possessing the other as the good overwhelms thoughtfulness. When unrealistic expectations are not met, the bubble bursts, the sizzle fizzles. Remedies are tried. Reality remains recalcitrant, to which one must resign or retreat into new fantasies. Often enough the marriage, intended to be lasting, ends, leaving a measure of bitterness and cynicism.

If marriage is to be lasting, it must be built upon friendship. Friendship, like marriage, is a reciprocal relationship which is lasting and shares the deepest concerns. To not be able to share one's deepest concerns with another is less than true friendship. And if the friendship does not last, it calls into question if the person was a "true" friend. If friendship is reciprocal, lasting, and shares the deepest concerns, then those concerns must be about what truly is the good.

Things other than the good, put in the place of the good, will not last for a person, and all the more so between two persons, each inclined to pursuing one's own subjective vision of the good. Friendship that is lasting is the effect of mutual commitment to the good. True friendship is as rare as true commitment to the good. When one is inculcating the good in another, the relationship is not reciprocal. It may be a relationship of love, which need not be reciprocal. Marriage requires more than friendship, but it must at least be based on friendship, if it is to flourish and not merely survive. Feelings based on fantasy about the other decline in time. Feelings based on the beauty of the pursuit of truth and goodness increase in time. Since the good of friendship is not the good of romantic love, and since marriage as lasting must be based upon friendship, the marriage must be based upon the good and have the good as its chief end.

2. The nature of persons is opposed to separating sex and love.

A person is a union of body and soul and cannot be reduced to a mere body, as a sex object, without degrading the other as a person. Respect of personhood is opposed to casual or recreational sex, to prostitution, to rape, and to pedophilia, all of which reduce a person to a sex object. Self-loathing naturally results from participating in this conduct. It can be persisted in only by deadening one's conscience and darkening one's mind.

3. The full union of two persons is opposed to polygamy (having more than one wife) and to polyandry (having more than one husband).

It is not possible to have a full union with more than one spouse. Polygamous relations are less than marriage, although they may be called so. Polygamy inevitably denies full personhood to the other. If all partners were regarded as equally and fully human, then all would have equal rights.

If one person can have multiple spouses, then all can have multiple spouses. The logic of polygamy, which denies the exclusivity of the marriage relation, permits each man to be married to every woman and each woman to be married to every man. In effect, it makes the notion of marriage absurd. It becomes polyamory, the having of as many sexual partners as one pleases, which separates sex from commitment that comes with love. The pattern of animal mating goes with animal life, not with human life, which seeks the good for man as a rational being.

4. Marriage, as lasting, is opposed to divorce, except for adultery, or willful desertion which cannot be remedied.

Marriage is constituted, that is, sealed, by sexual union. A marriage not having been sealed by sex can be annulled as if it never existed. Marriage can be broken by adultery, in which the sign and seal is given to another. Marriage likewise can be terminated when the sign and seal are withdrawn, even when not given to another, in the desertion of the marriage bed. As a public institution in which Church and/or state are involved, desertion of many kinds, terminating in the desertion of the marriage bed, may be remedied by counsel from Church or state, which counsel is to be sought before a final decision is reached. One has the right to divorce for adultery or desertion, but one is not required to do so, since restoration of the relation is possible.

Given the moral and natural evil in the world, the person who enters thoughtlessly into marriage may as thoughtlessly seek to leave when suffering arises. The suffering is a call to stop and think, and thoughtless persons seek merely to avoid suffering, not to learn from it. This thoughtlessness is guarded against by the counsel of family and friends, and by the requirements of state and Church when, by professing an oath or vow, the obligations of marriage are made explicit and witnessed to by others. There are legal and moral consequences for violating the marriage contract and one's vow. One is bound by a vow to accept certain consequences (for better or worse, till death do us part), even if one has thoughtlessly taken the vow. Grounds for divorce are limited by one's vow. Attempts to avoid limits by avoiding the involvement of state and Church, and family and community, cannot avoid inherent consequences, which are destructive, when passion in divorce is unbounded.

5. Sex as a natural union is opposed to what is unnatural.

Biological and spiritual factors move a man and woman both to express mutual love and procreate by a natural sexual union, even when a natural union is not procreative. A sexual union is between two persons. What is not between two persons is unnatural. A sexual union, by virtue of being a union, is both mutual and simultaneous. What is not both mutual and simultaneous is unnatural. Mutual and not simultaneous is unnatural. Simultaneous and not mutual is unnatural. What bypasses the natural procreative act is unnatural, even when the procreative effect or intent is not present. Act, effect, and intent are morally distinguishable, and often are separable and separated.

One may intend conception and act without effect. One may not intend and act with or without effect. Does the intent by use of contraception to separate act from possible effect make the act itself unnatural? Since there is no change in the act itself, with or without the intent, the act is not unnatural.

6. The good for marriage is opposed to companionship or children as the good.

One may seek marriage because one feels lonely, or feels more vulnerable being alone. One may have companions without marriage and one may be married without companionship. Companionship is friendship, which is the effect of mutual commitment to the good. Seeking friendship directly, as in seeking happiness directly, rather than as an effect of the good, is contrary to the nature of things and to human nature, and will therefore naturally be frustrated. Marriage should be based on friendship, which is based on the good, but friendship does not have to result in marriage.

The good for marriage is not children. Persons are not the good, but the good is by and for persons. One is not obligated to have as many children as one can, but one is obligated to maximize the good for all persons, including the children one may have. Persons who choose to marry or not to marry must make that decision in relation to the good, all things considered, for their particular case. Decisions about the number and frequency of children must be made in relation to the good.

Separated from the good, discussions about having children and the use of contraception become mired in feelings produced by ill-informed conscience, locked in half-truths of antinomies. Without the good, moral discussion inevitably freezes into the pattern of legalism vs. antinomianism. Procreation without the capacity to nurture for the good, and abstaining from procreation as a hindrance to the pursuit of one's own happiness, both deny that the good is by and for persons. Having children is not an end in itself, but is to be understood in the context of the work of dominion, the end of which is the good.

7. Marriage, as lasting, is opposed to disregard of the order which protects it.

There is a natural order for marriage which protects it. In this order, what comes after requires what comes before. Marriage is for the good and one must therefore first seek the good for oneself. To seek the good as the knowledge of God is the love of God. To seek the good for oneself is love of self. If one has come to know and to possess the good, one can and will seek the good for the other. This is love of neighbor, a love which often is not reciprocal at first. Should the other become committed to the good, one can then seek the good, as friends, with the other. Friendship is the effect of mutual commitment to the good and is the basis of the lasting relationship of marriage. From among those who are committed to the good, one is to find one's complement, a person suitable as a life partner. Not every friend is suitable, and not every one initially attractive is suitable. Attraction should be based on knowledge of what is relevant. It is notoriously difficult to acquire this knowledge in a manner that is emotionally safe for those who are emotionally vulnerable. Traditionally, courtship which involves a process of oversight has been the guard against romantic fantasy. The traditional role of the man as protector and provider required that he have a proven ability to endow the family with financial stability. Preparation for vows and the exchange of vows make explicit the commitment and expectation of each for the marriage. Finally, there are the sanctions of the civil law for the one who violates the marriage contract. Historically, the guilty party in a divorce lost property rights and the right of oversight of offspring. Since the 1960's, civil sanctions were nullified by no-fault divorce, adding to the current increase in the dissolution of marriage.

CONSEQUENCES OF MORAL LAW 7

Ordinary infidelity (lack of commitment to the other) is rooted in and reveals spiritual infidelity (lack of commitment to the good). Marriages die without the good. The effects are felt throughout the family and can persist and accumulate in social pathologies through generations. With sufficient breakdown of families, the culture crumbles from within and is replaced from outside by war, famine, and plague. Entire civilizations have ceased to exist in this way. The time and boundaries of nations are determined by their seeking after the good.

Marriage for the good increases the good in one's own life, and in the lives of others, through generations. One can be fruitful and multiply, both physically and spiritually, so that the work of dominion can be done, in keeping with the view that the good is by and for persons. In marriage for the good, the visible reveals the invisible. The relation between man and woman reveals the relation between God and man, for better and for worse. As commitment to the good increases, fruitfulness (physical and/or spiritual) increases—fruitfulness that lasts through generations.

Chapter 17

———

Moral Law 8: Value and Talent

ORIGIN IN HUMAN NATURE

W E NATURALLY VALUE THINGS. No one values all things alike. If all things were of equal value (or of no value), there would be no distinction of good and evil, and of means and ends, and therefore no choice. If value were fully subjective, determined by existential choice, there would be no truth about the human condition to be valued, no obligation to authenticity, and no way to distinguish the absurd from the non-absurd. A truly valueless universe cannot exist for man. An absurd hero is merely a pose, nihilism a show. There is no escape from reason and from value.

ON THE NATURE OF VALUE AND TALENT

1. Value is a function of supply and demand.

When there is no demand, there is no value, as in the case of garbage. Not having value, it is said not to be owned, and therefore not to be anything that can be stolen. The atomic substance of anything can be processed and recycled and so made of use that is valued. But the original waste, as such, is not valued. Dirt, which is abundant in supply and not greatly demanded, has little value. Diamonds are said to be in great demand and in small supply, so they are of great value.

2. Demand is a function of one's view of the good.

How much a person is willing to pay (or to sacrifice) for something reflects that person's view of the good. View of the good can differ dramatically between two persons, while supply remains constant. Football fans may be willing to pay five thousand dollars for a front row seat at mid-field for a Super Bowl game. Another may be willing to see a video replay of the game. Both see the game, the only difference being that the first feels immediately the excitement of the crowd and its cheering. The first is willing to pay more because he values the excitement (the hoopla) of the game. The latter is able to see all the plays up close and in slow motion, repeatedly. He has a more thorough view of the game and the excellence displayed. For the first, hoopla is the good; for the latter, the display of athletic excellence is the good. In this case, what is valued differs and the supply differs, though the demand may remain equal, hence the amount spent differs.

3. Supply is a function of talent.

Human ability, grounded in knowledge, can change the supply as well as the need for services. Inventions of engines and development of electric power have changed the amount of human labor needed to accomplish a task. Demand for space is altered by telecommunication. Inventions of new materials have made others obsolete and technology has increased supply of materials, services, and goods, faster, cheaper, and more efficiently. Nuclear power alters the need for fossil fuels and new technologies may discover sources that are practically unlimited. As talent is developed and exercised, dominion is increased. As dominion is increased, knowledge as means and as an end in itself is increased. The more knowledge spreads, the more it increases in depth and breadth.

4. Talent is an ability to achieve some aspect of the good.

Talent is grounded in the uniqueness of one's being and is in each person. The origin of talent therefore is from the origin of one's being. It is not from self, or parents, or society. No one has, nor can have, all talent. One cannot by oneself achieve the fullness of the good, yet each one needs the good in its unity and fullness. Talent is given to each, for the good, which is for all. Therefore, talent is given to each for all.

5. Talent is known by interest and ability.

Differences among persons emerge from birth. They are not environmentally determined, but the extent of development is affected in part by one's total environment. As human beings develop, their uniqueness, interest, and ability, become more pronounced. Some aspects of reality capture one's interest. Interest leads to investigation and discovery, and an ability to master relationships in the area of interest, which leads to greater interest and knowledge and ability. Usually this develops into one's area of specialization in education and in career.

The uniqueness of one's personhood is developed upon the basis of which aspect of one's triune personality is dominant for that person: thought, feeling, or will. There is a recurrent recognition of the triune aspect of human personality in differing worldviews. In the Great Commandment, one is to love God with the whole heart—mind, soul, and strength. There are the differing offices of prophet, priest, and king, connected with the different aspects of the heart. The New Testament speaks of knowledge, holiness, and righteousness, connected to these aspects of the heart and to these differing offices. Disciples have divided along these lines as followers of Paul, Apollos, or Cephas. Greeks speak of truth, beauty, and goodness. Hindus speak of the yoga of knowledge (*jnana*), devotion (*bhakti*), and action *karma*). Modern European history has unfolded from a period of rationalism to romanticism to pragmatism. Talent, grounded in human personality, is to be classified according to the triune distinction in human personality.

Discernment is needed to classify talent appropriately. Faulty classification is both burdensome and oppressive. All philosophers are not the same. Within the field of philosophy there are different areas, functions, and styles. Teaching philosophy is not doing philosophy. Scholastic system-building is not critiquing foundation. Intuitional approaches are not analytical approaches. Plato is not Aristotle; Kant is not Hegel; Descartes is not Derrida, in epistemological orientation. Yet all might agree on the need and desire to engage with basic questions using reason. An athlete who excels in action may do so because of "a fire in his belly." And his talent is not to achieve excellence in act merely, but to exhort others to excellence, knowing that fire which motivates from deep within.

6. Talent is developed through the effort of others as well as through one's own effort.

Talent does not originate by human will but is developed by human will. More often than not, talent is hardly developed due to lack of human will. Parents and teachers, given the limits of circumstances and worldview, discern and develop talent in its early stages. Personal desire and effort complete its development. The accumulated cultural achievement, both material and intellectual, is the base from which one begins development. Poverty, in both senses, hinders development of talent. All families and cultures are not equally endowed, and some worldviews are inimical to development. For what a person achieves, there is a debt owed to one's forebears, and through them, to all mankind. But personal effort is essential in order to go farther than current levels of cultural achievement, and to add to it. And society in turn owes a debt to that person.

7. Talent is developed fully only in the vision of the good.

In a society well endowed with opportunities for development through education, a person may neglect those opportunities or not use them fully to develop one's talent. Persons with the highest education in the highest offices may fail to come to a knowledge of the good, and therefore talent, which is an ability to achieve some aspect of the good, fails to be exercised toward the good, and so comes short of its fullest development and achievement. Pressing challenges to achieving the good are ignored or avoided because the goal of the good is not in view. Without belief that basic things are clear, reason will not be exercised to show this clarity. Without insight, confidence, and compassion, a researcher will not persevere to achieve a medical breakthrough. Faith as understanding and insight, hope as confidence that the problems can be solved, and love as compassion for those who suffer, are virtues necessary to achieve the good and to find the means to it.

8. Talent is irrepressible. When it is fully developed, it forms its function.

It finds ways to come to expression in service to others. It not only survives; it cuts new channels; it devises new ways to express itself and it overcomes. The development of talent is the expression of dominion, the achievement of mastery. It is accomplished not in an abstract, theoretical manner, but in the context of love, that is, in seeking the good for others.

MORAL LAW 8

One is to develop one's talent in pursuit of the good in service to others. Failure to do so is to take from others what is of value that belongs to them. Value is a function of supply and demand. Supply is a function of talent. Talent is an ability to achieve some aspect of the good. Talent is given to each for all. Talent is not of oneself, by oneself, or for oneself. It is for others. There is therefore a moral obligation to serve others through the use of one's talent. As one has received from the commonwealth of mankind, so one is to contribute to and increase this commonwealth. The one who receives and does not give is one who only takes from others, and never offers anything in return to others. How inhuman a person would be who never had received from this commonwealth is hard to imagine. There is an obligation therefore, not only not to harm or to destroy the wealth of others, public and private, but to contribute to it according to one's capacity, that is, one's talent.

APPLICATIONS OF MORAL LAW 8

1. Development of one's talent is opposed to the neglect of one's talent through sloth or greed or pride.

There are common obligations and necessities of life which require attention, sometimes at the expense of developing one's talent. Obligations to provide for one's necessities as well as obligations to parents, and children, and to community in emergencies, are prior to focus on one's talent. These are not culpable sources of neglect. But there is often failure to be diligent in education, or to allow money and prestige to dictate choice of career, or to limit use of one's talent. In the name of cultural identity, and the equality of all cultures, one may resist the influence of advanced cultures which have benefited from the cultural history of mankind. In that case, cultural pride and fear and ignorance inhibit wholesale development of talent. A clear view of and desire for the good eliminates these barriers, and allows a discerning selection from what is and what is not in accord with the good, from the various cultures of mankind.

2. Use of talent for the good is opposed to the misuse of talent for what is not good.

Many have used philosophical abilities to advance worldviews which are not built upon what is clear. Medical abilities have been used to advance death as well as life. Thieves have used their cunning for crime rather than for crime prevention. Talent used for the good is a virtue; talent used for evil becomes a vice. Artistic talent has been used to flatter rather than to reveal our human condition, and has been used to pander to our baser instincts. Reporters and writers have served propaganda rather than truth and justice. Scientists and educators have not left their students more enlightened by failing to identify operating presuppositions. Valor has been used to brutalize rather than to protect human life. Evil may be done in ignorance, but ignorance, in light of clarity, is inexcusable. One need not accuse for ignorance, but neither should ignorance be excused. Culpable ignorance, by grace, can be forgiven.

3. The origin of talent is opposed to absolute ownership by man.

God, as the Creator of all, owns all absolutely. Man is steward, having received talent which is grounded in the uniqueness of one's being. Through the work of dominion, which is historically cumulative, talent is exercised to increase the supply of that which has lasting value. The origin and social development of talent is opposed to capitalism. Capitalism affirms that man individually owns absolutely, that man is not a debtor to the common good which made the development of talent possible. The origin and individual development of talent is opposed to communism. Communism affirms that man collectively owns absolutely, that it does not require individual effort to develop one's talent, that man is entirely a product of his social-economic environment. Capitalism and communism are antinomies. They share a common assumption that man owns absolutely. Both agree that the creator of value is the owner of value. They differ as to what or who the creator or the determiner is.

For communist theory, as an outworking of naturalism and environmental determinism, human consciousness is wholly determined by the process of dialectical materialism, operating through social-economic forces in history. It would follow from this that the historical collective is the creator of value and therefore the state, as the embodiment of the collective, owns and distributes as it wills what is of value. There is no debt proportionate to effort owed to the individual, beyond need. The principle "from each according to his ability; to each according to his need" does not factor in individual effort or lack of it: "If a man does not work, then he does not eat" and "Each man is rewarded according to his own work." The individual is merely a subordinate (and dispensable) part of the collective whole. Here, the whole endures when the individual ceases to be. Here, there is no personal, individual immortality, responsible for and rewarded by the good.

Capitalism does not notice sufficiently the nature, origin, and social development of talent. It notices the individual and the individual's effort in developing talent, by which value is created. It notices supply and demand in a phenomenological way, without attempting to give an ontological account of the origin of man's being and talent. It takes the individual for granted and explains the whole as an aggregate of individuals, which is non-existent without the individual. As each individual pursues self-interest, understood in acquiring pleasure and avoiding pain as the good, the process is guided by an invisible hand as it were, to the benefit of others. In capitalist theory, there is no sense of debt or need for a sense of debt beyond that which is explicitly contracted. Development of one's talent in pursuit of the good, in service to others, is not obligatory. Here, there is no limit to the accumulation of wealth, except what the free market allows, and an informal expectation of charity from a sense of *noblesse oblige*.

The attempt to mitigate the excess inherent in going to the right or to the left by a synthesis of the two (as in socialism) fails to deal with assumptions generating the antinomy. In socialism, man individually owns some things absolutely, as private property, and man collectively owns some things absolutely, namely the public means of production. Indiscriminate labor, not talent, is thought to be a source of value. In socialism, man (individually or collectively), not God, is absolute owner. Acquiring pleasure and avoiding pain is seen as the good, not the effect of possessing what we believe is the good. Stewardship, as the alternative, cannot be understood and put into practice without understanding value in relation to the good, and the origin and development of talent in relation to supply.

4. Talent, as the source of supply, is opposed to social policies which are based on finite supply.

Supply is the function of talent. Population policies based on food supply must reckon that food supply can and has changed in the development of dominion. Population can and should be limited by the willingness to exercise dominion, actual and at least near-term potential. It should reckon also that social pressure and suffering can and have been stimuli to greater dominion through the development of talent. Emphasis is to be placed on the development of talent in the pursuit of the good, not merely technological advance apart from the good. What is to be sought is moral rule, not merely natural rule. There is presently a finite supply of energy from fossil fuel. But there are other sources, some of which are renewable and practically unlimited, awaiting development through the exercise of talent. Talent can also limit demand through greater efficiency in use of resources and in lessening the demand for those resources. To permit burial of the inventions of talent and the buying of patents to be used in ways that serve special interests, rather than public interest, should be disallowed by public policy, or at least made a matter of public information and decision making.

5. The need for effort in developing one's talent is opposed to economic policies and social practices which create disincentives to effort.

Incentives are not only financial or primarily financial. But money, as a medium of exchange, can serve the end of personal growth and enrichment. Economic policies which redistribute wealth apart from effort and responsibility by various taxation programs, or which debase currency by inflation, undercut some incentives which sustain hard work. Social instability through war, crime, and corruption, ordinarily hinder development of talent. Lack of a free market hinders exchange and allows unfair competition by monopolies or subsidies which are undue burdens. Envy and resentment toward those who achieve above others are likewise dampeners on effort. To create a culture and climate favorable toward effort, a worldview and a set of social practices are required. Cultures vary significantly in supporting and achieving a work ethic favorable to personal and social progress. There is a culture of poverty which cannot be removed by external financial aid, which fails to address the lack of incentive to effort.

6. Talent, as an ability to achieve some aspect of the good, is opposed to wasteful spending of resources which do not advance the good.

There is a very close connection between the view of the good and how we spend our money, time, and energy. Consumerism occurs in inverse ratio to seeking the good. The less of the good we have, the more consumer items we desire. Consumerism encourages self-indulgence and the loss of self-discipline, which is necessary for the development of talent. If we are unleisurely in order to be leisurely, this leisure is the occasion of contemplation and reflection, which is the basis of culture.[1] This leisure is not the indolence of a leisured class, or an escape from the work of the bourgeoisie, nor withdrawal from the active life to a contemplative life. Rather it is a reading of the divine revelation in all that comes to pass. Frugality here is being disciplined for the good; it is not the parsimoniousness of self-centeredness. Where grace is lavished in wisdom, it serves the good without waste.

7. Talent used in service to others is opposed to the unlimited accumulation of wealth by what indebts others.

There are inherent limits on ownership and on being indebted to another. A person is not property to be bought and sold. Property is owned by persons. A person cannot cease to be a person. Therefore, a person cannot be owned by another as property in perpetuity. Persons cannot increase their wealth by enslaving others as property, that is, indebting others in perpetuity. Every person stands in need of some property as a means of livelihood, which can be passed down to succeeding generations as one's patrimony. One's patrimony may not be permanently alienated by another in order to increase wealth.[2] One may get legally, but one may not be entitled to morally, what a person's present bargaining power permits. To press one's present advantage in contracting with the disadvantaged constitutes oppression—taking advantage of another. Prices and wages reflect a present aggregate view of the good, in which extremes balance each other without correcting each other. Artificial blocks to correction may be legally removed, but sometimes only catastrophic changes bring the needed correction when legal correction fails. The more the good is embraced by all, the more prices and wages will reflect true value, and the more talent in each will be developed and be recognized and rewarded by all.

---

1. Josef Pieper, Alexander Dru, and T.S. Eliot, *Leisure: The Basis of Culture* (Indianapolis, IN: Liberty Fund, 1999).

2. In Mosaic Law, the land as the source of wealth was, like talent, given by God, in this case to each family, as an original patrimony. It could not be sold, and, if indebted or rented, must be restored to the original family line that owned it, at the end of every fifty-year period. All debts were to be cancelled in the fiftieth year of Jubilee. There was thus, in biblical law, a built-in limitation on the accumulation of wealth by what indebts others (see *Leviticus 25*).

CONSEQUENCES OF MORAL LAW 8

The neglect or abuse of talent increases the poverty of life for all. The good as comprehensive must be corporate, cumulative, and communal. It is the work of all human beings throughout history. The distribution of mankind's cultural achievement varies greatly in time and place in groups and in individuals. It varies also in kind, in the difference between natural goods and the moral good. Contribution to the increase in knowledge cannot be made without the benefit of past accomplishments of others. The enjoyment of these benefits cannot be experienced beyond the degree of one's understanding. And lasting enjoyment can be experienced only in relation to increasing understanding of what is ultimate, that is, of the infinite and the eternal.

One may be highly educated and wealthy, yet poor in possessing understanding of basic things. Without contributing to the good (assuming the opportunity), one cannot enjoy the good. If one is not pursuing the good, one is pursuing something else in the place of the good, a replacement of the good, and therefore takes away from the good for oneself and for others. This setback does not have to be a permanent loss for others. It is possible that while some increase in the experience of the good in their lives, others increase in the experience of emptiness in their lives. Emptiness is ultimate poverty.

The use of talent for the good, conversely, increases the richness of life for all. Richness is proportional to fullness understood in its unity. This richness is fulfilling and inexhaustible and transformative. The more it is sought and shared, the more it increases in each person and for all persons. This richness is not separable from persons, but is experienced in and through all persons who seek the good.

Chapter 18

MORAL LAW 9:
TRUTH AND JUSTICE

ORIGIN IN HUMAN NATURE

THERE IS A MORAL LAW CONCERNING JUSTICE. Justice has to do with our relationship to other human beings generally. It is grounded in our conception of our being. We conceive ourselves to be equal as humans. We are born equal in humanity. Early in life, and quite spontaneously, the cry for justice arises: "It is not fair; he got more than me." In justice, equals are to be treated equally. Equality is not a denial of differences in what distinguishes us as human beings; rather it is an affirmation of what is common to all human beings. Differences are to be treated relevantly, not arbitrarily. Persons of the same age, or the same citizenship, all other things being equal, are to be treated in the same way. Even when a theory of human origin would advocate the superiority of some over others (vs. all men are created equal), the principle that equals are to be treated equally still stands. Justice is an ineradicable notion in all human beings requiring equal treatment of equals.

ON THE NATURE OF TRUTH AND JUSTICE

1. Ultimate justice is ontological.

Justice has an ontological aspect as well as a social aspect. Where consequences are inherent to an act, justice is ontological, that is, in the being of things. To deny one's nature is inherently self-destructive.

Denial of one's reason has the inherent consequence of meaninglessness. While socially-imposed consequences may be avoided, ontological justice is inescapable, unless there is reason to believe divine mercy can bring redemption.

2. Social justice is first distributive, then contractual, and then retributive.

By what means can we speak of a fair distribution of the necessities of life within a nation? How are earth's resources distributed among nations? How are the times and boundaries of nations set? Some have suggested by the spoils of war. But the strength and wealth of a nation are a function of its cultural values and worldview. If that is the case, ontological justice penetrates to determine aspects of social justice, as far as national boundaries and bounty are concerned. And ontological justice is beyond the sphere of human administration. When human justice fails or reaches its limits, ontological justice still operates. It is inviolable even when it may be questioned. A just nation will secure the distribution of the necessities of life to all its citizens, from generation to generation (consider debt limitation and Jubilee redistribution in ancient Hebrew law).

Contractual justice is maintained when human beings keep their agreements or contracts, whether in business, or in marriage, or between generations—whether these agreements are explicit or implicit. Agreements are entered into willingly and not under duress or deception. Employees may limit their duress by collective bargaining if it does not limit the freedom of any by intimidation. Distributive justice maintains a degree of social equality, thereby setting conditions for contractual agreements. The courts are to uphold contractual justice by imposing sanctions appropriate to the injustice done.

Retributive justice maintains equality by correcting harm done apart from distribution and contract. Payment is proportionate to the harm done. It is the principle of *lex talionis*—an eye for an eye. When applied to murder, it is life for life. Arguments against capital punishment must first show the invalidity of the principle of retributive justice (see *Moral Law 6, Application 6*). More often than not, utilitarian considerations are substituted for deontological ones. Or mercy is made to override justice, without the satisfaction of justice.

Retribution as a form of justice seeks to maintain the principle that equals are to be treated equally.

3. Full social justice is both preventative and corrective.

In a court of law where correction for injustice is sought, the means by which correction is sought is through knowledge of the truth. Witnesses are called who must swear to tell the truth, the whole truth, and nothing but the truth. The process of hearing is orderly, protected by sanctions for contempt of court and perjury. But the courts only correct injustice; they do not prevent the injustice which they seek to correct.

4. Truth is necessary and sufficient to correct injustice in court.

The assumption of the process in the courts is that truth is necessary and sufficient for correcting injustice. It assumes also that the truth can be known by a deliberate process, which allows for cross-examination and submission of evidence, for the elimination of prejudicial persons on juries, and for recusal of judges. The principle of justice is clear. When all the relevant facts are known, when all things hidden are brought to light, when all obfuscation is removed, the application becomes clear also. The scales of justice are balanced, in the name of equality. Lady Justice, sword in hand, is impartial, blindfolded to irrelevant differences. The sight of justice being done by the power of truth is awe-inspiring; it is worthy of respect.

5. Truth is necessary and sufficient to prevent injustice in a culture.

While correcting injustice in a court of law is an ideal, correcting and preventing injustice in a culture is a higher ideal. As truth is necessary and sufficient to correct injustice, so it is necessary and sufficient to prevent injustice. But the truth which prevents injustice goes to a deeper level. Courts deal with truth that is legally relevant. Preventing injustice must deal with truth that is morally relevant. It deals with truths by which we define our status and dignity, and hence our equality as persons. It deals with the assumptions of a worldview. It therefore must deal with the whole truth in a philosophical sense.

6. Full justice requires knowing and speaking the whole truth.

Knowing goes beyond merely believing. Speaking goes beyond merely declaring. It must communicate, overcoming obstacles to hearing. The whole truth must address worldviews and their assumptions in which injustice of inequality has been embedded for centuries, even for millennia. Men and women are the same in some respects and different in other respects. Neither sameness nor difference can be ignored or denied in the name of justice and equality. The quick easy fix of equality based on ethical relativism, grounded in academic skepticism, is not the whole truth.

7. Knowing and speaking the whole truth to prevent injustice is a function of the whole of one's life.

Everyone is called to be a faithful witness to the whole truth. To know the whole truth requires us to rationally assess the challenges of one worldview by another, beginning with what is more basic. It requires us to understand how worldviews come to expression in cultural practices. It requires us to be aware of injustices which may be justified within a worldview and to challenge that justification. Because certain practices have been upheld by many for long periods of time, so as to seem according to the nature of things, they are not thereby justified. Nor is the shout of every rabble-rousing ruffian against tradition worthy of consideration. Going to the right or to the left is not an option. Long-term ongoing care is necessary to know and to speak the whole truth.

MORAL LAW 9

No one is to do injustice directly or indirectly. Everyone is called to do justice. Everyone is called to be a faithful witness to the whole truth. Silence in the face of injustice is to condone injustice. Not to know the truth is tacitly to participate in a lie. And not to speak the truth is to speak a lie by silent assertion.[1] This is the big lie of the silent majority, which prevails in cultures for ages and which makes injustice possible. To avoid lying in small personal matters while going along with the big lie, approved by the many, out of fear of social disapproval (political correctness), is to strain at gnats while swallowing camels.

APPLICATIONS OF MORAL LAW 9

1. Truth and justice are opposed to ignorance as excusable.

It is easy to excuse oneself by saying "I did not know" or "I could not know." What is to be known is the falsehood of worldviews used to justify oppression. It could be naturalism and evolution used at any or every step to support survival of the fittest and superior race of Nazism, that led to the Holocaust. It could be naturalism and dialectical materialism used at any or every step to support Soviet Communism, that led to the Gulag. It could be spiritual monism and cyclicalism and reincarnation used at any or every step to support castism, that led to outcastes. It could be the lack of reason in fideism and this-worldly literalism used at any or every step in support of triumphalism (state-supported religion), that led to inquisitions and jihads. In any and every such case, ignorance is inexcusable, for if we seek, we can know what is clear and remove oppression justified by false worldviews.

2. Truth and justice are opposed to fideism.

Fideism is not knowledge. Fideism declares to be true what it believes to be true, without offering rational justification for its truth. It thereby nullifies its witness to the truth, for why should unsupported testimony require the assent of any rational being? Zeal is no substitute for knowledge. Declaration is no substitute for discussion and taking thoughts captive. Conflicts continue and injustice continues in slavery of many kinds, and in infanticide and genocide supported by propaganda and ideology, based on false worldviews. If truth is neces-

---

1. Mark Twain, "My First Lie and How I Got Out of It," in *The Man Who Corrupted Hadleyburg and Other Stories and Essays* (New York: Harper and Brothers, 1902), 167.

sary and sufficient for justice, the first call is to know the truth and to make the truth known. Fideism does not do this.

3. Truth and justice are opposed to privacy in public affairs.

They are opposed to privacy in decisions affecting public affairs. It is opposed to privacy for special interests to influence public decisions. Bribery and resultant corruption are recurrent in history and in some places, at times, have become endemic. Whole nations can languish in their grip. Businesses hide their unjust activity for the sake of gain and to avoid lawsuits. The right of citizens and consumers to know requires laws in support of full disclosure and access to information regarding decision-making in public affairs. Avoidance of these laws and concealment of information is evidence of the sufficiency of truth for justice. In the perennial temptation to unjust gain by the works of darkness, the fear and avoidance of public disclosure can only be overcome by a greater fear of the unavoidability of ontological justice: What shall it profit a man if he should gain the whole world and lose his own soul?

4. Truth and justice are opposed to restrictions on freedom of speech.

They are opposed to closed societies, restricted public forums, and prohibited books. A closed society does not allow the right to freedom of speech. It does not allow challenge to the prevailing power structure. To rule by might is not to rule by insight. Illegitimate authority defends itself by creating laws which prevent open discussion, a practice enforced in many countries today. What is not politically correct today is not supported through use of "soft power" exercised in hiring or in the use of air time. Diversity today does not include diversity of ideas. Books that challenge current assumptions are not banned or burned in this enlightened age; they are simply not published. Any authority, not grounded in reason, whether secular or religious, will succumb to the temptation to use power and force to restrict freedom of speech, in order to avoid the challenges of reason. It quickly becomes Leviathan, the use of force in the place of reason, the expression of the Beast.

5. Truth and justice are opposed to the abuse of the freedom of speech.

The right of the freedom of speech is the right of rational discourse. It is opposed to slander, contempt, harassment, and incitement to violence, as expressions of rational discourse. Speech, as expression of thought, is by its nature rational and is subject to rational constraints. Ideas oppose ideas. Slander and harassment oppose persons, not ideas. They oppose the messenger, not the message. They show lack of counter-argument, or despair about knowing or about the power of truth. It is a restriction on the freedom of speech, rather than an exercise of free speech, to slander and harass others. Contempt and violence extend slander and harassment. Striking another literally or symbolically through contempt or rage is not rational discourse and hinders the freedom of others. Self-immolation by starvation, or by fire or bomb, is a desperate act of suicide, not martyrdom. It despairs over the power of rational discourse. Non-violent demonstrations can call attention to acts, but discourse can get to the assumptions, and it is assumptions that must be addressed. Therefore, discourse must be protected, especially against its subversion by pseudo-discourse.

6. Truth and justice are opposed to false advertising.

False advertising hides knowable cost. This is in contrast to hidden costs not yet knowable. It is opposed to profit-making by withholding information regarding possible harm from the product sold or activity engaged in. There is a moral obligation not to cause harm to others, more so knowingly, still more so to minors, and yet more so for profit. There are varying conditions affecting responsibility for knowing the truth and for making the truth known. It is not simply "buyer beware." All protection is not simply paternalism. Warnings are placed on labels for products sold, often as a protection against expensive lawsuits. Lawsuits are difficult, and while they may correct an injustice in part, knowing the truth can prevent harm. Those who take advantage of the weakness of others, hiding the cost of harm, and those who harm the environment at cost to others, are to be brought into the light. Only by hiding can some things be done and only by exposure can these things be undone.

7. Truth and justice are opposed to public exposure of what is private.

Knowing and speaking the truth does not give license to the invasion of privacy. Some things are private and what is private is situational, dependent on factors of relevance. There is both a right to privacy as well as an obligation to privacy. Governments, business, and media may not seek out information on the private affairs of private citizens. Nor may confidence with lawyers, clergy, or doctors be revealed, if no criminal activity is involved. Nor should confidence with friends or family be betrayed, either casually, or for profit, or out of spite. Nor should a person make a public spectacle of oneself out of sheer inanity. The public has a right to be spared exposure to physical and spiritual nakedness and indecency. The corollary of saying what is public should be made public is that what is private should be kept private.

CONSEQUENCES OF MORAL LAW 9

An unfaithful witness shares in injustice and its consequences. As human beings, we are obligated to fellow human beings both to not do injustice and to prevent injustice from being done. If we can prevent murder or stealing, even by calling privately for help, we ought to do so. And if we treat equals equally and desire justice for ourselves, then our obligation extends to all. To passively allow injustice when we can do something about it is to participate in injustice. Failure to know and to speak the truth is to be an unfaithful witness to the truth, which prevents injustice. Falsehood, not opposed in its early stages, gathers strength as it grows and becomes more and more oppressive, until it can be stopped only by war. All participants in war suffer directly or indirectly, including the relatively innocent civilian population who failed to know and to speak the truth. The earlier falsehood is removed, the greater is the injustice prevented.

A faithful witness brings about justice by knowing and speaking the truth. A just society is no small ideal. Peace accompanies justice, and in peace human lives can flourish. Tolerance based on relativism, grounded in skepticism, compromises justice. Skepticism denies that some things are clear and thus compromises truth. It redefines justice by compromising the equal status of all human beings. By maintaining the clarity of basic things, the responsibility for knowing what is clear is upheld, and with that responsibility, an accountability of each to all, which prevents injustice and brings about justice.

Chapter 19

———

MORAL LAW 10:
SUFFERING AND THE GOOD

ORIGIN IN HUMAN NATURE

WE ARE BORN CHANGEABLE. We can change in what we think about good and evil. Suffering arises when we think we cannot possess what we believe to be the good. Since the good by nature is inalienable, being intrinsic to human nature, it cannot by external circumstances be hindered or removed short of ending one's rational existence, at which point moral accountability ceases. To believe that one cannot possess the good is to not only not understand, but to misunderstand good and evil.

ON THE NATURE OF SUFFERING AND THE GOOD

1. The good is not virtue.

The good is not virtue, whether natural, moral, or instrumental (see earlier discussion in *Moral Law 1*). Virtue is the means to the good; it is not the good. A good will (for Kant) is morally good; it cannot however be considered the good. Life and health are both means to the good and conditions for receiving the good. The good is both by and for persons, but persons are not the good. Intellectual playfulness (wit and humor) and contemplation are activities by which one possesses the good and intrinsic to that possession (as form is to content), yet are to be distinguished from the good. Wit and piety are good as virtues, but neither wit nor piety is the good. Wit without piety and piety without knowledge can harm. What gives content and unity to the virtues is the good.

2. The good is not happiness.

Happiness is the effect of possessing what we believe is the good. Lasting happiness is the effect of possessing what truly is the good. It is a sign, not the reality; it is the effect, not the cause. Even if it is intrinsic to the good, it is not identical to or to be identified with the good. The good is joyful and is to be enjoyed, but enjoyment is not the good, nor can it be sought directly as the good. Friendship is the effect of two persons knowing each other to be committed to the good, allowing a sharing of life in the deepest sense. Friends seek the good together and for each other; they do not seek the other as the good. Peace is the effect of the virtue of justice, seeking the freedom of all to pursue the good. No effect of virtue or of the good is identical with the good. Hedonic ethics and virtue ethics in their several forms are not teleological ethics.

3. Suffering is of two kinds, intrinsic and extrinsic.

Suffering is of two kinds, intrinsic and extrinsic, resulting from evil of two kinds, moral and natural. We wish to distinguish kinds as well as degrees of suffering, and to make the connection between suffering and evil generally, as well as between the two kinds of sufferings and the two kinds of evil.

If there were no evil, there would be no suffering. To explain suffering, one has to understand evil, both moral and natural. As the good cannot be conceived apart from human nature, likewise evil—moral evil—cannot be conceived apart from the good, and therefore apart from human nature. Natural evil, on the other hand, is not moral evil. Since it is not inherently connected to human nature, it easily appears to be random and gratuitous, serving no purpose. Since it is not inherent in human action or in nature (natural evil is not merely natural), its origin must be accounted for in considering what purpose, if any, it serves.

4. Moral evil is, at root, an act contrary to our nature as rational beings.

Since the good for a being is according to the nature of that being, evil is what is contrary to that nature. Evil for man, as a rational being, is to neglect, avoid, resist, or deny reason in the face of what is clear about basic things—about God and man and good and evil. What begins as neglect, in not seeking, grows and develops until it reaches the denial of reason in the course of epistemological and moral self-justification. Since it is clear to reason that only some (God) is eternal, God as Creator of human nature determines good and evil for man. Evil for man consists therefore in human autonomy, which is to put oneself in the place of God to determine good and evil (see *Moral Law 1*). The good is no longer the knowledge of God, which is avoided and resisted in order to preserve one's autonomy, but whatever the self in its non-rational or anti-rational autonomy arbitrarily determines to be good or evil.

5. There are consequences inherent in going against the needs and requirements of our rational nature.

Without reason, there is a lack of understanding and a misunderstanding of the nature of things, and therefore of their meaning. Without reason, there is no meaning. Meaninglessness is inherent in neglecting, avoiding, resisting, or denying one's reason. Meaninglessness is experienced as emptiness of life. The more conscious and consistent autonomy is held, the more arbitrary all distinctions and choices become, and the more empty life becomes. The need for meaning remains, but meaningless activity cannot satisfy this need. The excess one goes to in order to fill the emptiness gives no satisfaction, but rather brings boredom. A person persisting in autonomy avoids acknowledging that meaninglessness and boredom are self-inflicted. The meaninglessness of life is explained away (rationalized) by a futile hope, or by blaming circumstances or others. The spiritual torment of meaninglessness, boredom, and guilt, are the inherent consequences of moral evil, as the denial of one's nature as a rational being. The demands of one's rational nature continue to be felt in all the conditions of spiritual death. This is the fundamental inherent connection between moral evil and human suffering.

6. Natural evil is another source of human suffering.

Natural evil consists of circumstances producing toil and strife, and old age, sickness, and (physical) death. Natural evil (discussed earlier under the problem of evil, Chapter 8) is not original in the creation of the world by an all good and all powerful Creator. Nor is natural evil inherent in moral evil. Therefore, natural evil is imposed. It is imposed by God, not arbitrarily, but after moral evil and because of moral evil. The just consequence of moral evil is by creation inherent to moral evil and is not imposed. Therefore, natural evil is not punishment. The necessary and just consequence of moral evil is spiritual death, not physical death. Physical death is a sign of spiritual death. It is imposed by God as a call back from moral evil and spiritual death. It is a call to stop and think.

7. The call back from moral evil is redemptive, not punitive.

The call back from moral evil ends with physical death. Death is the last, enduring, universal, and final call back from moral evil, encompassing every degree of moral evil. It calls back from not seeking, from self-deception, and self-justification. While natural evil is universal in death, it varies in intensity throughout history in the forms of famine, war, and plague. And it may vary from culture to culture and individual to individual. Natural evil serves multiple purposes in relation to moral evil. It serves to restrain (outward expressions of) moral evil, to recall from moral evil (not seeking and not understanding), and to remove moral evil remaining in those who have turned back from moral evil, in order to bring them to a fuller measure of the good.

MORAL LAW 10

We are not to be discontented in pursuing our own view of the good, but to be content in pursuing what truly is the good. Discontent is the beginning of suffering due to a faulty conception of the good. Neither happiness nor virtue is the good. Contentment is the evidence that one has an established understanding of the good. What is called for is a sustained effort to know the good and the means to the good, given the epistemological and existential implications of moral and natural evil.

APPLICATIONS OF MORAL LAW 10

1. Understanding the good is opposed to envy of others in their circumstances, abilities, and honors.

Envy is discontent with one's lot compared to others. It covets what belongs to others as if that were the good, or necessary for the good. Those not honored envy those who are honored. Those who don't have envy those who have. Not having is viewed as a matter of self-worth and breeds resentment and more. Those who have can as easily pride themselves as being better than others. But the good is inalienable, intrinsic to one's choice, and cannot be taken from or given to a person. Since the good is by and for persons, and the worth of persons is different in kind from the good, ontological not ethical, a proper view of the good will disallow both envy and pride, both vain-striving and complacency.

2. Understanding the good is opposed to stoicism, as a hardening of oneself, to avoid suffering seen as useless.

This stoicism is of a particular kind, in a specific context. It is not the enduring of hardship in pursuit of the good, with hope. The hardening of oneself to avoid suffering, or the grim bearing of suffering as a duty without hope, or with resignation, or with indifference, is the failure to see the moral purpose of natural evil.

3. Understanding the good is opposed to resentment, complaint, and bitterness, under circumstances which are seen as a hindrance to the good.

Natural evil in all forms of toil and strife, and old age, sickness, and death, are often seen as a waste of time and energy. They are not seen as a sign of spiritual death and as a call back from moral evil, or as a preparation for dealing with hard spiritual realities. Physical war is an expression of and an analogy for spiritual war. Digging up physical roots is an analogy for digging up spiritual roots. War, famine, and disease lose meaning if they reveal nothing. Nothingness (nihilism) as mere waste naturally engenders bitterness.

4. Understanding the good is opposed to discouragement in hardships in contrast to patience and perseverance in hope.

The virtue of courage, by which hardships are endured, depends on hope of progress toward the good, which hope depends on understanding the good and the means to it. That evil is deceitful, desperate, and deadly, that it is permitted to work itself out fully in every aspect of human life in world history, that the conflict is age-long and agonizing, is not the common expectation. Nor is it commonly understood that evil is made to serve the good, and that the good expressed through the mastery of dominion overcomes evil. So, the loss of heart results from a deficient view of good and evil.

5. Understanding the good is opposed to the self-indulgence of hedonism to escape the emptiness of one's life, or to console oneself in pain.

Happiness or pleasure is not the good; lasting happiness is the effect of possessing what truly is the good. The good is comprehensive, inexhaustible, ultimate, and transformative, and therefore satisfies unendingly (see *Moral Law 4*). What is finite by itself cannot satisfy. Even in excess it does not satisfy, but leaves the seeker empty and bored at best, and more so in pain. An effect of possessing the good cannot be sought in place of the good, nor can it be a satisfying substitute for the good.

6. Understanding the good is opposed to cynicism, which sees the reality of (some aspects of) evil without seeing the reality of grace.

The cynic believes he is being true to reality by not blinking at evil. By grace, the sun rises and rain falls. Nations come and go, but by grace mankind goes on. The order of creation is upheld through Providence by common grace. And natural evil restrains, recalls from, and removes moral evil by redemptive grace. Mankind has been through its worst. It has been upheld and good has progressed over evil. The apocalypse brings not the annihilation of all life, but comes with the removal of all evil. Evil by nature is self-destructive. Left to itself, it collapses on itself. What is meaningful cannot be shaken. What is meaningless self-destructs. The fundamental reality in creation is infinite goodness, which makes evil to serve the good. Where evil abounds, grace more abounds.

7. Understanding the good is opposed to fatalism, a resignation to natural evil seen as merely natural, not imposed as a call back.

Serenity is sought in the acceptance of the inevitable. But what is thought of as inevitable depends on one's worldview. Destiny has been located in biology, in geography, in sociology, in culture, in the stars, or in divine decrees. Fate has been used to excuse responsibility for seeking change. But natural evil, as a call to stop and think, calls for change, at least in taking responsibility for one's own thinking. And a change in thinking is the basis of all other change. To take responsibility for not seeing what is clear about God and man and good and evil makes all the difference in the world.

CONSEQUENCES OF MORAL LAW 10

To those who do not seek the good, suffering from natural evil is avoided as meaningless. The lack of seeking and understanding spirals downward into ever-increasing meaninglessness. Everything becomes wasted, even one's call back through suffering. The utter dread is that this spiral does not end, that there is no worst.

To those who seek the good, all things are seen as working together for the good. Suffering serves a redemptive purpose, realized through ever-increasing understanding. Nothing fails this purpose in those who seek understanding. Evil deepens the revelation of divine justice and goodness and, by seeking, what is revealed is understood. This understanding is the good, which transforms and unifies and beatifies.

CONCLUSION

I F THE DERIVATIONS AND APPLICATIONS of the moral law have been shown, then there is a moral law which is *clear* since it is grounded in human nature, *comprehensive* since it governs all choices directed to the good, and *critical* since its consequence is a matter of life or death. The moral law is *universal*—for all human beings, and *perpetual*—for all time. It is also *total*—for all areas, and for all aspects of life (the inward thought as well as the outward act). The moral law is *teleological*—aimed at the good, which is the source of unity within the law itself, as well as the source of unity for all mankind. Since love seeks the good for another, the requirements of love and the moral law are one and the same.

If the moral law is clear, then some things are clear. The basic things are clear. The basic things about God and man and good and evil are clear to reason.

—

APPENDICES

—

PRESUPPOSITION OF PHILOSOPHICAL FOUNDATION:

The Principle of Clarity and Common Ground

THE FOLLOWING IS A BRIEF EXPLICATION and defense of the opening lines of *Philosophical Foundation*. The Principle of Clarity states: Some things are clear. The basic things are clear. The basic things about God and man and good and evil are clear to reason.

SOME THINGS ARE CLEAR

The opening words affirm that some things are clear. This affirms the Principle of Clarity as a necessary condition for all thought and discourse, and therefore as *common ground* for all that follows. Skepticism denies that some things are clear. By implication, skepticism affirms the contradictory that nothing is clear. A more formal statement of the proof that some things are clear is as follows:

Argument 1:

1. It is clear that contradictory statements cannot both be true and cannot both be false (at the same time and in the same respect).
2. The contradiction of "some things are clear" is "nothing is clear."
3. If nothing is clear, then no distinction is clear—in general, no logical distinction between *a* and *non-a* would be clear (*a* being a variable for any particular distinction, basic or non-basic).

If no distinction is clear, then:
  i. the basic distinction between *being* and *non-being* is not clear, and
  ii. the basic distinction between *true* and *false* is not clear, and
  iii. the basic distinction between *good* and *evil* is not clear.

4. If no logical distinction is clear, then no distinction is meaningful (*reductio ad absurdum*), and therefore no meaning is logically possible. (e.g., If there is no distinction between *true* and *false*, then *true* and *false* would lack meaning.)

5. If meaning is not possible, then thought and therefore talk are not possible (nihilism). To think or talk or act is to make distinctions and therefore is to affirm meaning. (If there is no concern for consistency, there is no possibility of dialogue and discussion ends.)

6. It is not the case that there is no meaning. Nihilism is not existentially possible—we cannot consistently live and give up thinking or talking (which is self-referentially absurd). Either we stop thinking and talking, or we are inconsistent and are hypocrites.

7. Therefore, the original "nothing is clear" is not possible and the contradiction "some things are clear" must be true.

Symbolically and more succinctly stated:
[abbreviations: C (some things are clear); M (there is meaning); N (nihilism—thought and talk are not possible)]

$\sim C \supset \sim M$ if nothing is clear, then meaning is not logically possible (from 3 & 4)

$\sim M \supset N$ if meaning is not possible, then thought and talk are not possible

$\therefore \sim C \supset N$ therefore, if nothing is clear, then thought and talk are not possible

$\sim N$ nihilism is not existentially possible—we cannot give up thought and talk

$\therefore C$ therefore, some things are clear

THE BASIC THINGS ARE CLEAR

Argument 2:

1. Thinking by nature is presuppositional: we think of the less basic in light of the more basic.

    i. At the level of concept, we think of the finite and temporal in light of the infinite and eternal. Our most basic beliefs are about our most basic concepts.

    ii. At the level of judgment, we think of truth in light of meaning, and meaning in light of reason. We must know what a statement means before we can say whether it is true or not. Reason as the laws of thought (identity, non-contradiction, and excluded middle) is the test for meaning.

    iii. At the level of experience, we think of (interpret) experience in light of basic belief. No experience is meaningful without interpretation—appearance is not reality.

    iv. At the level of argument, we think of conclusion in light of premises.

2. If the more basic is not clear, then the less basic cannot be clear, and therefore nothing is clear.

3. It is not the case that nothing is clear (some things are clear—from Argument 1 above).

4. Therefore, the basic things are clear.

Symbolically and more succinctly stated:
[abbreviations: BTC (basic things are clear); C (some things are clear)]

$\sim BTC \supset \sim C$ if basic things are not clear, then nothing is clear

$\sim \sim C$ it is not the case that nothing is clear (some things are clear)

$\therefore BTC$ therefore, basic things are clear

THE BASIC THINGS ABOUT GOD AND MAN AND GOOD AND EVIL ARE CLEAR TO REASON

This assertion has two parts: (a) the basic things are about God and man and good and evil; and (b) the basic things are clear to reason.

Argument 3a: the basic things are about God and man and good and evil

1. The basic things are about our most basic judgment.

2. Our most basic judgment is about our most basic concept (i.e., existence—either temporal or eternal). Eternal existence is more basic (ontologically and epistemologically) than temporal.

3. Therefore, our most basic judgment is about what is real/eternal (i.e., about God)

4. Therefore, the basic things are about God.

5. Since the basic things are clear (from Argument 2), it is clear what is eternal (i.e., whether or not God exists).

6. If some things are clear about God, then some things are clear about man (i.e., human nature).

7. If some things are clear about man, then good and evil are clear (based on human nature).

8. Therefore, the basic things are about God and man and good and evil.

Symbolically and more succinctly stated:
[abbreviations: BT (basic things); MBJ (most basic judgment); G (what is eternal/God); M (man/human nature); g · e (good and evil)]

BT is MBJ	basic things are about our most basic judgment
MBJ is G	our most basic judgment is about what is eternal/God
∴ BT is G	therefore, basic things are about God
G ⊃ M	if some things are clear about God, then some things are clear about man
M ⊃ g · e	if some things are clear about man, then good and evil are clear

∴ BT is G · M · g · e   therefore, basic things are about God and
                         man and good and evil

Argument 3b: the basic things are clear to reason
[abbreviations: R (reason); P (what makes thought possible); MB
(what is most basic)]

1. R is P   Reason, as the laws of thought, makes thought possible.
2. P is MB   What makes thought possible is most basic (in the
               order of thought).
3. ∴ R is MB   Therefore, reason is most basic (in the order of thought).
4. Therefore, since basic things are clear (from Argument 2), the basic
   things are clear to reason.

Therefore, the basic things about God and man (metaphysics) and
good and evil (ethics) are clear to reason (epistemology).

APPLICATION OF COMMON GROUND AND
THE PRINCIPLE OF CLARITY

1. Ground is that on which one stands, and what makes a particular
   activity possible.
2. *Common* ground (CG) is that on which all parties in a dialogue
   must stand, and what makes thought and dialogue concerning
   the basic questions of philosophy possible. Therefore, all dialogue
   must begin with CG, and made explicit (not merely assumed) in
   order to be secured.
3. CG grows at each step, in agreement, in dialogue. It is not to be
   abandoned by any party later in the dialogue. Dialogue should be
   suspended if CG is called into question. The condition for suspension should be made explicit to all who participate in the dialogue
   and is to be resolved before resuming dialogue. Therefore, all parties share responsibility to uphold and promote CG.
4. CG assumes and requires the Principle of Clarity (PC), that some
   things are clear—that knowledge concerning basic things is pos-

sible. The burden of proof to show what is clear is shared by all based on CG.

5. PC is opposed to skepticism and fideism at the basic level, both which assume that basic things are not clear. PC as CG excludes what is logically and existentially impossible.

———

A RESPONSE TO THE CRITICS OF CLARITY:

Common Ground Applied to Avoid Meaningless Disputes

THE NECESSITY FOR COMMON GROUND

COMMON GROUND IS THE SET of epistemologically necessary conditions for thought and discourse. To engage in discourse without Common Ground (CG) is to engage in meaningless disputes.

CG consists of the following:
1. *Reason* as the laws of thought (identity, non-contradiction, and excluded middle) is the test for meaning and is self-attesting.
2. *Integrity* is a commitment to reason as a concern for consistency.
3. *Rational Presuppositionalism* (RP) affirms the necessity to address the more basic before the less basic.
4. *The Principle of Clarity* (PC) affirms: some things are clear; the basic things are clear; the basic things concerning metaphysics (about God and man) and ethics (about good and evil) are clear to reason (epistemology).

For skeptics, to deny CG is to deny any possibility of knowledge, which is self-referentially absurd. For theists, to deny clarity is to deny inexcusability (of unbelief) and the need for redemptive/special revelation.

OBJECTIONS TO COMMON GROUND AND RESPONSES

The following objections deny Common Ground. A response is made to each objection.

1. *Objection: Being* can come from *non-being*. Since laws do not apply to *non-being*, no law *ontologically* prevents *being* coming from *non-being*.

   Response: If *being* can come from *non-being*, then there is *logically* no way to distinguish *being* from *non-being*. It is a meaningless distinction. Since *being* and *non-being* is the most basic distinction, then all other distinctions resting on this are meaningless. If all words are meaningless, then all thought and discourse end.

2. *Objection:* We cannot know *a is a*; we may have an incorrigible memory lapse (fallibilism). Yet the claim *a is a* is probably true.

   Response: If there is no rational basis for certainty (re: *a is a*), there is no rational basis for certainty about anything, including probability.

3. *Objection: a is a* is pragmatically true, not logically true.

   Response:
      i. Can the logical contradiction (*a is not a*) be possibly true in any sense? If it makes no sense, then it is necessarily false and its contradiction (*a is a*) is necessarily true, not just pragmatically true.
      ii. What is pragmatically true is about "what works for me," or "what I like." Expressions of feelings are non-cognitive (neither true nor false) and not subject to discussion.

4. *Objection:* Nothing (including reason) is self-attesting; therefore, nothing is certain.

   Response: Pure skepticism is self-referentially absurd (SRA): is it certain that nothing is certain? Or, can any degree of certainty (probability) be distinguished with certainty?

5. *Objection:* Fideism: reason is not self-attesting; only Scripture is self-attesting.

Response:

    i. Which, of many, is the self-attesting true Scripture?

    ii. Why is there need for any Scripture?

    iii. Which interpretation of Scripture is self-attesting?

    iv. Scripture/special revelation (SR) *requires* clear general revelation (cGR) and reason; and cGR *requires* SR.

    v. Any thought requires reason as the laws of thought.

    vi. Scripture is the Word of God *written.* (From SR) the Word of God is in all men *first* as light, that is, reason.[1]

    vii. Since reason is self-attesting, (from SR) it would be the Word of God as reason that is self-attesting.

6. *Objection:* Reason is not self-attesting; only God is. ("When God speaks, you know"—affirmed in existential theology and in simple piety).

Response:

    i. No experience is meaningful without interpretation; and every interpretation must be tested for meaning (by reason).

    ii. The experience of regeneration is not self-attesting; it may not be known by oneself if one has had the experience.

    iii. Many make the claim that "God spoke to me," which claims contradict each other.

    iv. Since reason applies to the being of God (God is not both eternal and not eternal, at the same time and in the same respect), God cannot contradict himself. Miracles do not contradict reason, which is uncreated, but transcend the laws of nature, which are created.

7. *Objection:* The simple pious cannot be expected to know these things.

---

1. *John 1:4.*

Response:

    i. All can know what is clear; all can know foundational (grammar level) truths; all can grow to maturity.

    ii. It is not a matter of learning, but of seeking. Left to oneself, no one (learned or unlearned) seeks God.

    iii. All suffer under the curse/natural evil (of toil and strife, and old age, sickness, and death); therefore, all are being called to seek.

8. *Objection:* Higher Consciousness ("HC") goes beyond reason.

   Response:

    i. God's being is rational (not both eternal and not eternal, same time/same respect); God's "HC" is not beyond his rational being.

    ii. If "HC" goes beyond the laws of thought, it makes no assertion (it isn't is; it isn't isn't; it isn't both; it isn't neither). "HC" moves to silence.

    iii. "HC" without reason cannot distinguish itself from lower consciousness or no consciousness.

    iv. Only reason by RP can achieve the higher consciousness of unity of diversity.

9. *Objection:* If you can get *a* from *non-a*, you can get *being* from *non-being*.

   Response:

    i. A particular form of being is not identical with all of being (being as such).

    ii. It is not chicken (*a*) from the egg (*non-a*), but *being* (both chicken and egg—both *a* and *non-a*) from *non-being*.

10. *Objection:* You can get *being* from *non-being*, in quantum physics or in creation *ex nihilo*.

   Response:

    i. Quantum foam is not particle physics, but (like energy) it is not *non-being*.

ii. God the Creator is Spirit, not matter, but Spirit is not non-being.

11. *Objection*: To every argument an equal argument can be opposed. Therefore, judgment is suspended and mental tranquility is achieved (Sextus Empiricus).

    Response:

    i. *Some is eternal* is not equal in rationality to *none is eternal* (that is, all came into being from non-being).

    ii. Because *being from non-being* is meaningless (necessarily false, false in every possible world), *some is eternal* is necessarily true, and maximally clear, and certain.

12. *Objection:* There are uncaused events (Epicurus—the atomic swerve/*clinamen* theory).

    Response:

    i. If an uncaused event could happen once, it could happen more than once, perhaps often or always.

    ii. There is no way empirically to distinguish a caused from an uncaused event.

    iii. If thoughts can be uncaused events, then uncaused thoughts making distinctions about cause become rationally meaningless.

    iv. Talk about uncaused events is therefore SRA.

    v. SRA's are non-starters—they end thought and discourse before they begin.

13. *Objection:* Reason cannot get you very far beyond *a is a*.

    Response:

    i. Reason is *first* the test for meaning. What violates a law of thought lacks meaning; a meaningless statement cannot be true, but is necessarily false (by *reductio ad absurdum*).

    ii. The contradiction of what is necessarily false *must* be true.

    iii. We can know by reason that there *must* be something eternal and that *only some* is eternal; we can know by reason that the good for a being is according to the nature of that being.

    iv. Therefore, the basic things about God and man and good and evil are clear to reason (PC).

    v. The Principle of Clarity has substantial content that can be extended by the Principle of Rational Presuppositionalism, both of which are affirmed in Common Ground.

14. *Objection:* If some things are clear, and knowledge is justified, true belief (in the strong sense), you need to give a philosophical proof that *a is a*.

Response:

    i. There are several levels of "clear": self-attesting, self-evident, self-referentially absurd, and clear to reason.

       1) Reason, as the laws of thought, is self-attesting; it cannot be questioned because, as the laws of thought, it makes questioning (one form of thought) possible. No attempt has ever been made or can be made to prove the laws of thought by using (assuming) the laws of thought.

       2) Only reason is self-attesting and is therefore most authoritative.

       3) It is self-evident that we think (use the laws of thought) and it is self-evident that there are laws of thought—reason in itself *is* the laws of thought. What is self-evident needs no proof because it is immediately evident and known without inference.

       4) It is clear that something exists (vs. nothing exists). To deny this is SRA (self-defeating vs. defeated by another).

       5) It is clear that the self exists (vs. *Advaita*) since the denial involves a contradiction and it is SRA.

       6) It is clear that there must be something eternal since the denial involves a contradiction (by *reductio* argument).

       7) It is clear that the material world is not eternal (assuming common ground that the material world exists and the

definition of the material world). This is based on what is more basic by RP—that there must be something eternal.

8) It is clear that natural evil (physical death) is not original. This is based on RP—that only some is eternal and analysis of infinite power and goodness (what God could, would, and must do, and therefore actually did).

    ii. Proof applies to some things that are clear (#5-8); it does not apply to other things that are clear (#1-4).

15. *Objection:* A practical (pragmatic) proof is not a philosophical proof. An SRA is a practical proof.

Response:

    i. An SRA, like an uncaused event, is both a practical and a logical objection. An uncaused event implies *being* from *non-being*, which renders the logical distinction between *being* and *non-being* (and all other distinctions) meaningless.

    ii. We can neither cease to think (practical) nor think what is meaningless (logical).

    iii. Denial of the light of reason (life) leaves us in the darkness of meaninglessness (death).

    iv. Thinking is the most basic activity of rational life; one cannot think what is unthinkable/meaningless; one cannot live death. The need to think remains; the light shines in the darkness. An SRA is not only impossible in this world; it is impossible in all possible worlds.

16. *Objection:* I don't understand a word you are saying ("much learning doth make thee mad"—Festus to St. Paul[2]).

Response:

    i. Either the person does not understand because the words are without meaning and no one can understand.

    1) But many do understand. Are they all mad?

---

2. *Acts 26.*

2) Specify the criteria to distinguish meaning from no meaning—is it other than the laws of thought as the test for meaning?

ii. Or, there is an irrational antipathy and this is an *ad hominem*—speaking against a person rather than what is being said. In which case, we wait for a response to what is said.

17. *Objection:* This is not the way philosophy is currently done.

Response:

i. Styles in philosophy change. What is current now may not endure ages away. Styles depend on substantive differences. The styles of Plato and Aristotle arose from epistemological differences.

ii. A descriptive claim is not a normative claim of what philosophy should be.

iii. *Philosophical Foundation* offers an answer to the question "what is philosophy?" that is classical/essential and comprehensive.

iv. CG is the set of conditions which make thought and discourse possible. Critics of clarity must address CG in order to speak meaningfully.

18. *Objection:* We should be epistemically humble; lack of clarity/certainty is epistemically humble.

Response:

i. Submission to the Word of God is epistemically humble. The Word of God and Historic Christianity affirm clarity and inexcusability (sin).[3]

ii. Public criticism of persons without prior agreement on positions leads to *ad hominems* and is not epistemically humble.

---

3. Romans 1:20; *Westminster Confession of Faith, 1.1.*

19. *Objection:* Why should we be that concerned about clarity? Most are not. The concern is peculiar and exclusive.

Response:

    i. Clarity concerns meaning at the most basic level of thought. No meaning here affects loss of meaning everywhere (nihilism).

    ii. If there is no clarity, then there is no inexcusability (sin), and no need for the gospel of Christ.

    iii. *Argumentum ad populum* (most don't have that concern) must reckon with (a) no one (left to oneself) seeks God, (b) all are being called to stop and think through the curse (toil and strife, and old age, sickness, and death).

20. *Objection:* I believe it is clear, but I can't give a proof.

Response:

    i. Proof (for truth) is not relevant where there is a test for meaning. Meaning is more basic than truth. If there is no meaning, then there is no (possible) truth.

    ii. Self-attesting, self-evident, and self-referentially absurd are immediately clear by test for meaning (not by proof for truth).

21. *Objection:* If I don't see what is clear, how can I hold to the Principle of Clarity (PC)?

Response: Holding to clarity in principle (as part of CG) is not the same as showing what is clear. PC is a necessary condition for one's thought.

22. *Objection:* Why is CG necessary? It seems a merely arbitrary imposition.

Response:

    i. CG is the set of necessary conditions for thought and discourse; it (basic CG) begins with reason as the laws of thought and test for meaning, and ends with PC. CG extends to every level of dispute: more basic, then less basic.

    ii. If there is no meaning, then it is a meaningless dispute; we should avoid, by RP, meaningless disputes.

    iii. Meaninglessness is the condition of spiritual death—the wages (inherent consequence) of sin (not seeking, not understanding, not doing what is right).

    iv. CG is to be applied as universally as sin and spiritual death is universal.

    v. More so when dealing with matters that have been disputed.

    vi. Most so when dealing with a contentious person.

    vii. Everywhere and always, we should avoid meaningless disputes (chain and bind the adversary—the light shines in the darkness[4]).

23. *Objection:* There is always an unknown, therefore uncertainty, and therefore no clarity.

    Response:

    i. The unknown must be distinguished from the unknowable as well as from the known. An unknown at a less basic level does not affect or set aside what is known at a more basic level. In this sense, we know in part. Human knowledge is finite—it may grow forever and still be finite.

    ii. If any worldview is coherent in its essence (more basic), then non-essential (less basic) differences in that world may not now be known, and may remain an unknown, without unsettling what is known at the more basic level.

24. *Objection:* Clarity is neither possible nor necessary.

    Response:

    i. If clarity is not possible, then nothing is clear, and no distinction is clear, and no meaning is possible. If all is meaningless, then we should be silenced.

    ii. If clarity is not possible, then inexcusability is not possible, and therefore morality is not possible, and the gospel is not necessary.

---

4. *Revelation 20; John 1:5.*

25. *Objection:* Clarity is presumptuous—who has or can claim it?

   Response:

   i. Scripture claims it: What may be known of God is clear so that they are without excuse.[5]

   ii. The Historic Christian Faith claims it: The light of nature, and the works of creation and providence do so far manifest the goodness, wisdom, and power of God, as to leave men inexcusable.[6]

26. *Objection:* Clarity is mere philosophy (head knowledge); what is needed is more piety (godliness).

   Response:

   i. Zeal without knowledge is mere pietism; it is not true piety.

   ii. Holiness is based on truth: Sanctify them through thy truth: thy Word (Logos) is Truth.[7]

   iii. We are transformed by the renewing of our minds; knowing the truth sets us free.[8]

   iv. Knowing words is not understanding meaning; having the foundation (elementary truths) is necessary for spiritual maturity.[9]

27. *Objection:* Clarity has little to do with the psychological and practical necessities of life.

   Response: Natural evil consists of toil and strife, and old age, sickness, and death; it is intensified in war, famine, and plague. It is imposed by God to restrain, recall from, and remove moral evil; moral evil is to neglect, avoid, resist, and deny one's reason in the face of what is clear about God; natural evil is God's call to stop and think to see what is clear. The psychological and practical

---

5. *Romans 1:20.*

6. *Westminster Confession of Faith, 1.1.*

7. *John 17:17.*

8. *Romans 12:2; John 8:32.*

9. *Hebrews 6:1.*

necessities arise from the (as a) call to see what is clear, therefore clarity has everything to do with the necessities of life.

28. *Objection:* If it is so clear, why don't I see it?

   Response:

   i. Left to oneself, no seeks and no one understands what is clear.

   ii. If we don't have a concern for consistency and accept the necessity for clarity to have meaning and morality, we will not seek.

   iii. Seeing clarity requires a commitment to reason as the test for meaning.

   iv. Seeing clarity requires critical thinking applied to unexamined assumptions.

   v. Seeing clarity is cumulative; it is a step-by-step process from more basic to less basic.

   vi. In short, without CG we won't see what is clear.

29. *Objection:* Proof of what is clear is not persuasion.

   Response: Persuasion without proof is blind faith; it is based on pseudo-argument, not sound argument. Biblical faith has evidence for what is not seen.[10]

30. *Objection:* Clarity is not necessary for the good.

   Response:

   i. Clarity is necessary for the knowledge of God through the work of dominion.

   ii. Clarity is necessary to take thoughts captive and to disciple the nations.

   iii. Clarity is not necessary for the good, understood as a beatific vision of God in heaven or a return to a paradise.

   iv. Clarity is necessary for meaningful thought; without clarity, Christ and the cross is emptied of meaning.

---

10. *Hebrews 11:1.*

31. *Objection:* God is not like that—to hold people inexcusable.

Response:

    i. God will not hold him guiltless who takes his name in vain.[11]

    ii. Clarity and inexcusability are not imposed; inexcusability is inherent in clarity, and clarity is inherent in the order of creation.

    iii. Sin and death are not imposed; sin is inherent in clarity and inexcusability, and death is inherent in sin.

    iv. The wages of sin are inherent in sin; spiritual death (meaninglessness, boredom, and guilt) is inherent in sin (not seeking and not understanding).

    v. The wages of sin is spiritual death, not physical death (present and imposed) or hell (future and imposed).[12]

32. *Objection:* To know what is clear requires work. Salvation is by grace, not work.

Response:

    i. Reason is the most basic form of the Word of God that comes to man (the life of the *Logos* in man, as light, by which man sees/understands what is clear about God).

    ii. The Holy Spirit works by and with reason (the Word), not apart from reason. The Holy Spirit works to convince, persuade, enlighten, and illuminate the mind with sound argument, not apart from sound argument.

    iii. The use of reason to know what is clear is not opposed to or independent of grace, but is itself a work of grace. The use of and proper response to sound argument is not a purely natural occurrence, but is itself something of a miracle.

    iv. We die spiritually when we deny our reason. The Holy Spirit restores us to life by restoring the life of reason in us.

---

11. *Exodus 20:7.*

12. *Romans 6:23.*

33. *Objection:* I don't define knowledge as absolute certainty.

   Response: No one does insofar as *absolute* is associated with the divine. But humans can have maximal certainty about basic things, like *a is a* and *some things are clear* (e.g., There is no *being* from *non-being* (*being* is not *non-being*)).

34. *Objection:* I don't know clarity by reason, but by intuition (or, I know reason by intuition).

   Response:
   i. Meaning is more basic than truth.
   ii. Reason is the test for meaning. What violates a law of thought (*a is non-a*) has no meaning (self-evident).
   iii. The opposite of what is known by intuitional awareness (immediate/non-inferential) can still be thought and may be true.
   iv. The opposite of what is known by reason cannot be thought and cannot be true.

35. *Objection: God exists* is not necessarily true.

   Response:
   i. Contradictory statements cannot both be true and cannot both be false.
   ii. If the contradiction of *God exists* cannot be true, then *God exists* must be true.

36. *Objection:* I don't have to prove (it is clear) God exists. God (the Holy Spirit) can show it (by a miraculous sign?).

   Response:
   i. If a person knows basic things are clear from general revelation, they can show what is clear.
   ii. If a person knows what is more basic, they can show what is less basic.
   iii. Miraculous signs accompany truths of special revelation, which must be consistent with clear general revelation.

    iv. All persons are called to know clear general revelation and to show clear general revelation.

37. *Objection:* What is maximal clarity?

    Response:

      i. Maximal clarity is necessary and sufficient for inexcusability.

      ii. Doubt or denial of maximal clarity of basic beliefs leads to loss of all meaningful distinctions. If *being* can come from *non-being*, there is no meaningful distinction between *being* and *non-being*.

      iii. Rational presuppositional epistemology (vs. all non-RP) maintains thinking is presuppositional (the less basic in light of more basic) and some things are clear (vs. nothing is clear). Given RP, basic things are clear and are clear to reason (vs. various forms of experience).

      iv. Basic things are maximally clear (nothing clearer) (vs. absolutely clear), sufficient for inexcusability. Denial of what is maximally clear is a denial of one's rational nature (sin) and leads to spiritual death (meaninglessness, boredom, and guilt).

38. *Objection: Objection* to clarity based on pseudo-argument vs. real argument.

    Response:

      i. A pseudo-argument does not engage with a real argument.

      ii. Objections to a real argument will show it is either invalid or unsound.

      iii. Pseudo-arguments are informal fallacies that are irrelevant to a real argument.

      iv. A pseudo-argument is used to neglect, avoid, resist, and deny reason—a progressive hardening into anti-intellectualism (from walk to stand to sit in the seat of scorners[13]).

---

13. *Psalm 1.*

39. *Objection:* If I know what is clear, why do I have to show what is clear?

Response:

    i. A person may fail to know what is clear even while claiming to know what is clear.

    ii. A person may think they know what is clear by using an epistemological method other than rational presuppositionalism (e.g., intuition or common sense), which does not amount to objective (vs. subjective) proof.

    iii. If one knows what is clear, one should be able to show what is clear, and be able to overcome commonly held objections to what is clear.

40. *Objection:* Only God (and not self or others) can bring us to see what is clear.

Response:

    i. It is *not* in question that God, as Creator, ruler, and redeemer, convicts us of sin (of not seeking) and of the death of not understanding what is clear. What *is* in question is how God does so.

    ii. Inwardly: God restores the life (light) of reason in us to see the emptiness of life without God—this occurs when spiritual death in us (meaninglessness, boredom, and guilt) is seen as due to sin (not seeking and understanding).

    iii. Outwardly: How then shall they call on Him in whom they have not believed? And how shall they believe in Him of whom they have not heard? And how shall they hear without a preacher? And how shall they preach unless they are sent? As it is written: "How beautiful are the feet of those who preach the gospel of peace, Who bring glad tidings of good things!" But they have not all obeyed the gospel. For Isaiah says, "Lord, who has believed our report?" So then faith *comes* by hearing, and hearing by the word of God.[14]

---

14. *Romans 10:14-17.*

SUMMARY

1. Neither skepticism nor fideism can set aside reason.
2. Critics of clarity try to set aside reason to avoid discussion, which shows the inexcusability of unbelief.
3. The light of reason is irresistible: it cannot be overcome and it cannot be withstood.
4. Reason in man (made in the image of God) cannot be eradicated from human nature.
5. The light shines in the darkness and the darkness comprehended it not.[15] Reason is self-attesting.

For further response to objections that arise against Common Ground, please see the ongoing work at: https://thelogospapers.com

---

15. *John 1:5.*

GLOSSARY OF TERMS

ambiguity   a term is ambiguous if it has more than one meaning: equivocal—if it has two unrelated meanings (ring on a finger, ring of a bell); analogous—if it has two related meanings (blanket of snow or bed cover); all non-basic terms are also philosophically ambiguous, relative to basic belief; a term is univocal if it has only one meaning.

analogous   like in some respects and unlike in other respects.

antinomy   contrary positions both of which can be false at the same time because both share a common assumption—capitalism and communism; this-worldly and other-worldly; all is eternal and none is eternal; skepticism and fideism; virtue is the good and happiness is the good—a source of recurrent conflict within and between cultures.

argument   the third act of reason (see concept and judgment) in which premises are used to logically support a conclusion (see validity and soundness).

basic belief   a belief is basic in relation to another if it is assumed by that belief; material monism (all is matter) assumes that all is eternal; macro-evolution assumes all is matter; superior race assumes macro-evolution; naturalistic science assumes methodological naturalism, which assumes metaphysical naturalism (all is matter).

clarity   applied to basic beliefs; a belief is clear to reason if the contradiction is not logically or existentially possible; e.g., there must be something eternal; clarity is necessary for meaning, morality, and inexcusability; one knows what is clear if one can show what is clear; what is clear can be known by anyone who seeks to know.

common ground
the set of epistemologically necessary conditions for thought and discourse: 1) reason—as the laws of thought; 2) integrity—as a concern for consistency; 3) Rational Presuppositionalism—as critical thinking applied consistently; 4) the Principle of Clarity—as necessary for meaning and morality; to engage in discourse without common ground is to engage in meaningless disputes.

common sense
takes appearance for reality: the sun rises in the east; the earth is flat; the color of the ocean is blue; there is an external world; based on what is common to sense perception, rather than common sense as practical wisdom; it takes the condition/position of the perceiver for granted.

concept
the first act of reason (see judgment and argument); in a concept the mind grasps the essence of a thing or class of things; set in contrast to an image, an act of the senses; concepts are either well-formed or not.

contradiction
contradictory statements differ in quantity (all or some) and quality (is or is not); they cannot both be true and they cannot both be false, at the same time and in the same respect; *all s is p* is contradicted by *some s is not p*; *no s is p* is contradicted by *some s is p* (see judgment).

creation *ex nihilo*
affirmed by historic theism, it is the belief that God created the world out of no pre-existing substance; in contrast to dualism where creation is by forming pre-existing matter, and to pantheism—in which the world is a part of God; it is the basis of affirming the infinite power and wisdom of God.

deconstruction
recognizes the constructive use of reason by providing an internal conceptual critique of a position; does not apply critical analysis to test the meaning of basic beliefs upon which construction occurs; calls into question reason in itself based upon the mere subjective use of reason.

deduction   reasoning from what is more general or universal to what is less general or particular; from all men are mortal to Socrates is mortal; from saying it is true of all to saying it is true of each.

deism   belief that the world was created by God, but not actively ruled by God; God did not act after creation to bring about natural evil in the world, or to give any redemptive revelation to mankind (Voltaire and Thomas Jefferson).

deontology   a theory of ethics focused upon duty and virtue as the end of moral action, independent of and in contrast to consequences; affirmed by Kant; set in contrast to teleological ethics which sees virtue as means to the good.

determinism   the belief that every event has a cause and that given the cause the effect necessarily follows; in contrast to libertarianism; hard determinists affirm causality and deny libertarian freedom; soft determinists affirm causality and freedom as doing what one desires.

dilemma   in logic, a form of argumentation in which either of two alternatives available is unacceptable; used rhetorically to show how entirely unacceptable a position is.

dominion   the exercise of rule or authority given to mankind to develop the powers latent in oneself and in the creation; based on the principle that creation is revelation, it is directed toward the good as knowledge of God; set in contrast to domination as rule for self-interest.

dualism   the ontological position that reality consists of two distinct kinds of being—matter and spirit—both of which are eternal; affirmed in different forms of Greek thought by Plato and Aristotle; distinct from theism, although dualistic attitudes persist in popular forms of theism.

empiricism   the epistemological position that all knowledge arises from sense experience; affirmed by John Locke; Hume drew out its skeptical implications; assumed uncritically in some claims made in the name of science; radical empiricism includes inner as well as sense experience.

epistemology	theory of knowledge; a major branch of philosophy that deals with the questions "Is knowledge possible?" and "How do I know?"
essence	the set of qualities that all members and only members of a class always have; human essence is said to be both rational and animal.
ethics	ethics is concerned with giving a rational justification for an answer to the question "What is the good?" Ethics assumes choice, which assumes values and therefore the highest value, which is the good; what is sought in ethics is rational justification for one's view of the good.
evolution, naturalistic	a purely natural explanation of the development from non-life to life, to more complex life, to hominid, to human; macro (not micro) evolution; internal disputes exist over gradual vs. non-gradual process; external challenges exist over the scientific vs. philosophical status of evolution.
evolution, theistic	a synthesis of naturalistic evolution and belief in God; subject to criticism from both naturalists and theists as compromising essential features of each, and is therefore inadequate as a compromise position; it has been subject to revision in the direction of theism or naturalism.
ex nihilo	from no previously existing matter.
existentialism	focus upon the individual in an actual condition of crisis with respect to the absence of any rational way to choose; without God (Nietzsche, Sartre) or without reason (Kierkegaard), man is forced to authentic freedom; his existence precedes what he becomes by choice (essence).
faith	faith is applied to belief in general, which cannot be verified through sense experience; faith is not opposed to reason; as truth cannot be separated from meaning, faith cannot be separated from reason; faith grows as understanding grows; it is tested as understanding is tested.

fideism   holding a belief without proof; proof is seen either as
                     not relevant or not possible or may not actually be pres-
                     ent; belief may be either theistic or non-theistic; fideism
                     assumes basic things are not clear; belief without proof
                     based on understanding loses all meaning.

freedom   doing what I want or please or choose, all things con-
                     sidered; applied to the most basic level of thought, I can
                     use my reason if I want to; set in contrast to libertarian
                     freedom: if *ought* implies *can*, then *can* assumes *want*;
                     the want of a rational agent is always free.

friendship   friendship is reciprocal, lasting and shares the deepest
                     concerns; it is therefore the effect of mutual commit-
                     ment to the good; in contrast to other relations which
                     are not reciprocal, lasting, or cannot share the deepest
                     concerns because they are not based on mutual com-
                     mitment to the good.

**general   what can be known of God by all persons, everywhere,
revelation**   at all times, through the ordinary means of knowing;
                     in contrast to special revelation; the subject matter of
                     natural vs. revealed religion.

**good and   an inference of reason; what must be said, if other
necessary   things are accepted as true; applied to analyzing con-
consequence**   cepts, judgments, and arguments; used in critical, inter-
                     pretive, and constructive reasoning.

happiness   the effect of possessing what one believes to be the good;
                     not sought for its own sake as the good, but naturally
                     accompanying the possessing what is believed to be of
                     highest value; lasting happiness is the effect of possess-
                     ing what truly is the good.

hedonism   the ethical view that pleasure/happiness of one kind or
                     another is the good (Epicurus, Mill).

hermeneutics   the process by which the meaning of a text or an event
                     is understood; no experience is meaningful without in-
                     terpretation; in general, we interpret what is less basic in
                     light of what is more basic; we interpret our experience
                     in light of our basic belief or worldview assumptions.

induction	reasoning from observation of instances of things to a general statement about that class of things; from observing that some crows are black to the general statement that all crows are black.
informal fallacy	an attempt to persuade by pseudo-argument (through appeal to what is not rationally relevant) rather than to prove by sound argument: appeal to fear and pity apart from the good; appeal to authority or popularity rather than reason; speaking against the person vs. what was said, etc.
integrity	integrity is grounded in a concern to be whole or unified in one's being; specifically, it is a concern for consistency over and against inconsistency, which is manifest in contradiction in thought; double-mindedness in desire and hypocrisy in what we profess and what we do.
intuition	an immediate awareness one has, apart from reason and the senses, of the connection between a (natural) sign and what it signifies; e.g., smile and friendliness, beauty and goodness; misleading if one thinks the sign is the reality, or that the sign is always accompanied by the reality.
judgment	the second act of reason in which two concepts are joined by affirmation or separated by negation: *all s is p, no s is p, some s is p, some s is not p;* judgments are either true or false and may be simple or complex; a statement is used to express a judgment (or proposition).
knowledge	justified true belief.
libertarianism	a view of freedom where *ought* implies *can*; one is free if one could have done otherwise; related to causality, if my act was caused, it could not have been otherwise; libertarianism denies determinism (every event is caused) in order to affirm freedom (Kant, William James).

literalism   the belief that understanding a text is free of interpretive assumptions; that preceding layers of context are not necessarily relevant; that meaning is explicit only and not also by inference; that understanding language figuratively is to be avoided whenever possible.

love   love seeks the good for the other; love is a moral virtue, not the good sought for its own sake; set in contrast to romantic love in which the other is considered the good; in theism, to seek the good as the knowledge of God is to love God and to love oneself.

matter   that which has size and is not conscious; can be measured.

metaphysics   a branch of philosophy which deals with the question, "What is real or eternal?"; it deals with *ontology*—the nature of being, whether being is matter or spirit; it deals with *cosmology*—how the cosmos came to be.

moral evil   an act contrary to the nature of one's being; for man as a rational being it is to neglect, avoid, resist, or deny reason in the face of what is clear; it is the failure to seek and to understand and to do what is right.

natural evil   in the context of an all powerful and all good Creator, natural evil is not original in the creation, nor inherent in moral evil; it is imposed by God to restrain, recall from, and to remove moral evil; it consists in toil and strife, and old age, sickness, and death, and all amplifications of these in famine, war, and plague.

naturalism   the worldview of material monism: only natural forces explain all phenomena of nature; applied to human culture, it is called secular humanism: only human effort explains all social phenomena; in the sciences, methodological naturalism in explanation (all knowledge is through sense experience) is used to support metaphysical naturalism—there is no God, no spirit or soul, and no afterlife.

nihilism   the loss of all meaningful distinctions in epistemology, metaphysics, and ethics; the inherent consequence of skepticism—the denial of all clarity; a position which cannot be maintained with integrity.

ontology   the study of being.

philosophy   philosophy can be defined in terms of its several features: *area*—foundation and goal; *attitude*—love of wisdom; *method*—critical use of reason; *application*—self-examination; *system*—a worldview.

postmodern   a cluster of skeptical responses to claims to objective truth in modern thought; it is anti-foundationalism, anti-realism, and anti-essentialism; it assumes reason is not ontological or transcendental, nor is thinking presuppositional; it privileges the subjective aspects of interpretation.

pragmatism   a theory of truth: a belief is true if it yields satisfactory consequences (if it works); also, a theory of meaning: the meaning of a belief is the conduct it is fitted to produce (William James); claims to settle metaphysical disputes; assumes skepticism and that what works is common ground.

presupposition   what is assumed or presupposed in any given statement or belief; applied particularly to what is assumed in a person's *system* of beliefs or worldview; one's most basic belief about what is eternal.

prima facie   literally "on the face of it"; applied to epistemic justification, rights, duties, evidence, etc.; it leaves open the question of who bears the burden of proof and what is one's epistemic duty: is one obligated to search out objections before believing what is *prima facie* justified?

problem of evil   if God is all good and all powerful, why is there evil?; if God is all powerful, he could create a world without evil; if he is all good, he would create a world without evil; the problem is intellectual, to make sense of an apparent contradiction, and not empty basic terms of meaning.

rational presuppositionalism thinking is presuppositional; we think of the less basic in light of the more basic: less basic/more basic, truth/meaning, experience/basic belief, conclusion/premises, finite/infinite, etc.; reason is the test for meaning; if we agree on what is more basic, we can agree on what is less basic.

rationalism a reliance on reason as the source of knowing the truth; to be contrasted with reliance on sense experience or intuition or testimony; also, to be contrasted with reliance on reason as a test for meaning (rational presuppositionalism).

reason in its use reason in its use is *formative*—used to form concepts, judgments, and arguments, which are the forms of all thought; *critical*—used as a test of meaning; *interpretive*—used to interpret experience in light of basic belief; and *constructive*—used to construct a coherent worldview.

reason in itself reason in itself is the laws of thought: the law of identity—*a is a*; the law of non-contradiction—*not both a and non-a*; the law of excluded middle—*either a or non-a*; these laws make thinking possible; the common ground for all who think.

reason in us reason in us is *natural*—the same in all thinkers; *ontological*—applies to being as well as to thought; *transcendental*—authoritative, self-attesting, cannot be questioned but makes questioning possible; and *fundamental*—to all other aspects of human personality.

redemptive revelation scripture as redemptive revelation reveals how man is brought out of sin and death; scripture assumes all have sinned—no one seeks, no one understands, no one is righteous; all are in the state of spiritual death—meaninglessness, boredom, and guilt; redemption by vicarious atonement shows both divine justice and mercy.

reductio ad absurdum a form of reasoning which proves the truth of a position by showing the opposite cannot be true because it is reduced to logical absurdity; used to show there must be something eternal; used to show the strong sense of clarity necessary to establish inexcusability.

religion the belief or set of beliefs used to give meaning to experience.

science the attempt to increase knowledge of reality based on theory confirmed by observation in experiment; science is overextended and becomes a source of skepticism when it assumes empiricism, that all knowledge is from sense experience, or makes claims which go beyond experience.

sensus divinitatis the immediate awareness of divinity present in human consciousness; variously understood, ranging from a sense of dependence on a higher power to awareness of God as Creator and ruler, or as one having an innate sense of the qualities of infinite, eternal, and unchanging, which can only, upon analysis, be applied to God.

skepticism the epistemological view that knowledge is not possible, that nothing is clear; consistently held, skepticism leads to nihilism, the loss of all meaning.

Sola Scriptura a principle of authority which maintains that scripture is the only rule of faith and life; set in contrast to new revelations of the Spirit or traditions of men; not set in contrast to reason making inferences from scripture, nor to reason making judgments concerning circumstances common to human societies.

soundness an argument is sound if it is valid and its premises are true (see argument and validity); a rational person will believe the conclusion of a sound argument.

special revelation what is known of God through testimony and its transmission; usually contained in form of scripture; the subject matter of revealed theology in contrast to natural theology or religion.

spirit   that which has no size and is conscious (also known as mind, soul, or consciousness).

spiritual monism   the ontological position that all of reality is eternal and is spirit; set in contrast to material monism, dualism, and theism; matter only *appears* to exist; this reality may be absolute non-dual, beyond all qualities (Shankara) or qualified non-dual, where all is part of God (Ramanuja).

spiritual death   set in contrast to and analogous to physical death; the inward condition of meaninglessness, boredom, and guilt; inherent in moral evil as the failure to seek and to understand basic things that are clear to reason.

talent   an ability to achieve some aspect of the good; originating in one's being and unique in each; developed fully only in the vision of the good; it is given to each for all; the good, achieved by talent, is the source of lasting value and of the richness of life for all.

term   a word or group of words used to express a concept (see concept, essence, and ambiguity).

the good   the good is the end in itself, chosen for its own sake and not for the sake of anything else; it is the highest good (*the summum bonum*); it is the source of unity (in a person, between two persons, and between groups of persons); set in contrast to virtue as means to the good and happiness as the effect of possessing the good.

the principle of clarity   some things are clear, the basic things are clear, the basic things about God and man and good and evil are clear to reason; necessary for meaning and morality.

theism   belief in God the Creator who brought the universe and all things in it into being; God is a Spirit, infinite, eternal, and unchangeable, in his being, wisdom, power, holiness, justice, goodness, and truth; in contrast to deism, God in theism is both Creator and ruler of mankind in history.

tradition   a way of life handed down by and received on the basis of testimony, in contrast to reason, intuition, or sense experience; without critical analysis, traditions are affirmed to be equal, requiring radical pluralism, diversity, multiculturalism, cultural relativism, and tolerance.

transcendental   that which is higher; stands above; authoritative.

uniformitarianism   a principle which holds that the forces now operating in nature have always operated, and in essentially the same magnitude; a naturalistic assumption first used in geology by Charles Lyell, and in biology by Charles Darwin.

utilitarianism   holds that pleasure is the good and that we are to act so as to maximize the greatest amount of pleasure for the greatest number of people; proposed by Jeremy Bentham and John Stuart Mill; set in contrast to ethical egoism—one should seek pleasure for oneself first, and to deontology—duty for duty's sake.

validity   an argument is valid if its premises logically support the conclusion (see argument and soundness).

virtue   virtue is not the good, but the means to the good; there are different kinds of virtues: instrumental (money, house, car), natural (health, beauty, talent), and moral (wisdom, courage, love).

wisdom   knowing the good and the appropriate means to achieving the good.

worldview   how a person understands the world based on answers to the basic questions; each culture is shaped by a worldview held more or less consciously and consistently; a culture grows or declines as its worldview increases or decreases in its capacity to provide meaning.

SUGGESTED READING

(See bibliography for more information.)

1. Philosophy: Introduction and Historical Overview

Online Resource: Stanford Encyclopedia of Philosophy (SEP): https://plato.stanford.edu

Cambridge Dictionary of Philosophy 2nd ed., Robert Audi Gen. Ed.

A Critical History of Western Philosophy, ed. D.J. O'Connor

Eduard Zeller, *Outlines of Greek Philosophy*

Fredrick Coppleston, *History of Medieval Theology*

Etienne Gilson, *Reason and Revelation in the Middle Ages*

John Passmore, *A Hundred Years of Philosophy*

John Passmore, *Recent Philosophers*

Revolution in Philosophy, Ayer, Strawson, Warnock *et al.*

2. Epistemology

Irving M. Copi, *Introduction to Logic*

Raymond McCall, *Basic Logic*

Meaning and Knowledge, Ernest Nagel and Richard Brandt eds.

Empirical Knowledge, Readings from Contemporary Sources, Rodrick M. Chisholm and Robert J. Swartz eds.

Alvin Plantinga, *Warrant: The Current Debate*

3. Faith and Reason

Faith and Rationality, A. Plantinga and N. Wolterstorff eds.

Ronald Nash, *Faith and Reason*

Thomas Aquinas, *The Summa Theologica*

Cornelius Van Til, *Defense of the Faith*

R.C. Sproul, J. Gerstner and A. Lindsley, *Classical Apologetics*

J.P. Moreland and W.L. Craig, *Philosophical Foundations for a Christian Worldview*

4. Concerning Origins: Science, Religion, and Philosophy

Michael Denton, *Evolution: A Theory in Crisis*

William Dembski, *Intelligent Design: The Bridge Between Science and Theology*

Richard Dawkins, *The Blind Watchmaker*

Cornelius Hunter, *Darwin's Proof*

Phillip Johnson, *Reason in the Balance*

Daniel Dennett, *Darwin's Dangerous Idea: Evolution and the Meaning of Life*

Jonathan Wells, *Icons of Evolution*

5. Ethics

Great Traditions in Ethics, Albert, Denise, Peterfreund eds.

Plato, *The Republic*

Aristotle, *Nicomachean Ethics*

Alasdair MacIntyre, *After Virtue*

John Finnis, *Natural Law and Natural Rights*

J.S. Mill, *Utilitarianism*

Simone de Beauvoir, *The Second Sex*

Freedom and Determinism, Keith Lehrer ed.

6. Existentialism

William Barrett, *Irrational Man*

Soren Kierkegaard, *Fear and Trembling and Sickness Unto Death*

The Portable Nietzsche, Walter Kaufman ed.

Jean-Paul Sartre, *Existentialism and Human Emotions*

Albert Camus, *The Myth of Sisyphus*

7. Postmodernism

Jacque Derrida, *Of Grammatology*

John Ellis, *Against Deconstruction*

Richard Rorty, *Objectivity, Relativism and Truth*

The Foucault Reader, Paul Rabinow ed.

8. Worldview and Culture

Allan Bloom, *Closing of the American Mind*
Richard Hofstadter, *Anti-Intellectualism in American Life*
Samuel Huntington, *The Clash of Civilizations*
Rodney Stark, *The Victory of Reason*

9. Worldview and World Religions

Chandradhar Sharma, *Indian Philosophy, A Critical Survey*
Eliot Deutsch, *Advaita Vedanta, A Philosophical Reconstruction*
Robert J. Corliss, *The Vision of Buddhism*
Fredrick Streng, *Emptiness*
Holmes Welch, *Taoism*
Fung Yu-Lan, *A Short History of Chinese Philosophy*
Jacob Neusner, *The Way of Torah; The Life of Torah*
Sayed Hossein Nasr, *Ideals and Realities of Islam*
Oliver Leaman, *Islamic Philosophy, A Brief Introduction*
Ninian Smart, *Worldview: Cross Cultural Exploration of Human Beliefs*

BIBLIOGRAPHY

Albert, Ethel M., Theodore C. Denise, and Sheldon P. Peterfreund. *Great Traditions in Ethics.* 4th ed. New York: Litton Educational Publishing, 1980.

Alston, William P. *Perceiving God: The Epistemology of Religious Experience.* New York: Cornell University Press, 1993.

Aquinas, Thomas. *Summa Theologica.* Edited by Mortimer J. Adler. Vol. 19 of *Great Books of the Western World,* edited by Mortimer J. Adler. Chicago: Encyclopedia Britannica, 1955.

Aristotle. *Complete Works of Aristotle: The Revised Oxford Translation.* Edited by J. Barnes. 2 vols. Bollingen Series. Princeton, NJ: Princeton University Press, 1983.

———. *The Nicomachean Ethics.* Edited by Hugh Tredennick. Translated by J.A.K. Thomas. New York: Penguin Group, 2004.

———. *Philosophy of Aristotle.* Translated by Renford Bambrough, J.L. Creed and A.E. Wardman. New York: Penguin Group, 2003.

Askew, Richard. "On Fideism and Alvin Plantinga." *International Journal for Philosophy of Religion* 23, no. 1 (1998): 3-16.

Audi, Robert, ed. *The Cambridge Dictionary of Philosophy.* Cambridge: Cambridge University Press, 1999.

Augustine. *Concerning the City of God Against the Pagans.* Translated by Henry Bettenson. London: Penguin Books, 1984.

———. *Confessions.* Translated by Henry Chadwick. Oxford: Oxford University Press, 1991.

Ayer, A.J., W.C. Kneale, G.A. Paul, D.F. Spear, P.F. Strawson, G.J. Warnock, and R.A. Wollheim, eds. *The Revolution in Philosophy.* London: Macmillan, 1963.

Bahnsen, Greg L. *Van Til's Apologetic: Reading and Analysis.* Philipsburg, NJ: Presbyterian and Reformed Publishing, 1998.

Bailey, Alan. *Sextus Empiricus and Pyrrhonean Skepticism.* Oxford: Clarendon Press, 2002.

Barrett, William E. *Irrational Man: A Study in Existential Philosophy.* Garden City, NY: Doubleday Anchor, 1962.

Barrow, John D. and Frank J. Tipler. *The Anthropic Cosmological Principle.* Oxford: Clarendon Press, 1987.

Barth, Karl. *The Epistle to the Romans.* Trans. E.C. Hoskyns. Oxford: Oxford University Press, 1968.

Bartley, C.J. *The Theology of Ramanuja: Realism and Religion.* London: Routledge Curzon, 2002.

Beardsley, Tim. "Fossil Bird Shakes Evolutionary Hypotheses." *Nature* 322, no. 21 (August 1986): 677.

Beauvoir, Simone de, *The Second Sex.* Edited by H.N. Pashley, and Margaret Crosland, New York: Knopf Publishing Group, 1993.

Bennett, Jonathan. *Learning From Six Philosophers: Descartes, Spinoza, Leibniz, Locke, Berkeley, Hume.* Oxford: Oxford University Press, 2003.

Berkeley, George B. *Berkeley's Three Dialogues between Hylas and Philonous.* Edited by Colin M. Turbayne. New York: The Liberal Arts Press, 1954.

Berkouwer, G.C. *General Revelation.* Studies in Dogmatics. Grand Rapids, MI: William B. Eerdmans Publishing Company, 1955.

Bloom, Allan. *Closing of the American Mind.* New York: Simon & Schuster, 1988.

Boethius, V.E. Watts. *The Consolation of Philosophy.* London: Penguin Books, 1969.

Bradley, F.H. *Appearance and Reality.* Oxford: Clarendon Press, 1930.

Brueckner, Anthony. "Transcendental Arguments and Skepticism." *Mind* 52, no. 206 (Jan 2002): 117-123.

Bultmann, Rudolf. *Faith and Understanding.* Edited by Robert W. Funk. Translated by Louise P. Smith. London: CM Press, 1969.

Burtt, Edwin Arthur. *The Metaphysical Foundations of Modern Science.* Mineola, NY: Dover Publications, 2003.

Butler, Cuthbert. *Western Mysticism: The Teaching of Saint.* Whitefish, MT: Kessinger Publishing, 2003.

Byl, John. "General Revelation and Evangelicalism." *Mid-America Journal of Theology* 5 (Spring 1989): 1-13.

Calvin, John. *The Institutes of Christian Religion.* Translated and edited by Ford Lewis Battles. Grand Rapids, MI: W.B. Eerdmans, 1987.

Camus, Albert. *The Myth of Sisyphus and Other Essays.* Translated by Justin O'Brien. New York: Knopf Publishing Group, 1991.

Carus, Titus Lucretius. *On the Nature of the Universe.* Translated by Sir Ronald Melville. Oxford: Oxford University Press, 1999.

Chan, Wing-Tsit. *A Source Book in Chinese Philosophy.* Princeton: Princeton University Press, 1963.

Charnock, Stephen. *The Existence and Attributes of God.* Grand Rapids, MI: Baker Books, 1996.

Chisholm, Roderick M. and Robert J. Swartz, eds. *Empirical Knowledge: Readings from Contemporary Sources.* Englewood Cliffs, NJ: Prentice Hall, 1973.

Clark, Gordon. *Historiography Secular and Religious.* Nutley, NJ: Craig Press, 1971.

———. *Religion, Reason, and Revelation.* Hobbs, NM: The Trinity Foundation, 1995.

———, and John Robbins, eds. *Thales to Dewey: A History of Philosophy.* Volume 3, *The Works of Gordon Haddon Clark.* Hobbs, NM: Trinity Foundation, 2000.

Clark, Kelly James. *Return to Reason: A Critique of Enlightenment, Evidentialism and a Defense of Reason and Belief in God.* Grand Rapids, MI: William B. Eerdmans Publishing Company, 1990.

Clarke, Samuel and Ezio Vailati. *A Demonstration of the Being and Attributes of God and Other Writings.* Cambridge: Cambridge University Press, 1998.

Clatterbaugh, Kenneth. *The Causation Debate in Modern Philosophy 1637-1739.* London: Routledge, 1999.

Clifford, William Kingdon. *The Ethics of Belief and Other Essays.* Amherst, NY: Prometheus Books, 1999.

Copan, Paul, and William Lane Craig. *Creation Out of Nothing: A Biblical, Philosophical, and Scientific Exploration.* Grand Rapids, MI: Baker Academic, 2004.

Copi, Irving M. and Carl Cohen. *Introduction to Logic.* Boston, MA: Prentice Hall, 2005.

Copi, Irving M. and James Gould, eds. *Readings on Logic.* 2nd ed. New York: Macmillan, 1972.

Copleston, Frederick C. *A History of Medieval Philosophy.* Notre Dame: University of Notre Dame Press, 1972.

Corless, Roger J. *The Vision of Buddhism: The Space Under the Tree.* St. Paul, MN: Paragon House Publishers, 1992.

Cornford, Frances Macdonald. *Before and After Socrates.* Cambridge: Cambridge University Press, 1932.

Cornford, Francis Macdonald. *Plato's Theory of Knowledge: The Theaetetus and the Sophist of Plato.* London: Routledge, 2000.

Cornman, James W., Keith Lehrer, and George S. Pappas. *Philosophical Problems and Arguments: An Introduction.* Indianapolis, IN: Hackett Publishing Company, 1992.

Cowan, Steven B., ed. *Five Views on Apologetics.* Grand Rapids, MI: Zondervan Publishing House, 2000.

Craig, William Lane. *The Cosmological Argument from Plato to Leibniz.* Eugene, OR: Wipf and Stock Publishers, 2001.

Craig, William L. and Quentin Smith. *Theism, Atheism, and Big Bang Cosmology.* Oxford: Oxford University Press, 1995.

Darwin, Charles. *The Origin of Species by Means of Natural Selection: The Preservation of Favored Races in the Struggle for Life.* New York: P.F. Collier and Son, 1901.

Davidson, Herbert A. *Alfarabi, Avicenna, and Averroes on Intellect: Their Cosmologies, Theories of Active Intellect, and Theories of Human Intellect.* Oxford: Oxford University Press, 1992.

Davies, Paul. *Superforce: The Search for a Grand Unified Theory of Nature.* New York: Simon and Schuster, 1984.

———. *The Mind of God.* New York: Simon & Schuster, 1992.

Dawkins, Richard. *The Blind Watchmaker: Why the Evidence of Evolution Reveals a Universe without Design.* New York: W.W. Norton & Company, 1996.

Demarest, Bruce A. *General Revelation: Historical Views and Contemporary Issues.* Grand Rapids, MI: Zondervan Publishing House, 1982.

Dembski, William A. and Michael J. Behe. *Intelligent Design: The Bridge Between Science and Theology.* Downers Grove, IL: InterVarsity Press, 2002.

Dennell, Robin. "The World's Oldest Spears." *Nature* 385, no. 27 (February 1997): 767-768.

Dennett, Daniel C. *Darwin's Dangerous Idea: Evolution and the Meanings of Life.* New York: Simon & Schuster, 1996.

Denton, Michael. *Evolution: A Theory in Crisis.* New York: Adler & Adler Publishers, 1997.

Derrida, Jacques and Gayatri Chakravorty Spivak. *Of Grammatology.* Baltimore: Johns Hopkins University Press, 1998.

Descartes, René, Elizabeth Sanderson Haldane, and G.R.T. Ross. *A Discourse on Method and Meditations.* Mineola, NY. Dover Publications, Incorporated, 2003.

Deutsch, Eliot. *Advaita Vedanta: A Philosophical Reconstruction.* Honolulu: University of Hawaii Press, 1969.

———, trans. *The Bhagavad Gita.* New York: Holt, Rinehart and Winston, 1968.

Diehl, David W. "Evangelicalism and General Revelation: An Unfinished Agenda." *Evangelical Theological Society Papers* 36 (1987): 21-42.

Dilley, Frank B. "Is there 'Knowledge' of God?" *The Journal of Religion* 38, no. 2 (April 1958): 116-126.

Dirac, Paul. *Principles of Quantum Mechanics.* Oxford: Oxford University Press, 1982.

Drange, Theodore M. *Nonbelief and Evil: Two Arguments for the Nonexistence of God.* Amherst, NY: Prometheus Books, 1998.

Dray, William H. *Philosophy of History.* Upper Saddle River, NJ: Prentice Hall, 1992.

Dulles, Avery. *A History of Apologetics.* Eugene, OR: Wipf and Stock Publishers, 1999.

Dupre, Louis. "The Argument of Design Today." *The Journal of Religion* 54, no. 1 (January 1974): 1-12.

Egner, Robert E. and Denonn, Lester E., eds. *The Basic Writings of Bertrand Russell.* New York: Simon & Schuster, 1961.

Ehrlich, Paul R. *The Population Bomb.* Cutchogue, NY: Buccaneer Books, 1997.

Eldredge, Nyles. *Time Frames: The Rethinking of Darwinian Evolution.* Princeton: Princeton University Press, 1985.

Ellis, John M. *Against Deconstruction.* Princeton: Princeton University Press, 1990.

Empiricus, Sextus. *Selections from the Major Writings on Scepticism, Man, and God.* Edited by Phillip P. Hallie. Translated by Sanford G. Etheridge. Middletown, CT: Wesleyan University Press, 1964.

Fanon, Frantz. *The Wretched of the Earth.* New York: Grove/Atlantic, 2005.

Feuerbach, Ludwig. *The Essence of Christianity.* Amherst, MA: Prometheus Books, 1989.

Finnis, John. *Natural Law and Natural Rights.* Oxford: Oxford University Press, 1980.

Flew, Anthony and Alisdair MacIntyre, eds. *New Essays in Philosophical Theology.* New York: MacMillan, 1973.

Foucault, Michel, *The Essential Foucault.* Edited by Paul Rabinow, and Nikolas S. Rose, New York: New Press, 2003.

———. *The Foucault Reader.* Edited by Paul Rabinow. New York: Pantheon Books, 1984.

Freud, Sigmund. *Civilization and its Discontents.* Translated by James Strachey. New York: W.W. Norton & Company, 1961.

Gangadean, Ashok K. *Meditative Reason—Toward Universal Grammar.* New York: Peter Lang, 1993.

———. *Between Worlds: The Emergence of Global Reason.* New York: Peter Lang, 1998.

Geertz, Clifford. *The Interpretation of Cultures.* New York: Basic Books, 1973.

Geisler, Norman L. and Winfried Corduan. *Philosophy of Religion.* 2nd ed. Eugene, OR: Wipf and Stock Publishers, 2003.

Gettier, Edmund L. "Is Justified True Belief Knowledge?" *Analysis* 23, no. 6 (1963): 121.

Gilson, Etienne. *Reason and Revelation in the Middle Ages.* New York: Scribner & Sons, 1938.

———. *The Spirit of Medieval Philosophy.* Notre Dame: University of Notre Dame Press, 1991.

Gonzalez, Justo L. *A History of Christian Thought.* Nashville, TN: Abingdon Press, 1987.

Gootjes, N.H. "General Revelation in its Relation to Special Revelation." *The Westminster Theological Journal* 51, no. 2 (Fall 1989): 359-368.

Grabill, Stephen J. *Rediscovering the Natural Law in Reformed Theological Ethics.* Grand Rapids, MI: William B. Eerdmans Publishing Company, 2006.

Grant, Colin. "Anselm's Argument Today." *Journal of the American Academy of Religion* 57, no. 4 (Winter, 1989): 791-806.

Griffiths, Paul J. "How Epistemology Matters to Theology." *The Journal of Religion* 79, no. 1 (Jan., 1999): 1-18.

Guth, Alan. *The Inflationary Universe: The Quest for a New Theory of Cosmic Origins.* New York: Helix Books, 1997.

Harris, Sam. *The End of Faith.* New York: W.W. Norton, 2004.

Hart, Hendrik, Johan Van Der Hoeven, and Nicholas Wolterstorff, eds. *Rationality in the Calvinian Tradition*. Lanham, MD: University Press of America, 1983.

Hawking, Stephen W. *A Brief History of Time*. New York: Bantam Books, 1988.

Hegel, Georg Wilhelm Friedrich. *Lectures on the Philosophy of World History*. Translated by H.B. Nisbet. Cambridge: Cambridge University Press, 1975.

Heidegger, Martin, and Richard Taft. *Kant and the Problem of Metaphysics*. Bloomington, IN: Indiana University Press, 1997.

Heilbroner, Robert L. *The Worldly Philosophers: The Lives, Times and Ideas of the Great Economic Thinkers*. New York: Simon and Schuster, 1999.

Helm, Paul. *Faith with Reason*. Oxford: Oxford University Press, 2003.

Henry, Carl F.H. *God, Revelation, and Authority*. Waco, TX: Word Books, 1976.

Hester, Marcus. *Faith, Reason and Skepticism*. Philadelphia: Temple University Press, 1992.

Hick, John H and McGill, Arthur C., eds. *The Many-Faced Argument*. New York: Macmillan, 1967.

Hick, John. "A Philosophy of Religious Pluralism." In *Classical and Contemporary Readings in the Philosophy of Religion*, edited by John Hick, 418. Upper Saddle River, NJ: Prentice Hall, 1990.

———. *Faith and Knowledge*. New York: Cornell University Press, 1957.

Hintikka, Jaakko. *Knowledge and Belief—an Introduction*. London: Kings College Publications, 2005.

Hobbes, Thomas, *Thomas Hobbes: Leviathan*. Edited by Marshall Missner, and Daniel Kolak. Longman Library of Primary Sources in Philosophy. New York: Pearson Longman, 2006.

Hodge, A.A. *The Westminster Confession: A Commentary*. Carlisle, PA: Banner of Truth, 2004.

Hodge, Charles. *Systematic Theology*. Peabody, MA: Hendrickson Publishers, 1999.

Hofstadter, Richard. *Anti-Intellectualism in American Life*. New York: Knopf Publishing Group, 1966.

Hopkins, Gerard Manley. *Poems and Prose of Gerard Manly Hopkins*. Baltimore, MD: Penguin Books Inc., 1953.

Horgan, John. *The End of Science: Facing the Limits of Knowledge in the Twilight of the Scientific Age.* New York: Broadway Books, 1997.

Howard-Snyder, Daniel and Paul Moser. *Divine Hiddenness: New Essays.* Cambridge: Cambridge University Press, 2001.

Hoyle, Fred. *The Nature of the Universe.* 2nd ed. Oxford: Basil Blackwell, 1952.

Hume, David. *Dialogues and Natural History of Religion.* Edited by J.C.A. Gaskin. Oxford: Oxford University Press, 1993.

———. *Enquiries Concerning Human Understanding.* 3rd ed. New York: Oxford University Press, 1975.

———. *A Treatise on Human Nature.* Edited with an analytical index by L.A. Selby Bigge Oxford, Clarendon Press, 1888.

Humphreys, D. Russell and Ken Ham. *Starlight and Time: Solving the Puzzle of Distant Starlight in a Young Universe.* Green Forest, AR: Master Books, 1996.

Hunter, Cornelius G. *Darwin's Proof: The Triumph of Religion Over Science.* Grand Rapids, MI: Brazos Press, 2003.

———. *Darwin's God: Evolution and the Problem of Evil.* Grand Rapids, MI: Brazos Press, 2002.

Huntington, Samuel P. *The Clash of Civilizations.* New York: Simon and Schuster, 1996.

Inwood, Michael J. *Hegel Selections.* New York: Prentice Hall, 1997.

Isham, C.J., Penrose, R and Sciama D.W. *Quantum Gravity* 2nd ed. Oxford: Clarendon, 1981.

James, William. *The Dilemma of Determinism.* Whitefish, MT: Kessinger, 2005.

———. *Pragmatism.* New York: IndyPublish.com, 2005.

———. *The Varieties of Religious Experience.* New York: Routledge, 2002.

———. *The Will to Believe.* Sioux Falls, SD: NuVision Publications, LLC, 2004.

Jastrow, Robert. *God and the Astronomers.* New York: W.W. Norton & Co, 2000.

Johnson, Phillip E. *Reason in the Balance: The Case Against Naturalism in Science, Law and Education.* Downers Grove, IL: InterVarsity Press, 1998.

Kant, Immanuel. *Critique of Pure Reason.* Edited by Howard Caygil. Translated by Norman Kemp Smith. New York: St. Martin's Press, 1965.

———. *Fundamental Principles of the Metaphysic of Morals.* Translated by Thomas K. Abbot. Indianapolis, IN: Bobs-Merrill Co., 1949.

Kaufman, Gordon D. "Philosophy of Religion and Christian Theology." *The Journal of Religion* 37, no. 4 (October 1957): 233-245.

Kaufmann, Walter. *From Shakespeare to Existentialism—Essays on Shakespeare and Goethe; Hegel and Kierkegaard; Nietzsche, Rilke and Freud; Jaspers, Heidegger, and Toynbee.* Princeton: Princeton University Press, 1980.

Kierkegaard, Soren. *Fear and Trembling* and *The Sickness Unto Death.* Translated by Walter Lowrie. Princeton: Princeton University Press, 1954.

Kierkegaard, Soren. *Concluding Unscientific Postscript.* Translated and edited by Howard V. Hong and Edna H. Hong. Princeton: Princeton University Press, 1992.

Kung, Hans. *Does God Exist?: An Answer for Today.* New York: Crossroad Publishing Company, 1994.

Kuyper, Abraham. *Lectures on Calvinism.* Grand Rapids, MI: William B. Eerdmans Publishing Company, 1943.

Leaman, Oliver. *A Brief Introduction to Islamic Philosophy.* Cambridge: Polity Press, 2000.

Leibniz, G.W., *Discourse on Metaphysics and the Monadology.* Edited by George R. Montgomery, and Albert R. Chandler. Mineola, NY: Dover Publications, 2005.

Lessing, Gotthold Ephraim, and Henry Chadwick. *Lessing's Theological Writings: Selections in Translation.* Palo Alto, CA: Stanford University Press, 1957.

Levinton, Jeffrey. "The Big Bang of Animal Evolution." *Scientific American* (November, 1992): 267.

Lewis, C.S. *The Abolition of Man.* New York: HarperCollins, 2001.

———. *The Great Divorce.* New York: HarperCollins, 2001.

———. *The Problem of Pain.* New York: Macmillan, 1974.

Livingston, James C. *The Enlightenment and the Nineteenth Century. Vol. 1, Modern Christian Thought.* 2nd ed. New York: Prentice Hall, 1996.

Livingston, James C., Sarah Coakley, James H. Evans, and Francis Schussler Fiorenza. *The Twentieth Century, Vol. 2, Modern Christian Thought.* 2nd ed. New York: Prentice Hall, 1999.

Locke, John. *An Essay Concerning Human Understanding.* Edited by Peter H. Nidditch. Oxford: Oxford University Press, 1979.

Lubenow, Marvin. *Bones of Contention: A Creationist Assessment of Human Fossils.* Rev. ed. Grand Rapids, MI: Baker Books, 2004.

Lyell, Charles. *Principles of Geology*. Dehra Dun, India: Shiva Offset Press, 1989.

Lyman, Stanford M. *The Seven Deadly Sins: Society and Evil*. Lanham, MD: Rowman and Littlefield Publishers, 1989.

MacIntyre, Alasdair. *After Virtue: A Study in Moral Theory*. Notre Dame: University of Notre Dame Press, 2007.

Markus, R. A., ed. *Augustine: A Collection of Critical Essays*. New York: Doubleday Anchor, 1972.

Marx, Karl. *Capital*. Translated by David McLellan. Oxford: Oxford University Press, 1999.

———. *The Communist Manifesto*. Edited by Friedrich Engels. Translated by David McLellan. Oxford: Oxford University Press, 1998.

———. *Critique of Hegel's "Philosophy of Right."* Edited by Joseph O'Malley. Translated by Annette Jolin and Joseph O'Malley. Cambridge: Cambridge University Press, 1970.

Mavrodes, George I. "Some Puzzles Concerning Omnipotence." *The Philosophical Review* 72, no. 2 (April 1963): 221-223.

McCall, Raymond J. *Basic Logic*. 2nd ed. New York: Barnes & Nobles, 1952.

McLellan, David. *Marxism After Marx*. Hants, Wales: Macmillan Publishers Limited, 1998.

Mill, John Stuart. *Utilitarianism*. Mineola, NY: Dover Publications, 2007.

Millot, Jacques. "The Coelacanth." *Scientific American* 193 (December 1955): 37.

Moody, D.L. *The Best of D. L. Moody*, Edited by Wilbur M. Smith. Chicago, Moody Press, 1971.

Moore, G.E. *Selected Writings*. Edited by Thomas Baldwin. London: Routledge, 1993.

Moreland, J.P. and William Lane Craig. *Philosophical Foundations for a Christian Worldview*. Downers Grove, IL: InterVarsity Press, 2003.

Nagel, Ernest and Richard B. Brandt, eds. *Meaning and Knowledge*. New York: Harcourt, Brace and World, 1965.

Nash, Ronald H. *Faith and Reason: Searching for a Rational Faith*. Grand Rapids, MI: Zondervan, 1988.

———. *The Meaning of History*. Nashville, TN: B and H Publishing Group, 1998.

Nasr, Seyyed Hossein. *Ideals and Realities of Islam*. Chicago: Kazi Publications, 2000.

Neiman, Susan. *Evil in Modern Thought: An Alternative History of Philosophy.* Princeton: Princeton University Press, 2002.

Neusner, Jacob. *The Life of Torah Readings in the Jewish Religious Experience.* Encino, CA: Dickenson Publishing Co., 1974.

———. *The Way of Torah: An Introduction to Judaism.* 3rd ed. Belmont, CA: Wadsworth Inc, 1979.

Nietzsche, Friedrich. *The Portable Nietzsche.* Translated by Walter Kaufmann. New York: Penguin Group, 1977.

Noll, Mark A. *The Scandal of the Evangelical Mind.* Grand Rapids, MI: William B. Eerdmans Publishing, 1995.

O'Connor, D.J., ed. *A Critical History of Western Philosophy.* New York: Free Press, 1985.

Oliphint, K. Scott. *Reasons for Faith: Philosophy in the Service of Theology.* Phillipsburg, NJ: P&R Publishing, 2006.

Oppy, Graham. *Arguing about Gods.* New York: Cambridge University Press, 2006.

Packer, J.I. *Concise Theology: A Guide to Historic Christian Belief.* Carol Stream, IL: Tyndale House Publishers, 2001.

Paley, William, Matthew Eddy, and David M. Knight. *Natural Theology: Evidence of the Existence and Attributes of the Deity, Collected from the Appearances of Nature.* Oxford World's Classics. Oxford: Oxford University Press, 2006.

Passmore, John. *A Hundred Years of Philosophy.* Revised Edition. New York: Basic Books, 1966.

———. *Recent Philosophers.* Open Court Publishing Company, 1985.

Pearcey, Nancy R. and Charles B. Thaxton. *The Soul of Science: Christian Faith and Natural Philosophy.* Wheaton, IL: Crossway Books, 1994.

Peers, E. Allison. *Dark Night of the Soul: A Masterpiece in the Literature of Mysticism by St. John of the Cross.* New York: Doubleday Publishing, 2005.

Penelhum, Terence. *God and Skepticism.* London: Springer, 1983.

Penrose, Roger, C.J. Isham, and D.W. Sciama, eds. Quantum Gravity 2: a Second Oxford Symposium. Oxford: Clarendon, 1981.

Pieper, Josef, Alexander Dru, and T.S. Eliot. *Leisure: The Basis of Culture.* Indianapolis, IN: Liberty Fund, 1999.

Plantinga, Alvin, and James F. Sennett, eds. *The Analytic Theist: An Alvin Plantinga Reader.* Grand Rapids, MI: William B. Eerdmans Publishing Company, 1998.

Plantinga, Alvin, and Nicholas Wolterstorff, eds. *Faith and Rationality: Reason and Belief in God.* Notre Dame: University of Notre Dame Press, 1984.

Plantinga, Alvin. *God, Freedom, and Evil.* Grand Rapids, MI: Wm B. Eerdmans, 1994.

———. *The Nature of Necessity.* Oxford: Clarendon Press, 1974.

———. "The Prospects for Natural Theology." *Philosophical Perspectives* 5 (1991): 287-315.

———, ed. *The Ontological Argument from St. Anselm to Contemporary Philosophers.* Garden City, N: Doubleday Anchor, 1965.

———. "On Taking Belief in God as Basic." In *Religious Experience and Religious Belief,* edited by Joseph Runzo and Craig K. Ihara. Lanham, MD: University Press of America, 1981.

———. *Warrant: The Current Debate.* Oxford: Oxford University Press, 1993.

———. *Warrant and Proper Function.* Oxford: Oxford University Press, 1993.

———. *Warranted Christian Belief.* Oxford: Oxford University Press, 2000.

Plato. *Complete Works: Plato.* Edited by John M. Cooper and D.S. Hutchinson. Indianapolis, IN: Hackett Publishing Company, 1997.

———. *The Republic.* Translated by Francis Macdonald Cornford. Oxford: Oxford University Press, 1951.

Pojman, Louis. "Rationality and Religious Belief." *Religious Studies* 15 (June 1979): 159-172.

Polkinghorne, John. *Science and Providence: God's Interaction with the World.* London: SPCK, 1989.

Putnam, Hilary. *Reason, Truth and History.* Cambridge: Cambridge University Press, 1982.

Quine, Willard V. *From a Logical Point of View: Nine Logico-Philosophical Essays.* Cambridge, MA: Harvard University Press, 1980.

Radhakrishnan, Sarvepalli and Charles A. Moore. *Sourcebook in Indian Philosophy.* Princeton: Princeton University Press, 1967.

Reid, Thomas, *Inquiry and Essays.* Edited by Ronald E. Beanblossom, and Keith Lehrer, Indianapolis, IN: Hackett Publishing Company, 1983.

Rice, Richard, and John Sanders. *The Openness of God: A Biblical Challenge to the Traditional Understanding of God.* Edited by Clark H. Pinnock. Downers Grove, IL: InterVarsity Press, 1994.

Rorty, Richard McKay. *Objectivity, Relativism, and Truth,* Vol. 1, *Philosophical Papers,* Cambridge: Cambridge University Press, 1990.

Ross, David and John Lloyd Ackrill. *Aristotle.* London: Routledge, 2004.

Ross, Hugh. *The Creator and the Cosmos: How the Greatest Scientific Discoveries of the Century Reveal God.* London, Ontario: NavPress Publishing Group, 2004.

Roth, Michael D. and Leon Galis, eds. *Knowing: Essays in the Analysis of Knowledge.* New York: Random House, 1970.

Rowe, William L. *Philosophy of Religion: An Introduction.* 2nd ed. Belmont, CA: Wadsworth Publishing, 2006.

————. "Religious Pluralism." *Religious Studies: An International Journal for the Philosophy of Religion* 35, no. 2 (June 1999): 139-150.

Russell, Bertrand. *Our Knowledge of the External World.* London: Routledge, 1999.

Ryle, Gilbert. *The Concept of Mind.* New York: Barnes and Noble, 1949.

Sagan, Carl. *Cosmos.* New York: Random House, 1980.

Said, Edward W. *Culture and Imperialism.* New York: Knopf Publishing Group, 1994.

Sartre, Jean-Paul. *Existentialism and Human Emotions.* New York: Kensington Publishing Corporation, 2000.

Schellenberg, J.L. *Divine Hiddenness and Human Reason.* New York: Cornell University Press, 2006.

Schleiermacher, Friedrich. *On Religion: Speeches to its Cultured Despisers.* Translated by John Oman. Louisville, KY: Westminster/John Knox Press, 1994.

Shankara. *The Vedanta Sutras of Badarayana with the Commentary by Shankara, Volumes 1and 2.* Translated by George Thibaut. New York: Dover Publication, 1962.

Sharma, Chandradhar. *A Critical Survey of Indian Philosophy.* Delhi, India: Motilal Banarsidass Publishers, 1991.

Sheldon, Henry. *Unbelief in the Nineteenth Century.* Kila, MT: Kessinger Publishing, 2005.

Sire, James W. *Habits of the Mind.* Downers Grove, IL: InterVarsity Press, 2000.

Smart, Ninian. *Worldviews: Crosscultural Explorations of Human Beliefs.* Upper Saddle River, NJ: Prentice Hall, 1999.

Sommers, Christina Hoff and Sally Satel. *One Nation Under Therapy: How the Helping Culture is Eroding Self-Reliance.* New York: St. Martin's Press, 2006.

Spinoza, Benedictus de. *The Collected Works of Spinoza.* Translated and edited by Edwin Curley. Princeton, NJ: Princeton University Press, 1985.

Sproul, Robert Charles, John H. Gerstner, and Arthur W. Lindsley. *Classical Apologetics: A Rational Defense of the Christian Faith and a Critique of Presuppositional Apologetics.* Grand Rapids, MI: Zondervan, 1984.

Stark, Rodney. *The Victory of Reason: How Christianity Led to Freedom, Capitalism, and Western Success.* New York: Random House, 2006.

Strauss, Leo and Joseph Cropsey, eds. *History of Political Philosophy.* Chicago: University of Chicago Press, 2003.

Strauss, William, and Neil Howe. *The Fourth Turning: An American Prophecy.* New York: Broadway Books, 1997.

Streng, Frederieck J. *Emptiness.* Nashville, TN: Abingdon Press, 1967.

Suzuki, D.T. and C.G. Jung. *An Introduction to Zen Buddhism.* New York: Grove/Atlantic, 1987.

Talbot, Mark. "Is it Natural to Believe in God." *Faith and Philosophy* 6 (April 1989): 155-171.

Taylor, Mark C. *Tears.* New York: State University of New York Press, 1989.

Toynbee, Arnold J. and D.C. Somervell, eds. *A Study of History.* Oxford: Oxford University Press, 1987.

Twain, Mark. *The Man Who Corrupted Hadleyburg and Other Stories and Essays.* New York: Harper and Brothers, 1902.

Ullian, J.S. and Willard V. Quine. *The Web of Belief.* London: McGraw-Hill Higher Education, 1978.

Van Til, Cornelius and William Edgar, eds. *Christian Apologetics.* 2nd ed. Phippsburg, NJ: P&R Publishing, 2003.

Van Til, Cornelius. *Defense of the Faith.* Phippsburg, NJ: P&R Publishing, 1967.

Wach, Joachim. "General Revelation and the Religions of the World." *Journal of Bible and Religion* 22, no. 2 (April 1954): 83-93.

Webb, Stephen H. *American Providence.* London: Continuum International Publishing Group, 2006.

Weber, Max and Stephen Kalberg, eds. *The Protestant Ethic and the Spirit of Capitalism.* Oxford: Oxford University Press, Incorporated, 2007.

Welch, Holmes H. *Taoism: The Parting of the Way.* Boston: Beacon Press, 1971.

Wells, Jonathan. *Icons of Evolution: Science or Myth?* Washington, DC: Regnery Publishing, 2000.

Wheelwright, Phillip, ed. *The Presocratics*. New York: Odyssey Press, 1966.

Whitcomb John C. Jr., and Morris, Henry M. *Genesis Flood: The Biblical Record and its Scientific Implications*. Phillipsburg, NJ: P&R Publishing, 1961.

Whitehead, Alfred North. *Science and the Modern World*. New York: Simon & Schuster, 1997.

Williamson, Timothy. *Knowledge and its Limits*. Oxford: Oxford University Press, 2000.

Wittgenstein, Ludwig and G.E.M. Anscombe. *Philosophical Investigations*. Ames, IA: Blackwell Publishing, 2003.

Wittgenstein, Ludwig, G.E.M. Anscombe, and G.H. von Wright eds. *On Certainty*. New York: Harper & Row, 1972

Young, William. *Hegel's Dialectical Method*. Nutley, NJ: Craig Press, 1972.

Yu-Lan, Fung. *A Short History of Chinese Philosophy*. New York: Macmillan, 1948.

Zeller, Eduard. *Outlines of the History of Greek Philosophy*. Mineola, NY: Dover Publications, 1980.

INDEX

Abraham: analysis of his faith. *See* faith and reason

ad hominem. See informal fallacies

ad populum. See informal fallacies

Advaita Vedanta, 110

Anaximander, 29, 77, 135

appeal to authority. *See* informal fallacies

appeal to fear. *See* informal fallacies

appeal to pity. *See* informal fallacies

appeal to the unknown. *See* informal fallacies

Aquinas, Thomas, 133, 187

argument, 55

Aristotle, 141, 169, 180, 257; dualism, 132

astronomical data, 96

atonement, 191, 192, 193, 319

Augustine, 129, 327

Austin, Jane, 25

authority and insight: applications of moral law 5, 223; consequences of moral law 5, 229; on the nature of authority, 221; origin in human nature, 221; statement of moral law 5, 223

Ayer, A. J, 327

Bahnsen, Greg L., 327

Barth, Karl, 37, 328

beatific vision, 41, 72

Beauvoir, Simone de, 328

begging the question. *See* informal fallacies

Bentham, Jeremy, 179

Berkeley, George, 24, 85, 107, 108

Berkouwer, G. C., 328

biological data, 90

Bloom, Allan, 328

Boethius, 328

Bradley, F. H., 24, 106

brain in the vat, 106

Bultmann, Rudolf, 328

Calvin, John, 32, 34

Camus, Albert, 238

catastrophism, 89, 90

Charnock, Stephen, 329

clarity, 28

Clark, Gordon, 329

cogito ergo sum, 27

common ground, 5, 14, 35, 58, 287, 293

complex question. *See* informal fallacies

concept, 51

Copi, Irving M., 329

Copleston, Frederick C., 329

Craig, William L., 35

creation is revelation, 144, 187, 211

credo inquantum intelligō, 36

credo ut intelligam, 36

Darwin, Charles, 22, 38,
    88, 93, 93, 99
Davies, Paul, 96
Dawkins, Richard, 330
deconstructing
    post-modernism, 118
definition of knowledge, 49
Dembski, William A., 330
Dennett, Daniel C., 330
Derrida, Jacques, 106, 119,
    120, 135, 257
Descartes, René, 27, 107, 257
Deutsch, Eliot, 332
Dewey, John, 19, 106, 117
Dirac, Paul, 77
divine command theory, 181
dominion, 131, 211, 213, 219,
    252, 256, 282
dualism: objections to the appeal of
    dualism, 130

empiricism, 189
Epicurus: atomic swerve theory, 77
esse est percipi, 107
ethics: definition of ethics, 165
existentialism, 121, 179

faith and reason: analysis of Abra-
    ham's faith, 121–127; Kierkeg-
    aard's analysis, 123
Fanon, Frantz, 240, 331
Feuerbach, Ludwig, 331
Finnis, John, 175
Foucault, Michel, 19
Freud, Sigmund, 22, 81, 145, 240
friendship, 149, 175, 243,
    249, 252, 278

Gangadean, Ashok, 29
Geisler, Norman L, 332
geological data, 90
George, Robert, 175
Gettier, Edmund, 48, 50
Gilson, Etienne, 334
good (the): and God, 177; and hap-
    piness, 174; and human nature,
    175; and marriage, 252; and
    suffering, 277; and talent, 256;
    and the source of unity, 175;
    and virtue, 172; and work, 211;
    formal definition of, 171; ten
    characteristics of, 208
good and God: applications of
    moral law 1, 177; consequences
    of moral law 1, 182; origin in
    human nature, 171; statement of
    moral law 1, 177; the good and
    human nature, 175
gradual idealism, 203
Guth, Alan, 76

hasty generalization. See infor-
    mal fallacies
Hawking, Stephen, 76, 78, 96, 135
Hegel, 24, 37, 105, 122
Heilbroner, Robert L., 333
Herbert of Cherbury, 34
heteronomy, 180
Hick, John, 333
Hobbes, Thomas, 179
Hodge, Charles, 30
Hofstadter, Richard, 41, 333
Hoyle, Fred, 78
human dignity and rationality:
    applications of moral law 6, 234;
    consequences of moral law 6,

242; on the nature of human dignity, 231; origin in human nature, 231; statement of moral law 6, 233

Hume, David, 24, 26, 38, 85, 109; the problem of evil, 145–154

Hunter, Cornelius G., 334

Huntington, Samuel P., 334

incompatibilism, 66

inexcusability, 24, 33, 40, 140, 152, 157, 159, 168, 189, 193, 224

integrity and knowledge: applications of moral law 3, 202; consequences of moral law 3, 205; on the nature of integrity, 199; origin in human nature, 199; statement of moral law 3, 201

James, William, 66, 106, 117, 168

Johnson, Phillip E., 334

judgment, 54

kalam cosmological argument, 58, 75, 130

Kant, Immanuel, 28, 35, 122, 277; Copernican revolution, 105; deontology, 179; heteronomy, 180; libertarianism, 66, 167; on causality, 109; rationalism, 38; virtue and happiness, 174

Keats, John, 25

Kierkegaard, Søren, 123

Kuyper, Abraham, 189, 227, 335

Lao Tzu, 29, 135, 180

law of excluded middle. *See* the laws of thought

law of identity. *See* the laws of thought

law of non-contradiction. *See* the laws of thought

laws of thought: excluded middle, 10; identity, 10; non-contradiction, 10

Leibniz, G. W., 65, 335

Lewis, C. S., 240, 335

Locke, John, 24, 85, 105

logically possible worlds., 97, 134, 136

Logos, 15, 28, 39, 53, 116, 151

love, 7, 25, 45, 126, 152, 158, 172, 245, 284

love and fidelity: applications of moral law 7, 249; consequences of moral law 7, 253; on the nature of sex and love and marriage and the good, 245; origin in human nature, 245; statement of moral law 7, 248

Lucretius, 77

Lyell, Charles, 88

macro-evolution, 89, 90

Madhyamika, 115, 135

magisterial vs. the ministerial use of reason, 33

Marx, Karl, 19, 22, 37, 81, 145, 179, 234

material monism: general background, 71; the 1st argument: the material world is not eternal; 73; the 2nd argument: thinking is not motion of atoms, 80; the 3rd argument: the mind is not the brain - perception, 82; the

4th argument: naturalism is not based on science, 86
micro-evolution, 90
Mill, John Stuart, 179
moral law 01. *See* good and God
moral law 02. *See* thinking and presupposition
moral law 03. *See* integrity and knowledge
moral law 04. *See* work and hope
moral law 06. *See* human dignity and rationality
moral law 09. *See* truth and justice
moral law 10. *See* suffering and the good
most basic belief, 58

Nagarjuna, 106, 115, 116
Nash, Ronald H., 336
Nietzsche, 75, 106, 118, 119, 120, 146
Nirguna Brahman, 29, 135

Oliphint, K. Scott, 32, 34, 36
on causality and uncaused events, 63
Oppy, Graham, 159, 337

Passmore, John, 337
Peirce, Charles Sanders, 19, 117
philosophy, 9, 89; definition of, 3–8
Pieper, Josef, 264, 337
Plantinga, Alvin, 24, 32, 49, 50, 156
Plato, 14, 129, 131, 172, 180, 224, 338
post hoc ergo propter hoc. See informal fallacies
pragmatism, 117
pratityasamutpada, 115

presupposition, 56
principium cognoscendi, 14
principium essendi, 14

Ramanuja, 106, 111, 112, 113, 115
Rand, Ayn, 179
rational presuppositionalism, 57, 189, 293, 312
reason and argument, 51
reason in its use: constructive, 13; critical, 12; formative, 12; interpretive, 12
reason in itself. *See* the laws of thought
reason in us: fundamental, 15; natural, 14; ontological, 14; transcendental, 15
reason, definition of: reason in itself, 10; reason in its use, 11; reason in us, 14
red herring. *See* informal fallacies
reductionism, 27, 81, 224, 235
Reid, Thomas, 24
reincarnation, 102
Rorty, Richard, 17, 106, 117, 118
Rousseau, Jean-Jacques, 25, 180, 216
Russell, Bertrand, 78
Ryle, Gilbert, 85

Sagan, Karl, 71
Sartre, Jean-Paul, 122, 180
Schellenberg, J. L., 159, 339
Schleiermacher, Friedrich, 339
Schopenhauer, Arthur, 24
secularism, 199, 213
sensus divinitatis, 32

Sextus Empiricus, 66

Shankara, 29, 106, 110, 112, 115, 135

shunya, 115

Sire, James, 39

Skinner, B. F., 22, 81, 240

Sola Scriptura, 39, 195, 320

sources of fideism, 32–45; faith and reason, 35; knowledge and accountability, 32; ontology and epistemology, 34; piety and the intellect, 40; reason and hermeneutics, 39; reason and personality, 43; reason and the mysteries of the faith, 42; reason and the particular, 37; reason and the work of the Holy Spirit, 36; sensus divinitatis, 32; the magisterial vs. the ministerial use of reason, 33

sources of skepticism, 17–32; appearance and reality, 24; attitude as fundamental source, 31; construction and deconstruction, 20; empiricism, 26; intuition and certainty, 24; persuasion and proof, 23; pragmatism and skepticism, 19; relativism and tolerance, 21; reason and its uses, limits and limited uses, 27; tradition and transcendence, 22; truth and power, 19; worldview pluralism, 18

Spinoza, Baruch, 135, 340

Sproul, R.C., 178, 323

straw man. See informal fallacies

suffering and the good: consequences of moral law 10, 283

Suzuki, D. T., 115

teleology, 181

testimonium Spiritu Sancti, 36

the good and clarity, 175

theism: preliminary problems, 141; the free will solution, 154; the ironic solution, 156; the problem of evil, 145

theistic evolution, 98-109

there must be something eternal, 61

Toynbee, Arnold J., 10

truth and justice: origin in human nature, 267; statement of moral law 9, 270

truth and power, 19

uniformitarianism, 88, 89, 90, 93

value and talent: applications of moral law 8, 260; on the nature of value and talent, 255; origin in human nature, 255; statement of moral law 8, 259

Van Til, Cornelius, 32, 34, 188

Wells, Jonathan, 92, 341

Wittgenstein, Ludwig, 53, 119, 341

Wolff, Christian, 34

Wolterstorff, Nicholas, 323

work and hope: applications of moral law 4, 214; consequences of moral law 4, 219; hope and certainty, 213; on the nature of the good, 208; on the nature of work, 207; origin in human nature, 207; statement of moral law 4, 214

ABOUT THE AUTHOR

DR. SURRENDRA GANGADEAN was professor of Philosophy at Phoenix College and at Paradise Valley Community College for forty-five years. He regularly taught courses in Introduction to Philosophy, Logic, Ethics, Philosophy of Religion, History of World Religions, and Introduction to Christianity. For ten years, he taught courses in the History of Eastern Civilizations and in Interdisciplinary Humanities. In addition, he taught courses in Philosophy of Art, Philosophy of Literature, Philosophy of History, and Theology. He led seminar discussions for faculty, students, and the public in the Great Books Reading and Discussion Program. He received an M.A. degree in Literature from Arizona State University, an M.A. degree in Philosophy from the University of Arizona, and a Ph.D. in Natural Theology from Reformed International Theological Seminary. He presented academic papers and public lectures on the topics of Natural Theology and the Moral Law.

CPSIA information can be obtained
at www.ICGtesting.com
Printed in the USA
LVHW040343220723
752879LV00001B/38